This is not just another book on marriage. It wasn't until I was taught the principles in *Wife School* that I learned how wives are supposed to treat their husbands. I was blind to my harsh tongue and controlling spirit. Julie's witty humor will have you laughing out loud and her wisdom will leave you with a healthy marriage and a happy husband!

—Elizabeth Rosenblum, 33, married eight years, two children, Mentors High School Girls

The principles I have learned from *Wife School* have changed my marriage and therefore changed my life in unbelievable ways. I have gone from a "good" marriage to an "exceptional" marriage (which almost seemed unattainable and unrealistic). *Every wife needs to read this book.*

—Jenny Hendrix, 33, married seven years, five children

The principles in *Wife School* have changed my life. The wisdom and guidance have reversed the effect the world had on my marriage. Both my husband and I are truly grateful. God's ways are best, and I believe Julie has captured His design for the wife perfectly in this book.

—Emily Wilson, 33, married eight years, three children, Mentors Younger Women

In my twenty-six years of marriage, this is one of the best books I have read. I mentor a group of young mothers and would love for them to read *Wife School*. I found the story captivating. And I loved the character of the Genie. I wish I had one!

—Michelle Noah, 57, Christian school art teacher, married twenty-six years, four children, Bible Study Leader, Mentors Women

Wife School has been life changing for me in understanding that I have the ability to transform my marriage and my life by turning my focus from the imperfections in my husband to all he does that is right. *It is truly life altering.*

—Kendall Tashie, 50, married thirty years, six children, Bible Study Leader, Mentors Women

This is a game-changer in the world of marriage books. Incredibly insightful. I was reading *Wife School* at the pool, laughing out loud a bit, and this guy next to me asked me what I was reading. "Well, it's about marriage actually ... and it's *really* funny."

—Elizabeth Gullett, 29, Interior Designer, Married three years, Mentors High School Girls

Wife School is indeed a found treasure, like a magic lamp! Its truths are foundational and timeless and will transform any marriage relationship ... I wish I had met this Genie when I was a young bride! Julie's writing style is engaging and fun. I will be using this book as a teaching tool for every young woman in my mentoring ministry.

—Sheri Hogue, 51, married twenty-nine years, two children, Bible Study Leader, Mentors Women

I haven't even read half the book and I don't want to put it down! I wish I had read this when I first got married. I love the story line and the use of the Genie!

—Karen Jamison, 49, staff at Christian school, Married twenty-six years, five children

I really love the way this book is written. At first, I thought the Genie was going to be lame, but he makes the book so interesting! It's a story—not just another marriage book with rules. I was just thinking how I can't wait until this book is printed so I can lead a group of women through it.

—Lisa Womack, 46, married twenty-two years, three children, Bible Study Leader, Mentors Women

I love the way Julie used the story of Jessica to bring the reader in and keep them engaged in some pretty heavy stuff. I really learned a lot from reading *Wife School*, and I would recommend it to any of my friends, married or not.

—Emily Lee, 24, graduate student in Christian counseling, Married eight months

Amazing. Loved it! I think it is brilliant how Julie took what I thought was going to read like a self-help book, turned it into a fiction read, and yet taught at the same time. I will be buying copies for all women I love.

—Jennifer Sedory, 39, married eight years, one child

Wife School
Edition 2

Wife School
Edition 2

WHERE WOMEN LEARN THE SECRETS OF MAKING HUSBANDS HAPPY

Julie N. Gordon

MS, Marriage and Family Counseling

Table of Contents

Preface ·xiii

Dear Reader, please read these three remarks before
beginning *Wife School*: · xv

Part I   The Eight A's Every Wife Must Master · · · · · · · · · · · · · · · · · · · 1

Chapter 1   I Must Be Dreaming · 3

Chapter 2   First A: The Acceptance Lesson ·14

Chapter 3   Second A: The Admiration Lesson· ·30

Chapter 4   Third A: The Appreciation Lesson· ·39

Chapter 5   Fourth A: The Attention Lesson· ·45

Chapter 6   Fifth A: The Activities Lesson ·53

Chapter 7   Sixth A: The Approval Lesson ·57

Chapter 8   Seventh A: The Affection Lesson ·67

Chapter 9   Eighth A: The Authority Lesson · 79

Part II   Advanced Training for Wives· 93

Chapter 10   What to Do When Your Husband Fails or Has Adversity · · · · · · · · · · · · 95

Chapter 11   How to View Your Husband's Work from His Perspective · · · · · · · · · 102

Chapter 12   How to Correct Your Husband· 106

Chapter 13   How to Explain Anything to Your Husband· 111

Chapter 14   What to Do When Your Husband Mistreats You· · · · · · · · · · · · · · · · · 119

Chapter 15   What to Do When You Disagree about Parenting· · · · · · · · · · · · · · · · 129

Chapter 16   What to Do When Your Husband Has a Bad Idea · · · · · · · · · · · · · · · 134

Chapter 17   How You Contribute To or Diminish Your Husband's Reputation· · · · 139

Chapter 18   When Your Husband Doesn't Reciprocate or Try to Meet Your
             Needs · 143

Chapter 19   What to Do When the In-Laws Are a Problem · · · · · · · · · · · · · · · · · 151

Chapter 20   How to Wisely Handle Conflict with Your Husband· · · · · · · · · · · · · · · 157

Chapter 21   How to Be Attractive to Your Husband· 165

Chapter 22   How to Help Your Husband Be a Spiritual Leader · · · · · · · · · · · · · · · 171

Chapter 23   When There Are Many Things Your Husband Needs to Change · · · · · 178

Chapter 24   When Your Husband Doesn't Appreciate You · · · · · · · · · · · · · · · · · · 182

Chapter 25 When Your Husband Needs to Be Right ·186

Chapter 26 When Your Husband Is Critical and Complaining · · · · · · · · · · · · · · · ·193

Chapter 27 The End of Advanced Training for Wives ·202

Part III   How to Respond to Particular Struggles in Marriage · · · · · · · · · · · · · ·207

Chapter 28 When Your Husband Brags ·209

Chapter 29 When Your Husband Comes Home Grumpy or Doesn't Like
            His Work ·213

Chapter 30 When Your Husband Is Not Romantic· ·219

Chapter 31 When Your Husband Is Irresponsible ·226

Chapter 32 When You Want Sex More Than Your Husband Does· · · · · · · · · · · · · ·230

Chapter 33 When Your Husband Is Emotionally Needy· · · · · · · · · · · · · · · · · · · ·234

Chapter 34 When Your Husband Shows Interest in Other Women· · · · · · · · · · · ·237

Chapter 35 When There Is Conflict over Money· ·241

Chapter 36 When Your Husband Is Unskilled in Celebrating Your Special Days · ·244

Chapter 37 When Your Husband Doesn't Want to Spend Quality Time
            with You ·248

Chapter 38 When Your Husband Lies or Is Deceitful· ·252

Chapter 39 When Your Husband Doesn't Help Around the House· · · · · · · · · · · · ·256

Chapter 40 When You Work Outside the Home· ·262

Part IV   Conclusion · 267

Chapter 41   The Departure of Genie · 269

            The Turquoise Journal Lists · 273

            Acknowledgments · 275

            About the Author · 277

Preface

Having a master's degree in Marriage and Family Counseling, I have counseled and mentored women for over twenty-five years. Having also read over five hundred books on relationships during that time, the secrets that women need to know to make their husbands happy and their marriages sing have floated to the top. Marriage after marriage has been revolutionized as women have mastered the principles in *Wife School*. These precepts teach a woman how to love a man in a language he can understand.

Learning these principles takes time, as they are against many of women's natural inclinations. In my mentoring groups, I have discovered that often a year or more of being immersed in these new thought patterns is necessary for this monumental change to occur in a woman's mind-set. Even after much instruction, "tune-ups" are constantly necessary as women are prone to wander back to contentiousness (Gen. 3:16).

Granted, this is a lot of work. Wives must persevere in giving even in the face of her husband not reciprocating. *This is the man you were given to love*, and <ins>it is a</ins> <ins>woman's</ins> calling to <ins>"bring him good, not harm, all the days of her life"</ins> (Prov. 31:12). *Is it?* However, what is more important to a woman than an intimate, satisfying marriage? Very little, I have found. No woman has ever regretted the time she spent learning the principles that grow a satisfying and soul-stirring marriage.

Jessica, the protagonist in the story, is an example of today's married Christian woman who is on Facebook, watches *The Voice*, and is disappointed with her marriage. It is evident in the following story (by the protagonist's internal monologue) that Jessica is extremely misdirected in how to be a loving wife.

And in a way similar to how the authors of *Charlotte's Web*, *The Velveteen Rabbit*, and *The Lion, the Witch, and the Wardrobe* used toys and animals to speak profound truths, I have used a genie to convey wisdom in this story. He is not the goofy genie of Disney or the silly genie played by Shaq; this genie is a wise and relentless counselor who instructs the abrasive and messy Jessica how to transform her marriage.

The previous online lessons in *Wife School Online* have been collected and expanded into two volumes, *Wife School Advanced: Mastering the Art of Being a Wife, Vol. 1 and 2*. Each workbook is an eleven-week semester study to provide more in-depth practical help for wives, building on the principles in *Wife School*. The studies are designed for Women's Ministries, small groups, and individuals.

And now, let the magic begin as you and Jessica learn the lessons that lavishly renovate your marriages as you both enroll in *Wife School*.

Dear Reader, please read these three remarks before beginning *Wife School*:

1. *Wife School* is written in a story format to make it enjoyable. However, please get your colored pens and highlighters out and mark up this book. It will be imperative that you read—and reread—and reread again—the remarks of the Genie until the new thinking becomes your own. The Genie's remarks are announced in each lesson with a bold typeface so you can easily locate the Genie portion to reread.

2. The Genie asks Jackie to do assignments and keep them in her Turquoise Journal. Any notebook will do, but the importance of doing and accumulating these assignments is the difference between nominal and huge success. (Both volumes of *Wife School Advanced* include space for your Turquoise Journal Lists.)

3. Research has repeatedly shown that a group hugely contributes to success when trying to change behavior. Find some friends or women at your church and go through both volumes of *Wife School Advanced* as you read *Wife School*. Your marriage will permanently transform!

Dedicated to H

A woman who has been married to a man for over 30 years knows him very well. And what I know about you is that you are the most honest, kind, hard-working, sweet, generous, and fabulous human being on the face of the planet. My best achievement in life will always be "married well."

PART I
The Eight A's Every Wife Must Master

CHAPTER 1

I Must Be Dreaming

Tuesday, September 18

"According to this will, Jessica, your grandmother left you one thousand dollars." The lawyer continues to study the papers while I try to contain my shock.

"One thousand dollars? That's it?" I say as my voice rises with my blood pressure. My husband shoots me a glance to chill out, but no way am I calming down. Something is terribly wrong. It *can't* only be one thousand dollars!

I try to mask my semi-hysteria. "My three sisters all said Grandma told them they were each getting fifteen thousand dollars."

Now my husband stares down at the floor with his hand on his forehead. I've seen this move by Matthew before when he decides it's not worth fighting me.

"Sorry, Jessica, only one thousand dollars for you," the lawyer says. "But, yes, all three of your sisters get fifteen thousand dollars. It's very clearly delineated in the will."

Delineated? Why do lawyers use those big words? To show off, I guess.

"There's no mistake in the dollar amounts," the lawyer says. "However, there's one more item to discuss. The will says you are to receive this wooden chest." He picks up a mahogany box and hands it to me. "Your grandmother asked specifically that you open it when you were alone." He then hands me a silver key.

A small relief comes over me. Maybe Grandma left cash in that wooden box ... or jewels ... or stock certificates. She always kept it locked so we grandkids never knew what was in it. Grandma once said my mother was to get the wooden box, and I remember thinking, *Who cares who gets that piece of junk?*

When Mom died in a car accident three years ago, Grandma said she thought with the way things were going at my house, I would be the one who would need the box. I never thought much about that comment or the chest's contents—until now.

My husband stands up to leave, and the lawyer takes a call from his secretary. *One thousand measly dollars? Are you kidding me? There better be something good in that chest. Maybe bonds or a property deed.*

We walk to the car. Matthew is silent except a brief remark that he needs to get back to the office. Lately, he is quiet much of the time. Yeah, when he is on his computer doing things for work or he's bowling with his buddies, all is well with the world. But when I'm upset? Where is he then? Does he enter in? Does he help me shoulder my burdens? Couldn't he hurt with me just once? I shouldn't be surprised that I'm alone in my disappointment—he's rather consistent in this area.

I'm anxious to see what's inside the box. I remember the lawyer said to open the box when I'm by myself. But who is he to tell me what to do? After we get into the car, I set the box on my lap, take the silver key, and open the box. Holding my breath, I wait to see stacks of one hundred dollar bills. But instead what's in there? An old, brass lamp with a handle and a spout that looks like it belonged to Aladdin? No! Noooooooooo!

I'm livid. What is going on? Why would Grandma do this to me? If I had a brain injury, I couldn't get sympathy from Matthew, but nevertheless, I try. "What do you think about that, Matthew? Can you believe Grandma cheated me on the inheritance?"

"Jessica, it was Grandma's money. She can do what she wants with her money. If she wanted to give it to Allison, Chloe, and Jackie, that was her prerogative. This traffic is horrible, and I need to get back to work." He doesn't even glance at me.

Disgust rises in my chest. Isn't marriage supposed to include emotional support? Doesn't he know how much I was counting on that money for some new living room furniture? If he made more money, I might have more of the things I want. I spend hours and hours addressing wedding invitations to make a few extra bucks just so we can keep up.

It seems no matter what I say, Matthew tugs the other way. I'm getting pretty sick of this. If this is marriage—this separateness, this resentment, this aloneness—well, maybe I don't want it.

"That beats everything," I say. "One thousand dollars and a crummy old lamp. I'll never get that living room furniture. We can barely pay bills with your salary, much less buy me new furniture."

My remark cut Matthew. It *was* pretty rough, I admit. But maybe he'll realize he's not pulling his weight in this marriage. Maybe he'll realize he'd better figure out a way.

to make more money, help more around the house, take a bigger interest in the kids' and my well-being. It's certainly not the marriage I thought I was getting when I said my vows.

We pull up at his office, and he gets out without saying a word. He is void of energy, lifeless. I watch him slither into the building. Matthew used to be energetic and witty; now he is sullen and boring. What has he deteriorated into? What has our marriage deteriorated into?

I'm not going to cause a scene, but I'm going to park this car and march in there and tell him that I need a little more from this marriage. The nerve of him to treat me like this!

Walking into the building, I smile sweetly to greet the receptionist and start my descent down the hall to Matthew's office. When I turn the corner, I hear Matthew laughing from his office. Not just chuckling, but rip-roaring laughter, like he is at some wild fraternity party. What's going on? The guy was almost dead ninety seconds ago!

I round the corner and look into his office. There he is, leaning up against his desk, talking with a twenty-five-year-old Greek goddess. She has long, dark hair that is shiny and silky. Her skin could grace the spread of any Revlon commercial, and her figure, the worse of all, looks like J. Lo! Matthew's exuberant countenance falls in a nanosecond.

"Uh, Jessica, uh, this is Indigo. She is, uh, my new assistant and the, uh, new account executive here. This is her second week."

Matthew had mentioned a new assistant, but I thought she wore glasses, was fifty to fifty-five, and wore a size sixteen. I never thought she'd sport high heels and smell like the cosmetics counter at Macy's.

With perfect posture and hand extended, Indigo graciously walks toward me with great charm and confidence. "Matthew, we can finish discussing this later," she says, as she flips him a look and walks out of the room.

I am flooded with anger and fright. This man is not cold or lifeless at all; he's alive and kicking with blazing heat.

"I wanted to tell you, uh, Matthew, that dinner will be at, uh, seven. We're having meatloaf." He doesn't like meatloaf, but that's what I made.

"You came in here to tell me that?"

"Yes," I lie.

My stomach is in my throat. My *feet* are in my throat. I realize in a split-second how far our marriage has slipped. I see the colossal gap between who Matthew is around others—attractive *female* others, that is—and who he has become around me. Why, I haven't heard that laugh in *months*!

"The entire creative team is staying late tonight," he says. "We've got to get some fresh ideas for the new Marley account. That's why we hired Indigo. The firm is bringing in dinner, so don't worry about me."

Somehow, I manage to stagger out of there. Somehow, I manage to drive, even though my legs are shaking. The realization that Matthew is full of energy and life when he is not around me makes me feel drugged.

Thinking of Indigo's looks compared to mine makes my emotions nosedive even further. Of course, much of her looks are hair and makeup, but still. I'm average height, average weight, average hair (brown and to my shoulders)—just overall average looks. I do have nice skin and nice brown eyes (that are a little too close together). My teeth are straight and white (thanks to Crest Strips), but my cheekbones could definitely be higher. I'm average, though. Average. *Average.* And she rocks. Rocks. *Rocks.* And I *hate* it!

Now I am only marginally upset that Grandma left me a paltry one thousand dollars. The real fear is that gorgeous, skanky Indigo-woman is now around Matthew, and since our marriage is in the pits, he's especially vulnerable.

Wednesday, September 19

It is morning, and I hurry around to get the boys' lunches packed for school. I was awake when Matthew got home last night but pretended to be asleep.

"Have a good day at school, boys!" I say. "I've got a babysitter coming tonight because it's Meet-the-Teacher Night at school."

"Yeah, well, okay, I guess," Brandon, our nine-year-old, says as he grabs his backpack. Brandon has been getting in trouble at school for talking back to the teacher. It doesn't surprise me though. I mean, what kind of father is Matthew to the boys? Matthew is often preoccupied with his computer work at night and ignores the boys. If he spent more quality time with Brandon, I'm sure these behavior problems would subside.

How did I get myself into this marriage mess? And now, that J. Lo look-alike is added to the mix. He's going to work with her closely every day? I can hardly breathe. I hate him for not meeting my needs while at the same time I feel intense jealousy of his arousal for Indigo.

Brandon and Josh, his little brother, leave for the school bus. Affection for those boys washes over me. There are two people in this world I love to the moon and back, and they're my precious boys. The thought of them having a broken home stabs me. This wasn't the plan. Matthew and I were to live happily ever after.

"I'll see you later," my husband says, not even looking my direction.

"Okay," I reply, trying not to let my ocean-sized emotions tumble out.

"It might be ten before I'm home because the team has added an extra practice," Matthew says. "The bowling league finals are this weekend," he adds with an air of excitement as he opens the door to the garage.

"Matthew! Tonight is Meet-the-Teacher at the kids' school. Wasn't it on your calendar? I e-mailed you the date. What do you mean, an extra bowling practice? You're not going with me?"

"I know it's Meet-the-Teacher, Jessica. But it's the practice for the league's finals, and I have to show up. Anyhow, it's just a small event at an elementary school. I'm sure you can handle it. It's not their graduation, you know. What's the big deal?"

I know I shouldn't say anything, but I don't care. I have been severely wronged, and I'm not going to put up with it any longer.

"What's the big deal? The big deal is that you don't get it, Matthew. The big deal is that you put your bowling and your work and your new Mediterranean account executive and everything else in the world ahead of our children and our family. *That's* the big deal!"

He gazes at the floor for one long second. I should have left out the part about the "new Mediterranean account executive." But tough! He deserves this verbal whipping. He is a loser and half a man. Matthew calmly opens the garage door, exits, and closes the door quietly behind him.

Are you kidding me? I stomp to the door and throw it open.

"It's sad, that's all I can say, Matthew. It's really sad and pathetic." I slam the door.

I'm delirious with rage. Who in the world does he think he is? He doesn't have a *clue* about wives or relationships or running a family! Can I put up with this inconsideration, this selfishness, this lack of interest in our family any longer? Wouldn't it be better for the kids to go through a failed marriage than live in a home with such contempt between the parents?

Tears run down my cheeks as I throw in a load of laundry and seriously contemplate giving up on my marriage. I make the beds and load the dishwasher, feeling like I'm going to climb out of my skin. Then I have a strange realization that I'm barely able to admit: I don't want to throw away my marriage. I just want this marriage to be wonderful, but that seems utterly impossible. I want to love Matthew, and I want him to love me. But isn't this marriage too much of a mess to fix? How could we ever heal our marital problems? I have no idea where I would even begin. I feel hopeless.

I do more laundry and prep dinner ... sounds like a boring Facebook status. I cannot quit thinking about my anguish over my marriage.

Why can't Matthew change? Why can't he be different? He's aloof and distant. This is supposed to be my soul mate? I only want a few things from this short time on Earth and one of them is a soul-mate marriage. No wonder I am always hitting the chocolate. And how dare he light up and be excited by that tanned nymph!

Before starting my work of addressing wedding invitations, I decide to fold the last load of clothes. In the corner of the laundry room is Grandma's mahogany box. I decide to check inside the brass lamp. Maybe I acted too quickly. Maybe there are instructions about a bank security box inside the lamp. If we divorce, I will need every cent.

Taking the box to the den, I take the lamp out of the box and remove the cork from the spout. Up from the lamp comes a pillar of smoke. Immediately, I am petrified. Dropping the lamp on the sofa, I run into the hall to escape what I fear is going to be an explosion. There's no explosion, so I peek back around the corner.

Standing in my den is a dark, middle-aged, Mideastern man. He is around six feet tall and looks like he has worked out every day of his life. His tanned skin looks a little dry, like men who are sailors or who have played tennis without sunscreen all their lives. His eyebrows are a little on the bushy side, but they make his face interesting, and his gaze is his most surprising feature—soft and filled with kindness, free of any malice. Gold silk pants are topped with a white vest that is embroidered with gold thread, and a large turban populated with sparkly gems sits on his head.

He sees me, and motions for me to come to him. **"Do not be afraid. I am your genie and am now here to grant you one wish."**

How did this criminal get in? The doors are locked, and the alarm is on. Is this a dream? I slap my thigh, but I don't wake up.

"It's true," he continues. "I am your genie, and I'm here to grant you a wish, Young Jessica. What do you wish?"

How does he know my name? Who is this? My heart rate must be two hundred, but his calm eyes tell me that I'm safe. I slowly move toward him.

"Go ahead. Tell me your one wish, Young Jessica."

After ten more minutes of this repetitive dialogue where I question him, touch him, and slap myself again to wake up, I realize that if this is a dream, I will eventually wake up, so I might as well go along with his instructions.

"Okay, Genie, my one wish is this: I want an outrageously happy marriage!"

"Your wish is my command, Young Jessica. Would you like to begin the lessons now?"

"Wa—wa—wait a second. Begin wh—wh—what lessons?" I ask. "Can't you just say 'abracadabra' and make my marriage wonderful?"

"Of course I can, Young Jessica. But you would still have the same behaviors, attitudes, and thoughts, and in a matter of weeks, you'd be right back to where you are today. No, I'm not going to do a short-term fix. I am going to enroll you in my *Wife School*. I will teach you how to understand your husband and meet his needs. I will also instruct you in what a husband wants from a wife, which will win and keep the heart of your husband. When you master these timeless secrets, your husband will move toward you with great affection and openness to meeting your needs and desires."

"Waaaaaaait a second. Me? Me? I'm going to learn to understand *HIM*? How to love *HIM*? Why not make him understand and love *ME*?" Maybe I have a chauvinist genie.

"Although the Creator gave man the leadership in the home when He created man and woman," Genie says, "He gave woman a powerful ability, which is the ability to influence. As history has demonstrated, the power behind the throne is often the greater power."

I don't care about any history lessons, Turban Buddy, and it seems to me I'm getting the bummer end of this deal.

Genie continues. "The Creator has equipped the woman with knowledge and understanding to build and influence the home and the relationships inside it."

I'm not buying into this. He must not know my deadbeat husband.

"Women have much power," he says, "but her power is in her influence, *which must be bathed in meekness and humility*. Women not only do not understand the mind of a man, they do not understand their feminine role and the subsequent damage this misunderstanding does to the marriage."

Damage? Matthew is the one who damages our home by his neglect.

"Women are without adequate wisdom in knowing how to build the marriage relationship. This is what I will teach you, Young Jessica. First, I will instruct you how to make your husband outrageously happy in the marriage by truly understanding him and meeting his needs. Then he will turn with openness and new receptivity to meeting your needs."

I'll listen to what this charmer says for a little bit and see what he has to offer, but I'm not promising anything. I can always change my mind and back out, right? I mean, what do I have to lose? Anyhow, this is probably all a dream, and I'm getting ready to wake up any second.

"We will start now by learning the Eight A's that meet your husband's soul needs, the very oxygen he needs to breathe so he feels satisfied in his relationship with his wife. These Eight A's awaken affection in a husband toward his wife. By making these deposits into your husband's tank, he feels fulfilled in the marriage and you make yourself indispensable to his happiness."

And what about *my* happiness? Aren't we going to talk about that?

He continues. "The Eight A's are eight different types of deposits that you make into your husband's tank, that is, his emotional/psychological/soul tank. They are Acceptance, Admiration, Appreciation, Attention, Activities, Approval, Affection, and Authority. We will study the 8 A's' in that order. This is how to love a man in a language he can hear."

We keep talking about Matthew. I'm the one who is disappointed with this marriage. We need to talk about my needs!

He continues, "Wives often say to me, 'Genie, I'm a good wife. How dare he treat me like this!' However, I realize what these wives mean is that they cook for him, clean for him, do his laundry, and take care of his children. Although those activities are important, these women have no understanding of a man's true soul needs."

I am definitely a good wife if the cooking-cleaning-childcare issues are the standard. I'm not sure about this soul-need thing.

"When can we talk about Matthew making those deposits into my tank?" After all, that is what I'm really interested in.

"Every woman wants to be cherished, pursued, and loved," he says. "I have been teaching this course for thousands of years, and there's an order. I will teach you how to ask Matthew to meet your needs but in due time. First, you must learn how to meet his true needs. However, regardless of Matthew's response, *this is the man you were given to love.*"

The man I was given to love? Sorry, Bub, but I'm not very interested right now in doing the right thing because it is the right thing.

"The Eight A's make lovers and leaders out of laggards. They soothe a husband's anger as well as quiet his insecurities. You will become the queen of his universe. He will relax and welcome your input."

This genie is promising the moon. I know better than to fall for this.

"Men may admire women who keep a shipshape, tidy house. Men may applaud women who are clever or who run a big business. Being a gourmet chef may win their respect. But none of these qualities induce affection in a man toward a woman like the Eight A's. *A man has affection for his wife according to the care she takes of his soul, and that is done by depositing the Eight A's into his tank."* That's how a woman feels too.

These Eight A's sound more like a spell from *Sleeping Beauty* or *Harry Potter*.

"This is not a program to manipulate men into doing what the wife wants," says the Genie.

Why not? I'd go for that.

"What I teach wives," he says, "is not only to do and say the right things to their husbands, which cause husbands to regain affection for their wives, but I teach wives how to think differently about their husbands. Then the wife sincerely regains respect and affection for her husband. Over time, after learning the skills of how to treat a husband as well as how to think about him, the affection is real and grows. A cycle is started where affection in one spouse breeds affection in the other. These principles are truly magical and miraculous."

Who can believe that? I guess he has the answer to global warming, too.

"If you wanted to study car mechanics," he says, "you could start by looking under the hood and try to figure out what pipe goes to what. Or, you take a course in car mechanics and learn from people who already know engines."

Uh, I don't care about cars or engines, Mr. Hawaiian Tropic.

"Or," he says, "if you wanted to know how to be an astronaut, you would know that you must enroll in NASA and learn from the experts. You would never try to get to the moon without some instruction and assistance."

I'm not in kindergarten.

"It repeatedly surprises me," says Genie, "that even though much of a wife's happiness is dependent on her marriage relationship, she still tries to wing it instead of studying and mastering the art of being a wife. Women somehow think that romantic love alone should carry her marriage. The thought of learning how to understand and treat a man is infrequently considered a course to learn. Husbands, like train sets on Christmas morning, don't come assembled, and you need a set of instructions. I will give you the instructions."

This sounds like a pitch from an infomercial. I'm waiting for him to tell me that in three, no, in only two small payments, all this can be yours.

"That a woman *will* influence her husband and her home is not debatable," Genie says. "The foolish woman will influence her home by manipulating her husband. Conversely, a wise woman will influence and build her marriage by focusing on meeting the needs of her husband."

This is the way to say it, not "you have to meet his needs no matter what."

11

He keeps forgetting that *I*—me, myself, and *moi*—have needs. But I've wasted time before, so I guess I'll listen to what Mr. Beach Body has to say. "I'm ready to proceed when you are, Genie," I say.

"Then let's begin *Wife School*," Genie says as he circles his hand in the air and a beautiful turquoise book appears. The book has a gold oil lamp drawn on the cover.

"What's that?" I ask.

"This is your Turquoise Journal," he says. "Inside, you will find that I have written down eight different topics under which you will add your thoughts over time. We will only briefly refer to the first five lists today, but as you continue in *Wife School*, I want you to add to these lists."

I take the Turquoise Journal in my hand and open it to see what the heck he is talking about. There are different topics on each page, with numbers one through fifty written below each topic.

"As we discuss and learn the Eight A's over the next few weeks and months, we will also gradually fill in these lists. *It is by reviewing and adding to the Turquoise Journal lists that you will train your mind to think differently about Matthew.* The importance of this journal cannot be overstated."

Train my mind? Lists? Oh, dear, what have I gotten myself into? I pinch myself one more time to try to wake up from this dream. Pinching doesn't work. I thump my wrist. No, I'm still here with this genie.

"All husbands have a deep need to feel respect from their wives," he says. "I have discovered that faithfully filling out the lists in the Turquoise Journal profoundly assists a wife in regaining sincere respect for her husband."

This genie makes all sorts of wild promises and statements. Ha! I mentally throw down my gauntlet and silently challenge him to see if any of these Eight A's and this Turquoise Journal stuff could work on my despicable marriage and on me. I seriously doubt it.

Note to Reader—

A complete list of the eight exercises for the Turquoise Journal is located at the back of this book. An important aspect of a reader's success in Wife School is the written exercises that Genie asks Jessica to do. These exercises are actually based on the life-changing principles of 'cognitive restructuring,' which simply means, thinking different thoughts (Philippians 4:8). Genie instructs Jessica to use a Turquoise Journal to complete the written exercises he assigns her, although any notebook will do. This workbook portion of Wife School is nonnegotiable for maximum success.

CHAPTER 2

First A: The Acceptance Lesson

Still Wednesday, September 19

"*Wife School* is going to take time and energy," the Genie says. "I want you to be free to concentrate." He snaps his fingers twice, and on the breakfast bar appears a beautiful casserole of homemade manicotti, Matthew's favorite. (I know Matthew would like me to fix manicotti more often, but it takes so long to stuff those stupid shells.)

Nevertheless, having my own personal Rachael Ray in the kitchen is totally cool.

"The first A of the Eight A's that we are going to discuss is Acceptance," Genie begins. "I am going to teach you how to accept Matthew the way he is."

Well, that's a joke. No way am I accepting that heap of blemishes.

"The primary method to begin to accept a husband is to appreciate and focus on his positive qualities. Open your Turquoise Journal, and you will see the first list is entitled 'Strengths, Gifts, and Qualities I Admire in My Husband.' "

I look at the page and see there are blanks under the title, numbered one to fifty. Am I in fourth grade and getting ready to take a spelling test? Anyhow, I don't see why this exercise will help. Matthew's negative qualities certainly outnumber his positive ones. What about a list entitled "Weaknesses, Annoyances, and Disappointments" instead?

"Okay, I'll write down some strengths," I say, pretending to be agreeable.

Genie quietly stares at me, waiting for me to begin.

I pour myself another cup of hazelnut coffee and begin to scan my brain for any vestiges of positive qualities in Matthew. "Generous with the money he has, even though there's not enough. Loves the kids, even though he doesn't spend enough time with them—"

"*Positive* attributes only, please," Genie reminds me.

Because of my resentment toward Matthew, it's hard to think of positive qualities. However, I persevere and write as I talk out loud. "Let's me pick the movie; other people like him and trust him; he thinks I'm funny, well, used to," I say. I remember his laugh in the office yesterday when he was with Indigo. He hasn't laughed with me like that in a long time. (By the way, who names their child Indigo? It sounds like Delilah or Jezebel to me).

"Today I am only introducing the lists," Genie says. "But from now on, whenever you think of a positive quality or trait you admire in your husband, I want you to write it on List One. This list should grow to thirty, and then to fifty, and so on."

From now on? He's giving me a lifetime assignment? I don't mind a few lessons or a few lists, Mr. Ancient, but no lifetime assignments.

Making this list is like doing push-ups. "He takes us to church, he mows the yard, sometimes he plays catch with the boys," I write. I do feel the teeniest, tiniest twinge of guilt when I survey the list. Now I remember last summer when Matthew spent hours with the boys building a tree house in our backyard.

"All humans are made up of strengths and weaknesses, Young Jessica. When you focus on Matthew's weaknesses, it becomes difficult to have affection for him. When you focus on his strengths, you reverse that pattern."

I don't try to focus on Matthew's weaknesses. It's only that there are so many of them walking around, waving their little red flags.

"Envision your husband as a circle, half strengths and half weaknesses," Genie says. "Now do to your husband what the sun does to the moon to make a half-moon: it highlights half of the moon while half of the moon slips into darkness and obscurity. The dark side of the moon is still there, but it is not noticeable."

I didn't pay much attention in science. I was figuring out what I was going to wear to the football game.

"If you focus and think about your husband's strengths daily," he says, "you will begin to think of him in terms of his abundant strengths. The negative qualities won't upset you in the same way. What you're doing now is looking at Matthew like a term paper that a critical teacher has graded and written red remarks all over. You are focusing on the red remarks, his weaknesses."

A lot of mistakes, a lot of red ink.

"Women in general," he says, "have a hard time accepting their husband's imperfections. They intellectually know all husbands have partial strengths and partial weaknesses. But when the husband's deficiencies surface after marriage, they are surprised, as if they were cheated and didn't know this man was going to have flaws or certainly not to this degree."

Cheated. Bamboozled. Duped.

"When the husband reveals a negative tendency, which, of course, he inevitably does," Genie continues, "like complaining, dishonesty, moodiness, slothfulness, self-ishness, or a million other weaknesses, the wife is struck with the thought, *Am I going to have to put up with this the rest of my life?*"

Genies can read minds?

"The weaknesses of the husband become the lens through which the wife views him," he says. "The husband may have many great qualities, but his shortcomings stand out in her mind. She is now stuck with this man who is a huge disappointment to her and is a big project that she must begin to work on."

A big, *unwanted* project. I wanted a "soul mate" relationship, but instead, I'm married to this ... this ... well, this self-centered loser.

"Generally, men see their wives' faults and tend to overlook them, as long as there is not too much emotional turmoil and they get regular sex. Women, on the other hand, feel as though they have a personal responsibility to change their husband into someone better suited for life ... and certainly better suited for her."

Any reasonable wife would agree with that.

"It would be helpful," he says, "if brides knew that their expectations for Prince Charming are unrealistic and that actually this man is an average Joe with his own set of weaknesses. Wives are shocked when they realize that not only is this man not going to meet all of her needs, he is going to have some extremely annoying issues."

He's right. I didn't sign up for this kind of marriage. I signed up for rose petals and lace. I signed up for someone who is nearly perfect and adores me and meets my needs. This gargantuan disappointment was certainly not what I wrote on my order form for a husband.

"You know that you are half strengths and half weaknesses, too" Genie says. "You expect your husband to overlook your faults, but you don't want to overlook his."

This might not be nice to admit out loud, but I don't feel like my weaknesses are nearly as severe as his.

"This is why the Turquoise Journal is of paramount importance," he says. "This first list will remind you daily of Matthew's strengths. You must read your lists every day at the beginning of our program and continue to add to them. *Choosing to set your mind on your husband's strengths will eventually help you to view him primarily from this positive perspective instead of your current negative perspective of his weaknesses."*

I don't want to exercise daily nor do I want to read any dumb lists daily. I must say, my genie is a bit of a boss. I agree to start doing the Turquoise Journal thing, but I'm not sure I'll follow through.

Genie hardly takes a breath. "Women are annoyed with their husbands in this century for the same reasons that their female ancestors were annoyed with their husbands in the past: husbands procrastinate, are critical, selfish, inconsiderate, unethical, poor listeners, uninterested in the wife's concerns, grumpy, lazy, unromantic, talk too much about themselves, are guarded and don't share their real selves, don't spend enough time with the children, seek adventure and excitement instead of funneling that energy into the family, are needy and whiney, have egos that constantly need maintaining ... The list is endless."

Maybe I am too hasty in judging this genie. He certainly understands Matthew.

Genie's not finished. "Or maybe he likes to wear cowboy boots with his suits, doesn't tip enough, burps at the table, doesn't give you enough quality time, buys expensive cameras he doesn't need, sprawls out on the sofa watching sports, doesn't call and tell you his plans, is inconsiderate of how tired you are, is messy, likes to hunt and fish while you like book clubs, doesn't help enough with the housework, is not outgoing with your family ... There are a million things wives want to change about their husbands."

This Arabian might understand Matthew a lot more than I thought.

"Although men will rush into burning buildings," he says, "and go to war to protect their loved ones, their heroic and courageous natures are often ignored and instead their weaknesses, *especially their inadequate ability for emotional intimacy*, get the laser focus of the wife."

I need to high-five someone after that last statement, "inadequate ability for emotional intimacy."

"Men have outstanding built-in capabilities to provide for and protect their families," he says. "But again, women dismiss these gallant qualities because of their disappointment with the husband's deficient ability to be relational."

That's right—I want a deep, intimate relationship with Matthew. But instead, Matthew gives me the relationship of a worm.

"The best environment for husbands to live in whereby they can grow is one in which their tanks are full of the Eight A's. However, as I said, many wives do the opposite—they whine and are critical, which is the worst environment for others to grow and change."

I'm not sure how or why, but that last statement penetrated. I feel like someone told me I am pregnant again or that I was adopted. I have wanted Matthew to grow and change, but I've done the exact opposite of what he needs in order to do that. Good grief. Maybe I need this genie after all.

"For now," Genie says, "pretend you have a cemetery in your backyard and bury your husband's weaknesses, mistakes, and his disappointing ways. Stop demanding that he be unflawed. Stop demanding that he doesn't have a dark side."

A dark side? Now I'm waiting for him to tell me he's a friend of Yoda's.

I decide to wedge in a word. "Genie, can you give me an example of how a wife has accepted a weakness in a husband?" I'm going to need a lot of help if I'm supposed to learn how to accept Matthew's weaknesses.

"I was instructing a wife," says the Genie, "a couple of centuries ago whose husband was a brilliant lawyer in old England. His mind was keen in understanding the nuances of specialized law. He was outstanding in the courtroom. At home, his wife asked him to hang some pictures. Now, this wife's father was a fix-it genius, so therefore this wife thought all men should be able to repair things around the house. But the husband had absolutely no background in household or mechanical repairs and didn't know how to hammer the nail into the stud in the wall. The wife unwittingly said, 'Now that's unbelievable! A grown man who doesn't know how to hang a picture!' The husband got mad, threw down the hammer, and yelled, 'You should see me give a closing argument to a jury!' "

I laugh. I can see the whole scene in my mind.

"But after our Eight A's course," Genie continues, "this same wife forgot the nail incident and asked this same lawyer husband to fix a door that had fallen off its hinges. Of course, the husband failed, as he had no idea how to perform this mechanical feat. This wife suddenly remembered that all men have weaknesses, and that one of her husband's weaknesses was a lack of mechanical ability. She realized that this was an unmet expectation in her marriage, so she had a little private talk with herself."

"Then she said to her husband, 'Well, a brilliant legal mind like yours is so full of important legal thoughts that there's not room for small, unimportant things. I'll call a workman tomorrow. I won't bother you again with these household details.' She finally accepted that her husband was half strengths and half weaknesses and stopped focusing on his weaknesses. She realized that the man was a brilliant lawyer but a crummy repairman."

I understand that brilliant lawyers sometimes can't do household jobs, but how exactly does this relate to my accepting Matthew? I guess there are some things Matthew does right. He can organize an entire advertising campaign. He agonizes over the details and does a wonderful job. Also, I think about how courageous Matthew acted when there was a fight in the neighborhood between some teenage boys. Matthew, recognizing our preteen neighbor in the group, put himself (Matthew) in harm's way to protect the young boy, yet I only complained afterward that he was not trained to handle that. I didn't tell him how I admired him for his courage in protecting the young boy. No, I don't tell Matthew when I admire something; instead, I berate him for not scheduling more time with our boys and for buying the wrong milk at the grocery. I criticize him for not understanding my cycles and moods.

"Women spend much of their lives," Genie says, "trying to change their husbands with negative comments instead of accepting them and depositing the other seven A's. Whatever your man is, he is. Stop fighting the time the sun comes up. Your husband came with a package of weaknesses, and your job is to accept and overlook them."

I still have trouble overlooking that Celia Roberts didn't invite me to her birthday party in the eighth grade (although she invited my other best friends), so I'm sure I'm going to have trouble overlooking the stadium packed full of Matthew's weaknesses.

"For centuries," he says, "I have seen husbands move toward their wives with affection as women deposit the Eight A's. But regardless of your husband's behavior, you must always remember, *this is the man you were given to love.* This is the recipe for truly loving Matthew in a language he can hear, feel, and understand."

A recipe? He's now reducing marriage to a cookbook with a few recipes? This Eight A's thing sounds too simplistic.

"Look at List Two in your Turquoise Journal," Genie says.

I don't want to look at another list. I want cheesecake.

I turn the page and see that List Two is "Things Other Husbands Do Wrong," also with numbers one through fifty below the title. I'm not sure where Genie's going with this, but I can certainly list the faults of my sisters' and friends' husbands.

"This list makes you grateful for things that Matthew doesn't do wrong," he says. "For example, start with big things: He's not in jail; he's not on drugs; he's not an alcoholic; he's not physically abusive; he doesn't steal; he's not having an affair."

That voluptuous Indigo presses into my mind when Genie says "affair." At least he's not having an affair *yet.*

"I can do this list, Genie. My sisters' and friends' husbands have many obnoxious behaviors." I chuckle to myself when I think of them. Samantha's husband just bought a new boat when they are having trouble buying groceries. Roberta's husband won't stop talking and is always bragging, making up stories where he's the hero. Ashley's husband can't seem to stay employed. I quickly begin jotting down my thoughts.

"Most women can easily do this," Genie says. "And I see you're no different."

Matthew starts to look a little better in my mind as I write down my immediate thoughts of annoyances of other husbands. Yes, this is a good exercise. A teeny-weeny shift occurs in my feelings for Matthew as I realize there's a long list of things that he doesn't do wrong.

"No husband is perfect. Some men are better with the children," says the Genie, "but they may have problems with huge egos. Some men handle money better, but they are not as sensitive to spiritual issues. Other husbands are patient, but they may not be as exciting as others. No husband has it all. Each husband is a mixture of good and bad, and your job is to be the detective, find the good, and shine the flashlight of your mind on the good by reading and rereading your lists in your Turquoise Journal. Over time, this will change how you view Matthew, and you will learn to be grateful for all of his many positive qualities."

Maybe over time, but certainly not today.

"The expectations that a woman has from marriage are Herculean," Genie says. "She thinks she has found a handyman to fix the faucet, a date for every social event, a provider with a substantial income, a sage who will know how to love yet guide the children, and a lover who gazes into her soul."

Click the "thumbs up" icon for that description of a husband.

"But what she really has is a normal man, half strengths and half weaknesses, who has no idea that after he is married, his wife will immediately enroll him in her own Husband Improvement Course. Do you see that this superhuman she wants is already going to disappoint her immediately after the 'I do'? Do you see how her long list of expectations is going to be unmet? Yet women often continue to hold onto their expectations, are disappointed, and then angry. *A wife's anger propels a husband to withdraw*, and then we have a negative cycle in motion."

Is it possible I have too many expectations of Matthew? Yes, I admit I want love, affection, appreciation, a good living, spiritual leadership, emotional maturity, selfless giving, and for him to win Father of the Year. Is that asking too much?

"Be an overlooker, not a tabulator," Genie says. "After you consistently deposit the Eight A's, Matthew will turn back toward you and will be open to your influence. But for now, please accept him as he is."

I'm reluctant to accept these wrinkles around my eyes, and I'm likewise reluctant to accept Matthew's weaknesses. I wish there was a magic cream that could fix both.

"Even though my Eight A's wildly induce affection in a husband toward his wife," he says, "a woman's motive in her marriage should be to give and love without expecting anything in return because that's the nature of genuine love. But for now, I realize it will take you some time to grasp and embrace that level of loving."

You're dang right that I'm not ready to embrace "giving and loving" just because it's the right thing to do. The honest, deep-down truth is I want Matthew to love *me*. Adore *me*. Give to *me*.

Wow, even as I listen to myself, I know I'm wrong. I know that genuine love gives without the thought of getting back, like how I love my kids. A pain shoots through my brain as I consider that maybe I'm more to blame in this cold marriage than I realized.

"What I'm going to tell you now is going to be one of the most beneficial perspective shifts in your entire marriage," Genie says.

Yeah, right. And there's a new Lexus convertible outside that's mine too.

"At a deep and often unconscious level, a woman thinks her husband is hers to coach and maneuver. That is why she feels the freedom to try to remake him."

Can't we be finished with *Wife School* for the day? Isn't the bell about to ring?

"As we'd discussed, the most common area where women try to change men is that women want men to meet her craving for emotional intimacy," he says. "Women want their husbands to share their thoughts and feelings with them. They also want their husbands to inquire about their wife's thoughts and feelings. Women want verbal affirmation, nonsexual affection, gifts, kindness, and a lot of meaningful communication."

My energy returns with this list. Right on, Genie Baby. I smile and nod.

"As we've said, in order to get what women want, they correct, advise, hint, and suggest," Genie says.

Yes, that is often my strategy for trying to squeeze some emotional intimacy out of Matthew, but what else is a woman to do?

"Here is the difficult part to grasp, Young Jessica. Your husband wants something too, with the same intensity that you want emotional intimacy. Are you ready to hear it?"

Do I have a choice?

"It is this: Matthew wants to relax in the marriage and be who he is. He wants to enjoy your companionship *the way it is*, not be in an improvement class. He wants the security and comfort of being able to be himself, accepted the way he is, with no one trying to change him or criticize him. Do you see that your desire to grow, coach, and change your husband *is in direct opposition* to his desire to relax, be comfortable, and enjoy life the way it is?"

Is he saying that he wants me to accept Matthew's passivity?

"Men hate it when wives are relentlessly disappointed with them," Genie says.

Well, too bad. I hate it that I don't feel loved by Matthew. And right now, I'm very annoyed with this genie and his teaching.

"What husbands want is to be at ease in a reassuring and soothing relationship," he says. "They don't want to be prodded with a hot iron to change all the time."

I don't use a hot iron, but my tongue can leave a pretty mean sting.

"What most women don't understand is as much as she wants her husband to change and to work on emotional intimacy so she can feel closer, *he wants the opposite*—to relax in the relationship, to *not* have to work on the relationship, *to simply enjoy the wife's companionship*."

But I don't want that. I don't want his leave-me-alone stuff.

"Young Jessica, you have no idea how much input you give about everything."

Really? I thought I was just being helpful. I didn't know I was coming across as a hovering mother.

"Instead of correcting Matthew all the time, enjoy his good qualities of honesty and hard work. Appreciate how he takes out the garbage, is nice to your family, and is sexually faithful."

I can't even fathom shutting up and being content with things the way they are.

"Women are created with the tendency to focus on nurturing and growing relationships. Most men are not created to excel in those strengths to the same degree. Most men are created to focus, to put energy outward into the world, and to conquer their work. Demanding that a husband strongly desire emotional intimacy with you is wishing he was a woman."

Now that's plain stupid. I certainly don't want a woman. Yuck.

"It is incredibly perspective-altering for you to see that this tendency of a husband to not meet your needs for emotional intimacy is *not* personal against you. It is how most men act when they are untrained. The romantic comedies and romance novels don't sell to millions of men but rather to women. Men like action and suspense movies with women characters who think they are wonderful *the way they are*. Why do you keep bashing this man who is blind and deaf to your intimacy needs? Heavens! Yes, you eventually have to teach him, but first you have to step back and realize this man is not excessively selfish. He is not out to upset you but is simply acting like most men act *because they don't understand women and have no idea what women want and need*."

Well, Toga Man, you got that one right. Matthew doesn't get me, and it infuriates me.

"Women are resistant to understanding that as much as they yearn for this tender attachment with men, men are equally predisposed to not care about it. Why are you upset over something that almost all men have in common? It's like being upset that a four-year-old can't read. Most four-year-olds can't read. You have to teach them."

This thought of Matthew being a normal male and not getting me—instead of being a selfish clod—is new. I'm not sure I believe it.

"Once you consistently deposit the Eight A's, as I will say over and over, Matthew will begin to open toward you and eventually will be able to hear that you, the woman, want and need closeness and intimacy through talking, acts of kindness, and consideration. But not now, not today. You will need to master the Eight A's and make mega-deposits first."

This genie is saying that *I'm* supposed to learn how to meet Matthew's needs with these so-called Eight A's, and that this will open him to being interested in learning about *my* needs. When Genie asked me what one wish I wanted, I should have asked that Matthew be the one to change. I guess it's too late to revise my one wish.

"To the family, men bring courage, a desire to provide for and protect, and an outward focus on bettering the world. Women more often bring the ability to nurture and develop closeness in the family. *Stop being mad that men don't bring everything.*"

I start to soften to Genie's teaching, but then I become resistant again.

"It is not on Matthew's radar that you want emotional closeness," he says. "Matthew thinks, 'I bring home my paycheck. I am sexually faithful. Why do I have to work so hard to be verbally and romantically expressive over and over again? I don't need that, and besides, it wears me out. What's her problem?'"

"Yeah, Genie, he thinks my desire for emotional intimacy is a problem. Once he told me that my needs were the size of the Atlantic Ocean." The thought makes me sad as I remember how utterly misunderstood I felt.

"Once you meet all his Eight A's, if Matthew is like the thousands of men before him, he will open to what you need *just because you want it*. He will have positive emotions toward you and will want to please you."

That sounds like heaven, Matthew being emotionally intimate with me. But why am I letting this jeweled barefoot guy persuade me that there's hope for Matthew to do that? Matthew's not ever going to change and be open to me.

"I do realize it's difficult for most women to enjoy what they now have instead of looking at what they don't have," Genie says. "This is a skill most women need to develop, and that skill is to learn how to drop unmet expectations. Open your Turquoise Journal to List Three."

Reluctantly, I pick up my Turquoise Journal. This is some crazy dream I'm having. And besides, this whole Turquoise Journal thing is turning into a lot of work.

"List Three is 'Unmet Expectations I Have of My Husband,' " he says. "We will only get started on this list today, but go ahead, be outrageous, and begin to list everything you want from Matthew."

Fa-la-la, I can easily do this list. I write, "Listens well, admires me, romances me, highly considers my opinions, cares about what I want, interested in my dreams, interested in my comfort, tries to surprise and delight me, compliments me, works hard to grow relationship with the children, funnels his best energy into our home life—"

Genie stops me even though I'm only getting warmed up. "That's enough for now. You can add to the list as you think of other items. For now, I want you to imagine that Matthew was called away to an undercover Secret Service job in Asia. Because of the security and underground nature of the project, he will not return for four years. He's gone, but he's coming back. In the meantime, you have to take care of your own needs because you will not be in contact with him at all, not even on Skype or the phone. Think about your needs and how you would take care of them. You can assume that you will have adequate financial support during this time. Now, what kind of expectations would you have from Matthew?"

"I guess I wouldn't expect anything from him during that time," I cautiously say. "Precisely. After women get married, how incredible it would be if the woman didn't have any expectations except faithfulness and a living. How fabulous for the husband if she were delighted with him the way he was. However, when women marry, they usually have Moby Dick expectations of the husband. Let go of your expectations. Expect nothing from your husband except faithfulness and a living, and learn to enjoy what he brings to the marriage. This is accepting your husband the way he is."

This is so unrealistic. We are not making a Hallmark movie.

"Another mental exercise that is helpful is to pretend that Matthew gives you all those things you wrote on the list. I want you to write to the side of that list, 'Pretend expectations are met.' "

What? This is crazy. This *genie* is crazy. And *I'm* crazy for listening to him.

"Proceed to treat Matthew like he is meeting your expectations. What would that look like?"

I instantly think of Colin Firth's character of Mr. Darcy in *Pride and Prejudice* or Ryan Gosling's character of Noah in *The Notebook*. The thought of being married to a man who pursued me with such attention is invigorating. "I'd be affectionate and affirming," I say and smile.

"Do you see? That's what Matthew wants. Right there. That's it. Did you hear yourself? Affectionate and affirming. Add content and sweet, and you've got it."

Duh. *That* would be if I were married to Mr. Darcy, not Matthew.

"Someone has to start a new cycle in the relationship," he says. "Someone has to be the mature, giving person with *no expectations*. Someone has to go first. That someone is you," Genie says.

No! I say to myself, while I mentally stomp my foot. I still want Matthew to go first. My brain is fighting everything Genie says. These *Wife School* principles are polar opposite my natural inclinations.

"*Wife School* is almost adjourned for the day," he says. "But I want to quickly point out the next two lists that you are to fill out. List Four is 'Nice Things My Husband Says or Does.' "

This list thing is getting annoying. There are only a total of eight lists in all of *Wife School*, so I don't see why he has to introduce so many at first.

"When Matthew does something nice, such as listens well, offers to help you, smiles at you, goes places with you, gives attention to the children, says nice things to you, write it down. This exercise will help you remember the many things Matthew *does* bring to the marriage."

Focusing on anything nice about Matthew right now is a looonnnggg stretch for me.

"Does he open the door and let you walk through first? Does he give you money to buy groceries? Does he pay for the children to go to the dentist? Does he get the oil changed in the cars? Does he help you around the house? Does he give any attention to the children? Does he do the taxes? Does he pay the bills? Does he paint the house? You will be shocked at what he brings to the marriage if you pay attention."

Of course, Matthew brings *some* gifts to the marriage, just not the ones I want the most.

"Giving your husband the Eight A's will invoke elves to work in your husband's brain to turn his heart back to you, but you have to be patient. *Wife School* does not turn marriages around overnight."

Okay, you have two nights.

Genie continues. "Your biggest enemy will be self-pity. '*What about me? Why does this take so long? This isn't fair.*' That's how the masses think. Rise above your moaning, complaining, and being discontent. Think, '*Yes, I have a hard situation at the moment, but I have a plan. I will work my plan.*' "

Okay, Dr. Phil, relinquish the philosophy talks.

"The way the world was originally designed," he explains, "was that humans would get their approval needs met from the Creator. They would then be able to give to others *from their fullness*. But several years ago, there was some trouble in a garden, and now, instead of getting full from the Creator, you humans pull on each other to get your needs met."

What garden? What is he talking about?

"Instead of being responsible for your own needs and giving to Matthew," he continues, "you are angry that he is not meeting *your* needs. This discouraging situation can be completely turned around, though, by only one spouse. And that is what the Eight A's are all about—turning around the marriage through the wife."

I still don't see why the wife has to do all the work. And especially *this* wife. I mean, *I* was the one who got the genie.

"I know I have given you a lot to think about," he says. "But I want you to glance at List Five, 'Things My Husband Might Find Difficult to Accept in Me.' We won't work on this list today, but as time goes by, I'd like you to list tendencies or attributes in yourself that might make you unpleasant to a spouse."

Me? Matthew might be upset with *me*? In what ways? I doubt there will be much to put on *that* list. I pull my weight in this marriage.

"Although these lists initially seem like a lot of work, they are the means by which a wife's mind is renewed and trained to think differently about her husband. Filling out the Turquoise Journal lists is nonnegotiable in *Wife School*. By adding daily to your lists, you will be pleasantly surprised how you truly begin to accept Matthew in your heart. Be patient, Young Jessica. All Eight A's work together and don't happen overnight. I was around when Rome was built, and it wasn't built in a day."

"Genie, were you really around?" I ask, but presto, he's gone.

Perfect timing, though, because my brain is fried, and I need to get started on my day's work of addressing wedding invitations and I already feel depleted from information overload.

I open Pandora on my computer and opt to listen to Adele on the radio. "We could have had it all," she sings. The song touches something deep in me. I want my marriage to have it all. Is it possible that this genie has a program that really woos and wins back the hearts of husbands? Call me a cynic, but I'm pretty sure this is all baloney.

Later that night ...

After the Open House at school, I get the boys into bed and sit down in front of the fire. I love gas fires where you flip a switch and bazinga, it's lit. Kind of how a genie would do it.

Matthew is still bowling. Being without a husband tonight at the Open House was awful. But to be honest, there were a lot of single moms there. Maybe I should be grateful that I'm not a single mom. Not yet, at least.   Brandon's teacher said he talks too much in class, and Josh's teacher said he is having trouble with his reading. Why can't Matthew be more interested in the children's lives at school? Genie would want me to give up that expectation for now, I guess. Matthew *is* interested in teaching the boys to play football, though. I guess I'd better write that in my Turquoise Journal. Retrieving it, I scribble down that thought and begin to reread my various lists: "Takes care of our cars; brings his paycheck home; is nice to my sisters ..."

After reading the lists, I notice a tiny lift in my spirit toward Matthew. At least he is out bowling and not out with Indigo. The thought of that dark-eyed temptress sends chills down my bones.

Genie said that focusing on Matthew's strengths would adjust my attitude. Not that I think it will work like Genie says, reestablishing my affection for him, but maybe a slight adjustment. Accepting Matthew as he is and focusing on his strengths will be the most difficult thing I've ever done. It's in the same category of difficulty as giving up sugar for life. Speaking of sugar, I'm hungry, so I get up and get some trail mix with almonds, cranberries, and dark organic chocolate. Healthy sugar.

I continue to think about what Genie said today, that my depositing the Eight A's will enable Matthew to regain affection for me. Genie wants me to give Matthew the

Eight A's regardless of how he responds because Genie says it's the way genuine love works, giving without the thought of receiving. I'm not ready for that level of giving, but I am considering that Matthew will be more willing to meet my needs if I meet his first. (I am not the sea of virtue that I pretend to be.)

I guess I'm going to give this *Wife School* thing a try—at least for a while. So I'd better get practical. How would I think and act if I gave up the expectation that Matthew should have gone with me to the Open House tonight? For one thing, I'd have dinner ready to heat up. Secondly, I'd be sincerely interested in his bowling. I do want to talk about the boys' issues at school, but maybe that can wait until after we talk about his topics.

Upon hearing the garage door open, I begin to microwave his manicotti. Matthew sheepishly walks in.

"Hi," I say in a perky tone. "I've got some manicotti for you."

"You do?" he asks, surprised.

"It's almost ready. How was your bowling?" I say, forcing a fake positive attitude. I should have tried out for my high school plays.

Matthew is probably wondering what's going on. Usually he gets the cold treatment for displeasing me. "I had eight strikes in a row. It was thrilling, Jessica!" His face lights up.

My first thoughts are not nice. Not nice at all. I think, *Wow, who really cares about your stupid bowling?* and *That's more important than your children's education?* I try to remember the items on my Turquoise Journal lists. *Bury his weaknesses in the backyard*, I remind myself. *Shine the light of my thoughts on his good points, the half-moon strategy*, I think to myself.

"That's great, Matthew. Tell me about it." Who is this woman who hijacked my voice?

Setting his manicotti on the table, I sit down next to him while he talks about his night. He is beyond excited. Why can't Matthew be this excited about the boys and me? Genie will be pleased to know, though, that I am several notches up from my usual cool self when Matthew disappoints me like he did tonight.

Later, Matthew gets into bed and seems like he's waiting for something. Duh, that's a hard one to figure out. I take a very long time getting ready for bed. Finally, he's asleep. Tiptoeing over with great carefulness, I slide in, trying not to wake him. I'll have to deal with accepting his sex drive another day.

Matthew's text message ringtone beeps, but he doesn't wake up. Carefully sliding back out of bed, I again quietly tiptoe over to read the text that is on the top of his iPhone. It's from Indigo! "Finished the Smith account plan and am excited to show it to you tomorrow."

That invader! How dare she text him this late! And she hasn't even been working there two weeks! This is war, you French-manicured villain!

CHAPTER 3
Second A: The Admiration Lesson

Monday, September 24

As expected, when I confronted Matthew about Indigo and her motives, he went ballistic. He said she was the best assistant he's ever had, that my jealousy was ridiculous, and told me to grow up. I know I shouldn't have railed so heavily on him. Genie told me to get off his back. Okay, I failed Lesson One. Shoot me.

One of my younger sisters, Chloe, calls and wants to meet for lunch. Since I have three upcoming weddings that I am addressing invitations for, I know I should say no, but I don't. Although I like doing calligraphy (and heaven knows I need the money), my home business is extremely time-consuming and inhibits my daytime social life.

Chloe and I decide to meet at Jason's Deli because we like the salad bar with organic choices. Allison, my older sister, and Chloe, the sister right below me, are my best friends. Mom said she should have named me Brittany, because then we would have been the ABCs. We have a much younger, single sister, Jackie, in Nashville who we try to persuade to move back to Memphis all the time. We three Memphians continually plot her return. We are the Three Musketeers, and if Jackie would return, we would be the Fantastic Four. Jackie severely struggles with her weight, and it hurts me to think about it. She is incredibly bright, funny, and beautiful. I wish Genie would visit Jackie with a *Skinny School*.

Anyhow, what would I do without my Memphis sisters? We usually tell each other everything, so I am having trouble not telling them about my Mediterranean visitor. But come to think of it, their marriages aren't up for any Oscars either. Griping about our husbands is one of our favorite subjects.

Before my lunch date, I need to start preparations for dinner and get a few invitations knocked out. But sad from this morning's disagreement with Matthew, I decide to quickly read my lists in my Turquoise Journal instead. Genie was right that the lists would have a positive effect on my feelings for Matthew. I am curious what the other seven A's are. They'd better have some wizardry because this marriage is a solar system away from where it needs to be.

Suddenly, Genie appears in the kitchen. Waving his hand in the air, a gorgeous platter of some chicken concoction appears on the breakfast bar.

"It's Chicken Cordon Bleu, made with organic chicken and nitrate-free bacon. I learned how to make it in Paris last century," he says.

I extend one of my clenched fists toward him to knuckle knock as he looks at me rather strangely. Obviously, genies are not versed in the customs of the day.

"As I've said, while we're together over the next few months, I will be providing you with 'happys' so you won't get behind in your housework and life. It's part of the package."

I'm trackin' with ya, Genie, when you mention prepared food and housework.

"Have you ever played chess?" he asks.

"I thought about joining the chess club in high school because there was a guy, Randy Campbell, in the club I wanted to date," I say. "However, when I found out how complicated the game was, I changed my mind." In the past year, I heard that scoundrel had cheated on his wife and asked for a divorce.

"Good, you are familiar with the complexity of the game," Genie says. "Think of these lessons as learning chess. We will begin with learning how each piece moves. Then we will begin to discuss strategy. As you know, there are thousands of nuances to chess. My goal is that you become an eventual chess champion or, in this case, marriage relationship champion. Of course, you realize that does not happen overnight. You must work hard and be patient. Being a fabulous wife is a skill—much like chess—in that it must be learned and persistently practiced."

Dang. I was hoping for "Make Your Husband Eat Out of Your Hands in Three Insanely Easy Lessons" like some of the magazines promise at the grocery checkout.

"How have you been doing with the Acceptance lesson?" Genie asks. After my long explanation (in which I "forget" to tell him about my railing over Indigo's text message), I promise to continue writing in my Turquoise Journal. Genie is now ready to move on.

"Our lesson today is the second A, which is Admiration. Admiration is the cry of a man's soul."

He keeps forgetting I have a cry in my soul too.

He continues. "Man has a tank inside his soul that is wooed by and drawn to praise and admiration. Although the wife's primary motive should be to give the husband praise and admiration because he needs it, it is also helpful for the wife to know that a man is also *drawn to the one who praises him.* It's a secret every wife should know. If she cultivates this skill and daily admires her husband, it will tie strong heartstrings around her husband's heart to hers."

Praise? Admiration? How do you spit that out when you are resentful?

"Not only does your husband crave admiration, Young Jessica, but your husband's admiration tank has a hole, and it drains every day. You will need fresh deposits daily."

Is there somewhere on eBay where I can buy a plug?

"Every day, you will need to find time to have an 'admiration moment.' I'm not talking about a *general* statement like, 'You're a great guy.' No, you admire something *specific* about your husband. Then you follow up your specific statement with evidence that proves it. That's called the 'admiration paragraph.' "

"Good grief, Genie. How do I spit out all this mush if what I'm really feeling is strong disappointment with him? What I really want to say is, 'You don't meet my needs, and I'm sick of it.' " I even sound harsh to myself. I must be a delight to be married to.

"A wise woman brings her husband good all the days of his life," Genie says, "because that is her calling. However, giving your husband praise is not only the right thing to do, as I said, it turns his heart toward you."

Genie's harping on "doing the right thing because it's the right thing" again. This guy has a little Mother Theresa in him—which, to be honest, I know I need.

"Alright, so if I decide to give Matthew a 'daily admiration moment,' what would I say?"

"This is where your Turquoise Journal comes in," he says. "When you read it every day and add to it often, you will begin to accept Matthew's weaknesses and develop antennae for his good points. In the course of daily living, you will begin to notice things your husband does right. You will have plenty of material if you look for it. Continue to overlook his weaknesses, and start telling him about his good qualities."

"I need an example," I say impatiently.

"What does your husband do for a living?" he asks.

"He's an account executive for an advertising firm." I guess I won't mention that pesky assistant that should move to Southeast Asia.

"Let's say he tells you about a conversation he has at work," begins Genie. "You pay a lot of attention to the conversation because you are trying to find qualities and actions to admire. He mentions that he came up with the idea for the new ad campaign. You ask him all about it, what he thought of, what he told everyone, etc."

To be honest, I'm not very interested in Matthew's work. It's often the same thing, and I get bored listening to it. Therefore, Matthew doesn't talk about it much anymore. That I used to give him a lot of advice on how to handle things at work might also have something to do with why he quit talking about it.

Genie continues. "Listen carefully to all Matthew has to say, and at the end, you add, 'Matthew, where do you come up with all of these excellent creative ideas? And it's obvious your coworkers thought your ideas were great too. Your boss is really fortunate to have such a creative account executive.' "

My jaw drops. I'm expected to say sappy stuff like that? "He already knows I think he's creative. I told him when we were dating."

Genie laughs. "Yes, I'm sure you did. I'm sure you filled his tank back then. But that tank leaks out *daily*, remember? What have you told him *lately*?"

I seriously don't want to do this admiration-moment thing. Especially since I'm still frustrated and primarily focused on all his weaknesses.

"How do I do this when I'm upset with him?"

"You understand that not only is this the right way to treat a husband," he says, "but that eventually, these Eight A's will rebuild your marriage and your husband's affection for you."

I do want that.

"Okay, will you give me another example of an admiration moment, Genie?" I can see that I don't have this lesson down at all.

"What does he do with his paycheck?" Genie asks.

"He deposits it in the bank. We use it to pay bills and things we need. He doesn't spend much on himself. He pays for bowling, but his league play is inexpensive. All the guys on his team have a slew of fancy new balls, but Matthew keeps playing with the same old one and wears the same bowling shoes. He says he is saving for the boys' orthodontic work."

"You mean you have a husband who doesn't spend much money on himself and instead wants to save for things the children need?"

I'm a little ashamed of myself. Matthew does have several good qualities.

"You've got some good material to admire, Young Jessica. Next time Matthew goes bowling with his same ball and shoes, say, 'Matthew, it's so unselfish of you to wear those shoes and have that same ball so you can save for the boys' orthodontic work. I'm very grateful for a husband with self-control with his spending and who is so generous with the family.' "

I could *never* choke that out. *NEVER.* That's not me. AHHHHHG! I feel like my head is in a vice and someone is tightening the lever.

"Does he resent you staying at home with the children?" Genie asks.

Another point for Matthew. "He likes me being at home and taking care of our children."

"So your husband does have some virtue, doesn't he? Find it. Magnify it. Put it on a pedestal. Shine a spotlight on it. And do it daily, Young Jessica. A man needs an admiration moment' daily."

Well, of course, my husband is going to like this praise if I can spit it out. My ego could use a little padding and plumping too. I think about how I tried to look nice to go to dinner last week and came out of the bathroom, all spiffed up, waiting for Matthew to notice. All he said was, "I'll get the boys in the car." I remember my heart sinking and wishing that he would praise me more.

"So, what do I do again?" I ask. "I don't know if I can choke this stuff out. This is like doing sit-ups."

"Keep your antennae up," he says. "He gives you material all day long to praise and admire. You're simply not in the habit. You're thinking about everything he does wrong. This is the beginning of an entire program where you change how you think about Matthew.

"I've seen much harder marriage cases than yours turn completely around. You can do this. You've got the desire for a wonderful marriage. You can conquer this, Young Jessica. Lay bricks every day, and soon you'll have built a cathedral."

And I guess he was around when the great European cathedrals were built?

"Your assignment tonight is to find something that Matthew does well, admire him, and give evidence of it in a follow-up paragraph. Never admire without a follow-up paragraph that gives evidence. Expect him to be shocked and not know how to respond."

Ugh. This seems so hard. Can I do this? Am I sure I *want* to do it?

"Men like to be praised about manly things, Young Jessica. Don't tell Matthew how well he folds laundry or cleans up your kitchen. Examples of manly qualities are items associated with his job, his body build, his physical strength, his smart brain, his quick wit. Got it? This kind of praise is oxygen to a husband's soul. Wives have the power to keep refilling their husband's leaky tanks, and in return, the husband's heart is drawn to the wife. A wise woman builds her house with the Eight A's and keeps the husband's admiration tank very full."

This is so not fair. "Genie, won't Matthew think this is phony?" I ask, searching for any way out so I don't have to do this.

"Maybe at first he will wonder what is going on," he says. "But he will open to it after a while. You might even feel you're laying it on too thick, and that surely his ego tank is filled to the brim. However, the truth is, most women underestimate the enormous size of a man's need for admiration and probably only fill up the bottom part of the tank. Yes, women like to be admired and praised, too, but it is not with the same intensity."

"I thought that men are supposed to be humble," I say. "Why am I admiring this man who is supposed to be humble?" I again attempt to escape this assignment.

"Let the Creator humble him," Genie says. "You make him happy with your praise."

No matter what I say, this joker's got an answer.

"I know I'm going to run out of things to say, Genie," I moan.

"Not if you pay attention and search for things to praise. Matthew might be good at driving, at knowing if the ref made a good call, good at painting, good at trimming the bushes, good at paying the bills. The list is virtually endless."

"Are you sure Matthew wants to be praised for paying the bills?" I ask, thinking how ridiculous that suggestion sounds.

"Certainly, if you say it right. For example, after he pays the bills, you could say, 'Matthew, you take good care of our family. I love the way you are responsible and pay the bills on time. I think your responsibility to our family gives me a lot of security and peace."

Where does he come up with this stuff? Does any woman really say all that baloney?

"One more thing," he says. "I want to caution you to infrequently, if at all, praise other men."

"What? I have no idea what you're talking about." I'm such a liar. I know exactly what he's talking about.

"Your husband does not enjoy your discussing how talented another man is, what a good father someone else is, or how well another man provides."

I can hear the judge slamming down the gavel in the courtroom and yelling, "Guilty!"

"Women like to brag on other men," Genie says, "hoping their husbands will 'get it' and do likewise. Foolish wives say things like, 'Joe hires a housekeeper for his wife' or

'Joe likes to keep their lawn so tidy.' She thinks she is being clever and sending a message, but she is only sending her husband's affection out the door."

This hurts. Last week when we were in the front yard, our next-door neighbor, Todd, was mowing his yard with his shirt off, revealing a chiseled six-pack. I asked Todd about his workout and told him I thought he looked great. I want Matthew to exercise and get rid of the cage around his middle. I hoped Matthew would be inspired by Todd, but instead, he said he had to make a call and went inside. Honestly, am I this dumb?

"Men have a natural competition between themselves to see who is the biggest rooster in the chicken yard. Your husband doesn't need you commenting on how wonderful the other roosters are. He needs you to buoy his ego. Remember, his tank drains every night."

Did Genie hear me telling my husband about the new car a friend bought for his wife and how he also surprises her with designer jewelry? Uh-oh.

"Your husband wants to be a hero in your eyes. Did you know that praise is the main trick that seductresses use to lure men into sexual unfaithfulness? Men are starved for admiration, and a woman who gives it to him wedges a way into his soul."

Now that's scary. I wonder if that size-two Indigo has been whispering sweet praises into my husband's empty tank.

"And Young Jessica, remember that praise in public is worth five times what private praise is worth. Admire your husband in front of your friends, his coworkers, your parents, and your kids. It's a secret many wives don't take advantage of. And while we're discussing this, criticism in public is equally multiplied in its effect."

Choke. I remember making a joke last week at church in front of some friends about Matthew's snoring. It got a big laugh, but I remember the look on his face, too.

"Praise and admiration are a wife's secret sauce. Do not use sparingly."

Don't use sparingly? I'm not using this sauce at all.

"It's bowling night for genies. I'll be back soon." He grins.

"Do genies really bowl?" I ask, but too late. Mr. Middle East is gone.

I wonder if I can cough out any of this admiration stuff. UGGHH! This is torture!

Later that night

Dinner's over. The dishes are done. Allison, my older sister, texts me that she wants me to help her pick out some fabric for her bedroom draperies tomorrow. I need to say no because I need to dig into my wedding invitations, but again, I say yes.

The boys are taking showers, and Matthew is on the phone with a coworker, talking about a presentation they are going to make tomorrow.

I can hear Matthew from the kitchen: "Chad, I know everyone does it, and it would probably seal the deal, but I don't feel right about it. I'd rather we play by the rules."

When he hangs up, I decide to try to take a shot at my assignment, Admiration. Here goes.

"Matthew, sorry to listen in, but I overheard you talking about not doing something that you didn't feel right about."

He jumps in. Obviously, he is distressed. "Yeah, Chad says if we secretly offer NBA basketball tickets to the guy who is in charge of picking the ad firm, Chad thinks that guy will pick our firm. But this new potential client doesn't want his coworkers to know he's getting the tickets. It seems unethical to me. Also, it's such a large gift. Those tickets would cost around five thousand dollars. It feels to me like we're paying him under the table."

Choke it out, I say to myself. Do it. Go ahead.

"Well ... I'm very ... proud of you, Matthew. It takes a lot of ... courage ... to go against a coworker's desire and stand up for ... for what's right. And I know you have been ... trying to land this account for some time, and you really want it. I ... uh ... I'm glad you're a man who chooses honesty over money." There. I did it. And I'm still alive. Maybe it was sappy and not a very good paragraph, but at least it was an attempt!

Matthew stares at me. He doesn't look away quickly like he usually does. He keeps looking at me. I feel uncomfortable. "Thanks, Jessica. That was nice of you to say."

"Well, sure, it's true. Oh, excuse me. I think I hear the boys calling me. Be right back." I exit quickly. Whew, that was H-A-R-D. And I have to do this every day? My heart rate is up to about 180, I imagine. Maybe Genie and I can negotiate for every week instead of every day. I wonder if all the A's are going to be this hard.

But I have to admit Matthew did like it. I think I'll hang in there and see what other tricks Genie has to teach me. Two A's down, six to go.

Before I get ready for bed, I check my e-mail. There's one from Brandon's teacher, remarking how he is disturbing class with his excessive talking. I read it out loud to Matthew.

"Tell him to stop it or we'll take him out of football," he says.

That's it? Matthew thinks that will solve the problem? Just give this eight-year-old an ultimatum and be done with it? And he wants me to do it? Isn't he the father?

Isn't he the one who should get involved with this? Just throwing out these trite answers to very complex issues sends me into the stratosphere.

We argue and go to bed mad.

Not good. Not good at all.

CHAPTER 4
Third A: The Appreciation Lesson

Friday, September 28

Matthew and I never resolved the issue about Brandon's excessive talking at school.

I e-mail Matthew a reminder to buy his mother a birthday card. Genie asked me to stop coaching/directing Matthew, but I think he appreciates that I remind him about his mother's birthday. I'll ask him later.

Moseying into the kitchen, I start the daily grind of laundry and housework before I begin my morning's quota of addressing invitations.

The phone rings, and it is Jenny Kline, my newest client. She asked me to do a rush order for her daughter's wedding last week, which involves six hundred invitations. She said price was not an issue, so I told her I would do her invitations for two dollars each instead of the usual $1.50 since it is a rush order. She agreed. With that twelve hundred dollars coming in, I turned down the next two weddings and also put in an order for that new sofa I've been salivating over. I wonder what she wants.

"Jessica," she begins, "my wedding planner told me that I only have a budget of six hundred dollars for addressing invitations. I have found someone who is willing to do it for that price."

I gasp. Shocked, I respectfully say, "Jenny, I turned down two other weddings so I could do your rush job. We had an agreement of twelve hundred dollars because it was a rush order."

"As I said, I found someone to do them for a one dollar each, so see if you can get those other weddings back," she says and quickly gets off the phone.

I'm livid. I call both of the other women whose weddings I turned down, and they now already have other calligraphers. The nerve of Jenny Kline! The audacity! I call Matthew to let off steam and hopefully gain a little sympathy.

He answers the phone with, "I am really busy. Is this an emergency?"

"I'm very upset about one of my calligraphy clients," I begin.

"This doesn't sound like an emergency, Jessica. We'll talk about it tonight."

We hang up. Typical. I'm emotionally distraught, and he's not available. The thought that he doesn't know I already ordered that twelve-hundred-dollar sofa doesn't help my agitated emotions either.

Walking into the kitchen, I think of what I'd really like to say to Jenny Klein, but instead, I instantly notice that the wood floors in my kitchen and keeping room are beautifully waxed, glistening in the sunlight. Also, there is a beautiful platter of some yummy seafood-type pasta on the counter.

I hear a familiar voice. **"Ready for the Third A, Appreciation, or are you too upset from both of those phone calls?" Genie asks.** He is floating in the air in the corner of the room and then gently descends to the ground. The whole scene helps lift my mood somewhat.

"The pasta looks delicious, and the floors look magnificent," I remark, trying to hide any negativity from the two phone calls. Any gift of housework is an especially appreciated present in my book. Housework is a duty that if I could be free from it for life, in exchange, I would consider giving up a baby toe. Well, not actually. I love wearing sandals too much.

"I'm better now with your 'happys,' " I say, which is actually true.

"Get out your Turquoise Journal, Young Jessica. We are going to start another list."

Another list? So soon? Why does he force me to make these laborious lists? Anyhow, I don't want to appreciate Matthew since he can't comfort me in my distress.

"The new list is entitled 'One Hundred Things I Appreciate about My Husband,' " Genie says.

"Genie, isn't this like the list 'Strengths, Gifts, and Qualities I Admire in My Husband'?" I complain, trying to beg off doing this exercise.

"The lists are very similar, but there is a distinction. Admiration focuses on who a man *is*. Appreciation is more about what a man *does*. But you are right; these two A's are closely related."

I barely see any difference. Such tedious, tiny distinctions.

"Appreciation opens up a whole new category where you can make deposits into your husband's tank. You admire that he is athletic, but you appreciate that he regularly gets tune-ups for your car. You admire his ability to understand investments, but you appreciate when he changes the light bulbs in the high ceilings. Men love admiration, but they also ache for appreciation for the little daily things they *do*."

I tend to think about the little daily things he *doesn't* do.

"Humans like to focus on what's wrong," he says, "not on what is done correctly. I want to teach you this skill of focusing on what's right, on appreciating the positive things your husband does. It is, again, a skill that few wives have."

Genie thinks his little Eight A's are a sacred teaching of a secret society of some kind.

"So number your paper, and let's get started," he says. "Today, you'll think of twenty-five things you appreciate about Matthew."

Such a drill sergeant.

Nevertheless, I look at my beautiful floors and begin to dig around in my brain to think of things I appreciate about Matthew. Uh, well … hmmmm. Not much coming to mind.

"Oh," I say, "he changes the filters regularly. That's one." I write that down. "He takes us on yearly vacations. That's two. He lets me buy a lot of bedding plants because I love flowers, three." I'm on a roll.

"We are going to take the yellow highlighter of our minds and focus on what Matthew does right," he says.

This still seems like a repetition of the Admiration lesson, but I decide to let it go. I write down that Matthew showers often and smells clean, he takes the cars through inspection, he handles our grouchy, widowed neighbor, he likes to grill out, and he lets me buy healthy, expensive organic food.

"Young Jessica, the purpose of this assignment, as you probably know, is to illustrate again how much your husband does for you and the family. It is extremely common for wives to focus on the negative and what their husbands *don't* do for them."

It's hard to get very excited about his little pond of virtue when I am confronted with the ocean of his inadequacy.

"Whenever you notice anything your husband does that you appreciate, I want you to write it down on this list," he says. "You will be amazed at the vast amount of life that Matthew gets right."

Yeah, I doubt it.

"The difficult part," he says, "is that you are to appreciate Matthew *out loud* as he does things. Not only do you tell him what you appreciate, but I want you to tell him *why* you appreciate it."

Oh, no, that vice is squeezing my head again. Tighter. Tighter.

"For example," he says, "when you are on vacation, say, 'Thank you for doing most of the driving, Matthew. That is thoughtful of you to let me sleep.' Or when you are together getting gas for the car, say, 'How nice it is to be married to a man where there's always money in the bank to fill up the gas tank.' "

"It's soooooo haaaarrrrd to say those things out loud," I complain. "Not only do I have to appreciate him, but I have to tell him? Why? Why do you make this so difficult?"

"I'm not trying to make things difficult," Genie laughs. "I'm trying to teach you relationship skills that will endear you to your husband, skills that will arouse affection in him for you. I understand that changing patterns is very difficult, but once you start appreciating Matthew, it will get easier. This third A of Appreciation is a very important component in filling your husband's tank."

And admire him? And accept him? I'm about to hit the wall. Or hit something.

"Wives take a lot for granted, Young Jessica."

He's got this one backward. Matthew takes *me* for granted.

"Appreciation reverses taking your husband for granted. Appreciation highlights what your husband does that you benefit from or enjoy."

I appreciate that Matthew takes care of getting the rental car when we're out of town. I appreciate that he picks up the cleaning on Saturdays.

"Finish this list of twenty-five things you appreciate, and begin to articulate those items out loud to Matthew," Genie says.

I turn around, and Genie is gone. Genies need to learn that in this century it's polite to say good-bye.

Since Matthew is bowling tonight, I won't be able to try out my new lesson of Appreciation. Maybe tomorrow.

The next night, Saturday, September 29

I still haven't said anything to Matthew about anything I appreciate. Hey, these things take time.

Matthew and I decide to grill out. Both boys have a friend spend the night, and they are making forts in the playroom. Also, I still haven't told Matthew that I ordered that sofa. I push that unpleasant thought out of my mind as I remember that tonight I am supposed to try to give Matthew the A of Appreciation. Oh, dear.

Matthew is on the patio, flipping the hamburgers. In between flips, he walks around the side of the house. When he comes inside with the hamburgers, he says,

"There's a wasp nest on the corner of the house. I'm going to use the wasp spray and get it down after dinner."

So after dinner, he gets the wasp spray and goes after that nest. He runs in the house, and we laugh as we watch the wasps circle in the air in confusion and disarray.

Hearing Matthew and myself laugh together feels good. Sometimes I do like this man. Then I realize I haven't heard Matthew laugh like that since—well, since Infuriating Indigo was in his office. I can't let my mind go there; I am to concentrate on this third A of Appreciation. *Focus, Jessica*, I tell myself. *Go ahead. Say something appreciative.*

There's a lump in my throat. I know this is an Appreciation moment. *Go on. Get it out*, I tell myself.

"Matthew, thank you for taking care of that wasp nest."

"You're welcome," he says.

Now add a sentence telling why, I scream to myself. *Spit something out.* "I appreciate how you take care of scary things like that, and you don't ask me to do it."

The soft expression on his face shows that he is pleased. "I'm happy to take care of the wasp nests."

Huh. That wasn't so hard. Look at me. I did it. I did it.

Here is another new habit I have to form, looking for the little things and the big things that Matthew does and then figuring out a way to make "an appreciation sentence" out of it.

Tonight Matthew looked at the gutters and said he was going to clean them sometime soon. I will have to think about what to say when he does that. I don't want to overdo this thing.

The memory of our last dinner date suddenly comes back to me. Matthew took me out to a nice restaurant, and I fussed about how cold my food was and how expensive it was for what we got. "This tiny appetizer costs seventeen dollars?" I had said. I don't think I ever even thanked him or told him how much I appreciated his taking me out; I only complained. My stomach sinks as I think of my failure. I know Matthew has faults, but I must admit that I'm not as sweet as Snow White. I guess I'll have to write down "complains; unappreciative" under List Five, "Things My Husband Might Find Difficult to Accept in Me."

Wife School is wiping me out. Genie said to lay bricks every day and soon the cathedral will be built. I'm not ready to bet my shoe collection on this program, but I admit, I do see progress tonight.

Matthew shows me the card he got for his mother. "I really think it's great," I say. "Your mother will love it." It's a nicer card than he usually gets. I start to ask him whether he wants me to e-mail him reminders or not, but he doesn't give me time.

"Indigo was out so she offered to pick it out for me," he said.

Indigo?! His assistant is picking out his birthday cards for his mother? I wonder what else she is offering to do for him? I'm about to lose it, but I gain control and remember that I am to deposit the Eight A's before I start asking for what I want. What I want right now is for Indigo to be vaporized and disappear, like Genie disappears. Here I am trying to deposit the A of Appreciation, and he tells me that his cozy assistant is running his personal errands? Pathetic!

The boys are being especially noisy upstairs, so Matthew offers to play a game of touch football with all of them outside. Great, because I need some time to recover from this curvy adversary who seems to be moving in on my terrain.

I run a hot bath to soak my achy body and emotions. I take it back that things are better in the marriage. I again doubt that these A's are going to work. Yeah, maybe there was a softening in Matthew tonight, but there are a zillion miles to go before I'm happy with this marriage.

CHAPTER 5
Fourth A: The Attention Lesson

Tuesday, October 2

Because of the downpour, I drive the boys to school so they won't have to wait on the bus outside in the rain. Now I'm an hour behind with my day.

When I told Matthew about the unpaid sofa last night, he was annoyed, as could be expected. I messed up on that one, I admit. Matthew said we would now have to cut back on Christmas. Cut back on Christmas?? I didn't tell him, but we're *not* cutting back on Christmas. I mean, *I'm* not cutting back on Christmas. Doesn't he know how important buying Christmas presents is to me? Why can't we cut back on something I don't care about? Again, Matthew doesn't understand me.

I open the pantry to get the broom and, *voilà*, the whole pantry is organized and tidy. I smell a genie.

"You might want to check all your kitchen cabinets and drawers too," I hear a familiar voice say.

Being an unorganized person at heart coupled with a dislike of housework, I am thrilled to open kitchen drawers and see my spatulas neatly lined up. A personal organizer would charge me megabucks for this. Nice.

"How have you been doing in *Wife School*, Young Jessica?"

I raise my eyebrows. "Alright, I guess," I say, not wanting to tell him the whole truth.

First, I tell him the wasp story. He is pleased.

"Matthew cleaned out the gutters, and I was going to give him the A of Appreciation," I say, "but I couldn't get it out because I was still annoyed that he had worked at home for four hours on his new ad campaign that day. However, I did try to deal with my irritation. Therefore, I got out my Turquoise Journal, read my gratefulness lists, and reviewed the notes on Acceptance, Admiration, and Appreciation. Genie, reading those lists turned me around! Not only did I drop my unmet expectations and accept that Matthew was working from home, I praised him for being a good provider and thanked him for letting me stay home with the kids. Later, I even squeaked out a small 'thank you' for the gutter work."

"Bravo, Young Jessica!" Genie exclaims. "Great progress in *Wife School*!"

Should I tell him I complained to Matthew on Sunday about his again doing his office work at home? Nah, I'll keep that to myself. I can't be perfect overnight.

"Let's begin the fourth A, Attention," he says.

Being in *Wife School* is like being on a treadmill where the incline and the speed continue to increase.

"Making the deposit of Attention is something most wives are very good at before they get married," Genie says. "Before marriage, wives notice when their fiancée gets a haircut; they notice if he buys a new pair of running shoes; they see that his car is dirty, and they run it through the carwash. When the woman's fiancée is talking before marriage, the soon-to-be wife listens with rapt attention as if this man was the president of the universe."

I remember how Matthew told me about his advertising campaigns when we were engaged. I thought Matthew should win Marketer of the Year. Now I can barely listen without yawning.

"Something happens after marriage," Genie said, "and then it quantum quadruples when kids are born. The wife simply becomes interested in other things, mainly the children."

The children are my life.

"What about the husband becoming interested in other things?" I ask. "Matthew used to be more interested in my life when we were dating." This sock fits both feet equally well.

"It's true that Matthew doesn't give you the same attention, but we are working on the only person we can change, and that's you, Young Jessica."

I exhale deeply. I know he's right.

"It's time to give Matthew back that attention he craves. I want you to start listening like you used to and become interested again in the details of his life."

I need a shot of B12. Or maybe a Caffè Mocha from Starbucks.

"There are thousands of ways to demonstrate Attention, Young Jessica. One obvious way is to be interested in the nuances and details of Matthew's work. Other areas to be interested in are his hobbies, his food preferences, his leisure preferences, his thoughts, his opinions, his comforts, his feelings. The list is virtually endless."

What a bummer. Matthew semi-ignores me, and I'm to pay more attention to him. Last night, I was trying to tell Matthew about the pressure I was feeling as the PTA vice president. He starts giving me reasons why I shouldn't feel pressure since I volunteered for the job. That's what I needed? This is how I'm treated, and this genie still wants me to keep filling this bozo's tank?

Genie continues. "Let's talk about a man's job. For example, if he is a dentist, the husband comes home and talks about his root canals. A wife is interested if the office is hiring a new sexy hygienist or if the office is making more money, but she doesn't want to hear about his routine root canals. Most wives listen a little and then inject, 'I'm glad you figured that out. Can you go walk the dog?' "

I laugh. Nevertheless, I try to end Matthew's work stories early too. I feel for the poor woman whose dentist husband talks about bridges and fillings.

"Listening to your husband is like playing ping-pong," he says. "For example, Matthew hits the ball to you with something like, 'I had a bad dream last night.' Now it's your turn to not play or to return serve. If you don't play, you say, 'I don't like bad dreams either' and then the conversation is over. If you decide to return serve, you say, 'Tell me about it.' Giving attention to your husband means trying to hit the ping-pong ball back to him to get him more engaged."

Matthew told me last night that there were insects on the knockout roses, a subject I'm not interested in. I said, "Oh, that's too bad." Not a very good service return.

"Instead," Genie continues, "the wise wife who is depositing the Eight A's will say, 'Now tell me what you did' and 'What was it like?' and 'What did you do then?' She will pull him out, listening attentively and looking for opportunities to admire and appreciate."

This genie keeps adding bricks to my backpack.

"If the phone rings while you're listening to Matthew, preferably ignore the call. But if you don't, at least tell the caller you're talking to your husband and you'll call them back. If it's a call you must take, say to your husband, 'Oh, Honey, put a comma in that story, I'll be right back,' and then come right back and get him to pick up the story. For example, say, 'Okay, the patient started gagging, and then what?' Don't leave him hanging with his stories. Always let a husband finish his story. It's an important way for wives to pay attention to a husband."

Recently, Matthew told me he was frustrated the TV stations weren't running the right ads that he had placed. I remember saying, "Go on, I'm listening. I'm just typing this recipe out to send to my sister at the same time." Uh-oh.

Genie continues, "When Matthew tells his jokes or stories in a group and you've heard them a hundred times, sit and listen and laugh like it's the first time. You show the crowd how much you admire your husband by this attention. Many wives, upon hearing the beginning of a story that they themselves could tell while they are sleeping, will say, 'I've heard this before. I'll refill the chip bowl. Can I get anyone a refill on their drink?' That kind of remark will suck all the air right out of a man's tank."

It's as though my life story has been on YouTube and this Genie has watched the videos.

"Wives stop doing the little nice things they did before they got married," he says. "Return to those little favors. Fix his eggs exactly how he likes them. Get the oil changed in his car. Find ways to make him feel like a king. Serve him before the children. Ask his opinion. *He* wants to be the center of your life, not the kids, not your weight, not your decorating, not your sisters, not your social calendar, not your home business."

I can put him before some of that but not before the kids and *not* before my weight.

"Preparing food the way a husband likes has always been a way that women pay attention to men," he says. "Plopping some greasy fast-food fried chicken down on the table isn't the same as preparing one of his favorite home-cooked, healthy dinners."

I know Matthew doesn't like lima beans. I fix them anyway.

"All humans crave someone who is interested in their details," he says. "Humans want someone to know—and care—that they stubbed their toe, that their lunch in the cafeteria today was crummy, that they didn't sleep well, that they've always wanted a sailboat, that they love Harrison Ford, that they like red licorice, that they hate wearing neckties with big designs. Wives have a great advantage to fill their husbands' tanks with the A of Attention. It feels *phenomenal* to be intensely listened to and noticed."

When Matthew and I were reading the Sunday paper together after church, I asked him what section he wanted first. He said, "The Sports section, like every Sunday." Maybe he feels like I don't pay enough attention to him. I certainly know every jot and tittle about the children. Josh told me last night at dinner, "Mom, you know just how much pepper I like on my pasta, not too much and not too little." I remember thinking what a conscientious mother I am. Uh ... not so sure about the wife department, though.

Genie continues. "Especially after children, many wives take their husbands for granted. Instead of being on the very heartbeat of what's important to the husband, the wife is more and more inattentive to him. A wise woman will be as careful with her words and actions toward her husband as she was before marriage. She will strive to look nice when he is around, as carelessness in her appearance is a form of inattentiveness."

Does that mean I have to give up those comfy, slouchy pajama pants I wear around the house on Saturdays?

"A wife should save her best energy for her husband," he says. "She should plan pleasures and delights for him. This is the A of Attention at its best."

This assignment is going to earn an F, I'm afraid. When Matthew comes home, I feel like he should serve me or give me a break. Homemaking and kids are exhausting!

"Listen carefully, Young Jessica. Continually prove, by showing attention to your husband, that he is the most important person in the world to you. Make him feel like no one in the world comes close to caring and knowing everything about him as you do."

Indigo recently bought Matthew a shirt for his birthday, which was supposedly from the entire creative staff. The odd thing was she got the size right. (Clothing is waayyy too personal of a gift, but when I complained to Matthew, he disagreed because, even though she picked it out, it was from several coworkers.) Well, anyhow, I can't seem to remember if Matthew's neck size is seventeen or seventeen and a half. I shudder when I think of that supermodel.

"Stop looking at what you're not getting from Matthew," he says, "and focus on being a bright and happy song in Matthew's life. Run him a bath, and bring him something yummy to drink."

Matthew would fall over if I ran him a bath and brought him something yummy to drink. He'd think I had already had something to drink.

"Got to run. They're having a sale in Burma on turbans," and he's gone.

Acceptance. Admiration. Appreciation. And now Attention. Isn't that enough? And there are four more A's? Can I *do* this?

I want Baskin-Robbins!

The next morning, Wednesday, October 3

Matthew's at work, and the boys have left for school. I feel discouraged this morning. The truth is, I don't see much improvement in Matthew. Looking at the mess in the kitchen doesn't help my mood either.

I have tried to accept, admire, appreciate, and give attention to Matthew. But last night, Matthew was watching Sports Center, ignoring us and even telling the boys to be quiet when they wanted his attention. Seriously, I'm supposed to do all this giving while he throws us his crumbs? I'm not giving up *Wife School* yet, but admittedly, I'm severely discouraged.

My phone rings. It is Emily, a friend who, like me, is also an officer for the PTA at the kids' school.

"Camille, the president, is moving to Nevada next week because her husband got abruptly transferred," says Emily. "Since you are now the vice president, you will be moved up to president."

I'm stunned and annoyed. Because the VP job was supposedly easy, I agreed to take it. I certainly had no intentions of ever being the president, a job that requires hours of work and organization, not counting the huge responsibility and corresponding anxiety. My wedding invitation business stresses me out already. I also have some high-maintenance boys who are acting up at school and, worst of all, a husband who is still in preschool as far as being a satisfying husband.

Emily is having a baby around Thanksgiving, so she is ruled out. The other officer, Sherry, is a complete nitwit. I know she can't handle the job. Sherry can barely get to our officer meetings without being forty-five minutes late because she has to let her nail polish dry. I reluctantly agree to take the position. I feel cornered and resentful.

Walking into the kitchen, I smell soy sauce and ginger. Genie is sitting on the counter in my cleaned-up kitchen with some delicious-looking Oriental Chicken. Even the gift of a beautiful dinner and a clean kitchen doesn't cheer me up. I am upset over this PTA presidency, and I'm upset with Matthew.

"I heard your conversation about the PTA, Young Jessica," Genie says. "It is not a good time for you to take on more responsibility, but I do understand how you felt pressured. However, I can help you with a little abracadabra concerning your PTA responsibilities, so try not to worry about that. Let's talk about how things are going with Matthew."

Today I am too discouraged to hide it from Genie. I quickly move from the PTA presidency to what is really bothering me. "It seems to me that all you say is, 'Give, give, give.' I try to accept Matthew, but he criticizes my driving; I try to admire him, but he goes to sleep while I'm talking; I bring him coffee with just the right sugar and cream, but he forgets to call me to tell me he is running late at work. I am not sure that I am the right candidate for *Wife School*. I don't think these lessons are working for me. "

I am seriously thinking of telling Genie to go back to Babylon.

"And I'm tired of fighting the resentment I have for Matthew. When was the last time he admired or appreciated me? Why doesn't he work on our marriage and our family like he works on his job? The kids and I have needs, and he repeatedly fails us."

So there. Stick *that* in your turban.

"I was waiting for you to have this meltdown moment," says Genie. "You're right on time too. This is often when the wife considers abandoning *Wife School* after starting the Eight A's program. She has been dutifully working the program, and the husband is not responding the way she expects him to. So she thinks the program doesn't work."

Duh. Isn't that just what I said, Mr. Embroidered Vest?

"You humans take a long time to change," he says.

"I only have one lifetime, Genie," I say.

He ignores my comment. "You are at the fork in the road," he says. "The ground in Matthew's heart is being plowed and softened. The seed has been planted in Matthew's heart that you are a different wife. If you were a farmer and you planted in May, would you start yelling at the plants in June for still only being tiny, green shoots?"

"Of course not," I say. I'm impatient and these stories of his take a long time.

"As you know," he says, "it takes until fall before the plants are ready for harvest. Yet you are mad that Matthew is not ready for the harvest, and it's only June. Like I said, it takes humans time to grow and change. Give Matthew some room and time. Persevere. Keep watering, fertilizing, and nurturing the work of the Eight A's. The program is working, just not as fast as you'd hoped."

That's an understatement, Barefoot Boy.

"Sometimes these principles take months and even years before the husband is ready to cooperate. But isn't your marriage and your family worth your Olympian effort? What else in the entire universe compares to how you feel about your marriage and your family?"

He's got a point. And a very good point. What else do I care about on Earth that even remotely comes close to how much I care about my marriage and my kids? My family trumps everything else twenty-fold. True, it is a huge effort on my part to continue this Eight A's program. But it's worth it. It's definitely worth it.

I take a deep breath. I can feel strength returning to my core. I am ready to accept responsibility for the marriage issues and to stop blaming Matthew. I am ready to be a wise woman and build this house. Sure, I will fail in some of my efforts, but I know I can try again because, after all, like Genie said, there is nothing else in life that comes close to how much I care about my marriage and family. Nothing. Absolutely nothing. This goal of swimming the English Channel is worth all my efforts.

"I don't think we're ready for the next A yet, Young Jessica. I will give you a few days to process all this information, and then I'll be back with the next A."

Realizing that my marriage and family is my top interest and concern in life has given me renewed determination. Just because the progress is slow, I am not to be discouraged. I am now ready to persevere in making my Eight A deposits into Matthew's tank, *even in the face of his not reciprocating*. I am sowing seed. And whatsoever I sow, I know I will eventually reap. I can physically feel my motivation coming back.

"There's a fundraiser coming up at the school," Genie says. "Don't stress over that; I've got it all under control. Keep prioritizing your marriage." And he's gone.

What fundraiser? I had temporarily forgotten all about my new PTA presidency. My heart begins to sink at the thought. In what way is Genie going to help with my presidency?

Oh, how do I get myself into these messes??

CHAPTER 6
Fifth A: The Activities Lesson

Friday, October 5

The troops have departed to their respective assignments of school and work, and I am here alone with hours of work that I need to do for the fundraiser for the PTA. The last president had virtually done no work at all, knowing that she was going to be transferred. How low and irresponsible! Now I get to take the boxes of brochures and multiple handouts (that have to be assembled into packets for each student) and staple and stuff them into these large envelopes. I asked six other women to help, but all of them are busy. Seriously, how does this happen to me?

I head to the patio to enjoy the October morning as I staple and stuff. The gentle warmth of the sunshine feels a little soothing to my anxious soul, but not much. The thought of the upcoming deadlines for my wedding calligraphy business along with the tension I feel over this huge PTA responsibility keeps me from truly taking in the full beauty of the morning.

Even though I had a meltdown with Genie two days ago over my impatience with Matthew's nonreciprocation of the Eight A's, I have seen glimpses of their effects this week, and that thought perks me up a little. Matthew asked if I wanted to go to the Pink Palace Crafts Fair being held this weekend. Also, he patted me on the back in a nonsexual display of affection while I was cooking dinner last night. I appreciated those attempts to connect and wrote them down in my Turquoise Journal.

I look up from my stapling and stuffing and see a dark-skinned person around the side of the house. I get up to see what Mr. Bronze is up to. Around the corner of the house are beautiful yellow and purple pansies, planted in perfect precision.

"Your favorite fall flowers, Young Jessica," Genie says with a smile.

"They certainly are," I admit as we walk back to the patio. On the patio table are all my PTA packets, completely assembled. He wasn't kidding when he said he was going to help. That gift was equal to at least five hours of my time.

"We are now ready for the Fifth A, Activities," he says. "Please get your Turquoise Journal so we may begin."

I hurry to retrieve my Turquoise Journal, and Genie jumps right in.

"During courtship, it is common for women and men to participate in many recreational and enjoyable activities. They go camping, they root for their favorite team, or they attend lectures they both appreciate."

This I understand. Matthew and I had a blast when we were dating. We went to parks, attended plays and movies, and visited restaurants with different world cuisines.

"As you know," he says, "life settles in with its responsibilities, and somehow the fun and play go out of the marriage."

Our fun and play walked out of the marriage when the kids walked in.

"The couple become coworkers, not companions," he says. "There is housework, yard work, children, church, volunteer responsibilities, extended family, and other priorities that claim the couple's time and energy."

Exactly, I say to myself, *because those things need to get done.*

"Women will tell me," he says, "that marriage is at the top of their priority list. But when I ask them what they are planning and doing to keep the fun and play in the marriage, they are speechless."

Women are supposed to plan the fun and the play? Why not men? Why does this genie always pick on women?

"One reason," I blurt out, "is that Matthew and I are no longer interested in the same things. Genie, I don't think Matthew and I are compatible anymore."

"Nonsense," he quickly retorts. "There are many activities you can find that you both enjoy. It takes work, however, to discover them and then to plan corresponding activities. Couples still need to date after they are married."

Date after we are married? Is there time for that? Is there energy? Money?

"Many ideas come to mind," he says. "Start a dinner club with friends, plan a trip, or go to a seminar on investing. Plan a landscaping design together for your home. Admittedly, it takes a lot of thinking and brainstorming to find activities that you both enjoy."

Tell me something I don't know.

"Some couples like active or sporting activities," he says. "Some couples like plays, museums, or art shows. Some couples like to shop for antiques or go to cooking school together. There is no right or wrong activity. The key is to find activities that you mutually enjoy together."

I like books; he likes horseshoes. I like Zumba; he likes basketball.

"If the husband likes golf and the woman doesn't, let him golf with his buddies," he says. "If the woman likes shopping and the husband doesn't, don't beg the man to go."

I love shopping. Matthew says he would just as soon go to the dentist as go shopping.

"You have to keep your antennae up so you can discover mutually satisfying activities," he says. "Remember, too, that both of you change as you age. So your interests change. The marriage is a living organism. What works when the couple is in their thirties often no longer works when they are in their fifties. Even though you both might have liked camping years ago, maybe now camping taxes you."

Bugs. Dirt. Heat.

"It's common for couples to say, 'We've grown apart.' Sure people change, but with effort, couples can find new activities or resurrect old ones."

This guy doesn't let anyone off the hook.

"Open your Turquoise Journal," he says. "We will make a new list. It will be List Seven, 'Activities My Husband and I Might Enjoy Together.' List ten possible activities."

My brain is dead. I try to get the neurons to fly, but they refuse. This is harder than it should be.

"Oh! I thought of something!" I say. "We both enjoy the boys' sporting activities."

"Good. Write that down. Keep thinking."

"We enjoy ... uh ... playing cards sometimes, but not too often. We enjoy making the yard pretty together, but really, that job is too hot for me. Well, let's see, uh ... also, we enjoy ... uh ... well ... oh ... we enjoy taking our boys hiking!" I say as my mind starts to activate.

"Good, good. Continue," Genie prods.

"We like movies ..."

"Write down all of that," Genie says. "If you keep your antennae up for other ideas to add to that list, you will find them. There are multiple other activities that you both enjoy doing together. When you think of them, reach for your Turquoise Journal."

I think of the things that Matthew is interested in: bowling, rugby, cars, and guns. This list that Genie is proposing is a *mutual* list, so none of that junk gets on the list. Thankfully.

"I guess I could go to some University of Memphis football games," I say. "I like the cheerleaders and the marching band."

"Going to a football game is an occasional gift you could give to Matthew," he says. "But unless you truly enjoy football, it should not be on the list. *Mutual* is the key word."

"I just thought of something!" I almost yell. "Matthew likes concerts, and so do I!"

You'd think I had won maid service for a year.

"Booyah!" Genie says. He acts like I just figured out long division and he's the proud schoolteacher.

I will get online this afternoon and see what concerts are coming to town. I feel a large sense of relief, knowing that maybe there are more mutual interests than I realized.

"You need to take those PTA packets to school, and I need to pick up a new pair of satin pants my tailor has made for me." And Genie vanishes.

I drive to the school to deliver the PTA packets. Right before I pull into the parking lot, I notice a guy driving carpool wearing a cowboy hat. I remember that Matthew and I both like country dancing. We used to two-step when we dated. Quick-quick, slow-slow. Quick-quick, slow-slow. Another possible item to add to the list!

Fun and Play, looks like you guys are back!

I call Matthew to tell him about my new excitement over some ideas for activities together. As he picks up the phone, I hear him laughing, and I also hear a woman laughing. I recognize Infiltrator Indigo's voice. My heart sinks.

"Hello, Jessica?" Matthew says.

Now I think maybe our new activity together will be going to the divorce attorney. I'm so mad. I make up some lame excuse why I called and hang up the phone. Ugh! I'm discouraged again!

CHAPTER 7
Sixth A: The Approval Lesson

Friday, October 19

Rain is in the forecast, and that bums me out because tonight we're supposed to go to the Mid-South Haunted Maze at the Agricenter. Also, today's "to-do" list includes cleaning up the tipped-over garbage cans in the garage. We accidentally left the garage door open and some neighborhood raccoons made a colossal mess. And on top of that, I haven't seen Genie for two weeks. Is it possible he gave up on me and went back to Mesopotamia?

I've been in a tailspin with my calligraphy home business for the last two weeks. Every waking free second, I've been at the kitchen table, knocking out those invitations. I've addressed over eleven hundred invitations in two weeks. As busy as I've been, I've still daily read my Turquoise Journal and tried to give Matthew the five A's that I've been taught so far: Acceptance, Admiration, Appreciation, Attention, and Activities. Matthew has moved toward me a little but not nearly enough to make me satisfied with this marriage.

I grab some rubber gloves and a broom and head for the garage. I am definitely startled when I walk into it. Not only is the raccoon mess cleaned up, the lawn equipment is organized and the tools are stacked neatly on the shelves. Also the walls have been power washed as has the cement floor.

And there is Genie. "I need a towel," he says. "I got my turban wet while I was cleaning."

So I'm not abandoned after all. Hip hip hooray.

"Young Jessica, it's time for *Wife School*. Get your Turquoise Journal."

I follow him indoors. We sit at the kitchen table to begin. Proudly, I tell Genie about buying tickets for two different upcoming concerts for Matthew and me. *Wife School* points for me in the Activities category!

"Today we will discuss Approval, the Sixth A that fills up a man's emotional tank," Genie says.

Early this morning, I exercised to an Aerobic Boot Camp DVD. This session with Genie is my second boot camp of the day.

"What I am going to tell you today will dissolve the tension that Matthew has toward you and will subsequently move him toward you with the intimacy you want."

Now we're talking. I love the word *intimacy*. I want Matthew to listen carefully to me, and I want him to share his innermost thoughts with me.

"There is an overall approval rating spouses give each other in a marriage that is composed of the small, separate approval ratings added together," he says.

"This morning I fixed Matthew scrambled eggs and toast," I say. "Arriving at the breakfast table he said, 'I'm not in the mood for scrambled eggs.' I'm supposed to read his mind? I felt annoyed and unappreciated. He didn't approve of my breakfast, and therefore, it translated to his not approving of me as a wife."

I decided not to tell Genie what I *wanted* to say to Matthew, which was, "Oh, sorry, Honey. Maybe you'd rather have your eggs over easy *on your head*."

"That is a perfect example," Genie says, "of how spouses don't give each other approval in the small but important areas of life. If instead Matthew had said, 'Jessica, you are sweet to fix my breakfast every morning, and I really appreciate it. But this morning, my stomach is a little upset, and I don't think I can eat scrambled eggs. I hope it doesn't hurt your feelings if I only eat the toast.' "

What husband handles his wife like that, like a fragile Chinese teacup? Admittedly, it would be glorious.

"Later in *Wife School*," he says, "we will discuss how to explain things to your husband, such as when your husband hurts your feelings or you feel unappreciated, but for now in this initial stage, please overlook and forgive him for his remark."

Forgiving another's offenses is probably the hardest task that we humans are called to do.

"Let's begin by looking at examples of the different ways Matthew could—or could not—communicate approval to you. Spouses read between the lines to hear if the other spouse is communicating approval. I will give you several sets of sentences. Let's see what approval is—or is not—being communicated. Ready?"

Do I need to raise my hand in *Wife School* when I have the answer?

"If Matthew says, 'Weekends are boring to me,' what do you think?"

"I think he doesn't want to be with the boys and me," I say.

"Right. He is unknowingly communicating a lack of approval in that you are enjoyable to be with," he says. "What about this sentence: 'Weekends are a great refuge to escape the stress of the office'?"

"I would think that he enjoys being home and enjoys me," I say.

"Good. That sentence communicates a subtle approval of your ability to provide a home life that Matthew enjoys. Instead of saying he was not in the mood for eggs this morning, what if Matthew said after you prepared a home-cooked meal, 'The food in this restaurant, Jessica, is consistently delicious'?"

"I would love that compliment," I say, "because food preparation is important to me. I would feel like Matthew was satisfied with my cooking, which is a large part of my homemaking skills."

"Exactly," he says. "We communicate approval to our spouses in the countless small ways we interact. One more example: If before lovemaking, Matthew said, 'Have you been keeping up with your workouts?' would you feel his approval?"

I don't laugh. "I'm seriously insecure about my few extra pounds so that would cut deep."

And BTW, that lovemaking would be cut off for that night.

"And if before lovemaking, Matthew instead said—"

"Okay, okay, enough, enough. I get it," I say. Genie just doesn't understand that we Southern women get easily embarrassed with these explicit scenarios.

"Let's turn things around," he says. "How do you think Matthew feels when you say, 'Did you see the new mansion the McKensies bought?' "

I'm a little startled. I say things like that all the time.

"Uh, well, uh, would he feel I am not approving of his ability to provide?"

"He might," Genie says. "What about this: 'Joe takes his boys on father-son outings every month.' "

He's picking sentences I've actually said before. "Not funny, Genie," I say.

"I'm trying to illustrate how subtle this A of approval can be," he says. "Women have no idea they are sending messages to their husbands that he doesn't measure up, that he's not enough."

It's not my fault that men's egos are as fragile as eggs. Husbands should buck up and take it like a man should.

"What would be communicated to a husband if after leaving a Halloween party, the wife said to him, 'Do you know how much fun it is to go places with you? You are delightful company. I love the way you engage other people and ask their opinions'?"

I have never said things like that to Matthew, although Matthew is fun at a party. Okay, okay. So approval is not one of my fortes. I never said I was perfect.

"Giving approval in a marriage is essential because spouses subconsciously say to themselves, 'My spouse knows the real me. If my spouse thinks I'm a great (or a lousy) parent, it must be true.' Do you see why the approval of a spouse is life changing? Spouses have enormous power over each other's self-concept."

My self-concept is that I'm a crummy wife and don't know what to cook for breakfast.

"If your spouse thinks you're a bad driver," he says, "you will begin to believe his opinion. But think about the opposite: What if your spouse thinks you're great at handling the family's finances? What if your spouse thinks you are clever and delightful to be around? Galaxy –sized healing and affirmation can take place in spouses when genuine approval is given. Again, spouses think, *If the person who knows the real me thinks I'm awesome (or pathetic), I must be.* Therefore, giving—or not giving—each other approval in a marriage either heals or destroys."

Matthew knows the real me, and I don't feel his approval. And it hurts.

"I want to explain some principles about men to you that most women don't understand," he continues. "To begin with, you need to know that a man's worst feeling in the world is to feel inadequate about his abilities. This is different from a woman's worst feelings, which always involve being unwanted or unloved in relationships. As you know, a woman likes to share her problems with her husband because she is longing for connection and intimacy. But the husband often hears her problems as evidence that he is not doing an adequate job in providing for and protecting her."

"I didn't follow that, Genie."

"Let me try again to explain as you must comprehend this marriage destroyer. Women want to share their problems with their mates. It is how women feel close to others; they share their struggles. But men often hear these problems and complaints as citations against their abilities to make their wives happy. They tell themselves subconsciously, *If I were a good husband, she would be happy.*"

"That is so silly for the husband to think that. All the wife wants is to be close and share her thoughts and to hear his thoughts."

"Exactly," Genie says. "But men don't feel close by sharing thoughts. Men feel close by having sex and doing activities together. Men see women's constant need to share their problems as women being discontent. They feel that if they, the men, were 'enough,' a woman would be happy."

Oh, brother. The very thing a woman does to feel close pushes the husband away.

"Every time she complains," Genie says, "that it's hot in the house, her car is old, she is tired, or that she is sick of the same old Saturday night routine, he feels like he is not doing a good job in providing for and protecting her. His pain at feeling inadequate as a husband is tremendously upsetting to him."

"Come on, Genie. Surely not." I am having trouble believing men are this ridiculous. "I know it's hard for women to believe, but it's true," he says. "A man measures how well he is doing in the marriage by how happy and content his wife is. If she is not happy, especially with his performance—for example, if she's not satisfied with his lovemaking, social skills, income, fathering, etc.—he then feels like a failure. He measures his success as a husband by her approval of him."

This is absurd. Men are absurd.

"Most women have very complex natures and want to improve everything. Wanting improvement is truly a beautiful thing about women. However, guess how the husband hears her constant suggestions to improve things?"

"That he's a failure and not doing a good job as a husband?" I ask, incredulously.

"Yes, he feels inadequate. Can you imagine how a man feels if the wife is constantly talking about not liking the paint color of the living room or is upset over the neighborhood or doesn't like the way the husband's family celebrates holidays? He hears that he is inadequate in providing for and protecting her or else she would be happy. This is extremely painful for him."

This is truly insane that men feel that way. The wife is only trying to make life nicer for her family.

"Physical pain is not as upsetting to a man as emotional pain."

Heavens, this can't be true.

"And, Young Jessica, I have not told you all of it. When a man feels inadequate with his wife, he does the thing she hates the most: he pulls back and gives her even less relationship. This, of course, heightens her insecurities even more, and now she wants to talk about his failure to have more relationship. This boulder begins to roll downhill."

I can see it. Matthew and I do this dance.

"What is a woman to do?" I ask, stunned. "I mean, I want to share my struggles and thoughts with my husband, and that means sharing my problems. My problems cause me anxiety and I want him to enter into them with me and listen to me. I want us to share our problems and feel close."

"That is how *you* feel close, Young Jessica. Matthew feels close, as I've said, by having sex and sharing activities with you. You feel exactly like most women," he says, "and this tango between spouses is responsible for much of the eventual emotional separateness that describes many marriages."

"I'm feeling a little confused, Genie. I can't share my problems with Matthew or he'll feel inadequate as a man?" That's pitiful.

"That's not exactly what I'm saying. I'm saying that you must realize through what grid Matthew hears you and to make accommodations in your communication with him. What I want you to see and hear, as if it's in all caps and italic, is that Matthew will feel inadequate as a husband if hears or thinks that you are not happy in areas that relate to his provision. Therefore, before you complain, whine, or fuss, or as you would say, 'share your problems,' think about how to tell him your problems so that he doesn't hear you saying that he is inadequate in providing for you or protecting you. Your contentment and approval communicate that he's doing a good job as a husband. When you talk about not having enough money for a new sofa, he feels inadequate. When you tell him he doesn't spend enough time with the boys, he feels like a failure. When you criticize him for leaving his clothes out, he feels like he's not pleasing you. Whatever you say to him, realize that if there is no approval in it for him, he will feel that he is not good enough as a husband. And this negative feeling keeps him from being able to feel close to you. *A man needs a woman from whom he feels approval.*"

I stop and think of the thousands of little things I fuss about to Matthew that communicate I am displeased with him: he's not home enough, I'm unhappy with our income, I don't like the amount of time he talks to me, I don't like some of his friends, I don't like what he says to the kids, I don't like what he wears, I want us to be more involved at church, I want more help with the household chores, I want ... Oh dear, oh dear.

"A spirit of contentment is beautiful in a woman, Young Jessica. Contentment says 'I am happy with the portion I have.' It says to a husband, 'You are enough, and I am satisfied.' Most women do not understand this interaction between men and women and therefore unknowingly complain, whine, and suggest endless ideas to 'improve' their lives together. Wives have no idea what impact they are having on their husbands with this behavior. Their constant anxiety and list of 'ways to improve life' tell the husband he is not doing a good job, and he hears it as 'you're not enough for me.' "

Maybe this explains why Matthew likes to hide behind that remote and ESPN.

"The good news is," Genie says, "if a woman understands that a man takes any criticism or correction and uses it to feel inadequate, she has a huge advantage in being able to watch her words so she can reduce his feelings of inadequacy. When a woman understands that a man's sense of inadequacy is a normal male characteristic, she can develop compassion for him and guard her words that create this terrible feeling in him. This is similar to when a man understands the hormone escalation in a woman before her period; to be forewarned is to be forearmed."

I laugh but then sadden as I remember when Matthew missed the exit on the expressway on Saturday afternoon. I said, "Want me to start doing the driving?" And on Sunday, he asked me if his friend from college, Nate, could come for a visit, and I said, "I'm embarrassed for him to see our junky furniture. Can't you find some more money to give me to fix things up so I won't be embarrassed to have company?" What a prize I am.

"As I've said several times before, most husbands are content in the marriage if they get adequate sex and don't have to deal with too much emotional turmoil," Genie reminds me. "But wives are another story. You name it, they want it."

Genie is being unfair again. For example, I don't want ... well, I don't care about ... uh ... hmpf. I know there's got to be something that doesn't matter to me.

"Husbands can't perform up to their wives' galaxy-sized expectations. Wives do not intentionally mean to communicate a lack of approval to their husband, but nevertheless, frequently the husband feels like the wife is never satisfied."

I've heard those exact words from Matthew's lips.

"The principle of giving husbands approval," he says, "is so powerful that this one A alone will transform a marriage. Wives can't be reminded too often that having unmet expectations zap the affection out of a marriage whereas being content and giving approval fill the husband's tank and enable him to feel affection for you."

It's time for some down-home honesty. "Genie, how in the world does a woman 'give approval' and 'become content' when the man's weaknesses repeatedly slap her in the face? I think it sounds real nice to say 'give up your expectations,' but in real life, how does a woman do that when her emotions are negative toward this man who disappoints her?"

"Give me a concrete example, Young Jessica."

Here goes. I'm all-in now. The mask is coming completely off.

"I don't like how much time and energy Matthew bowls instead of funneling that into the family. I don't like the lack of affection and intimacy I get from Matthew. I don't like that he hired a sex kitten for an assistant. And that's only scratching the surface." I feel a tsunami coming on.

But Genie is not fazed. I thought he would let out a deep sigh or say I'm too hard of a case. His eyes have more gentleness now than ever.

"I completely understand," he says. "You are no different from the millions of other wives in the universe. Your nature is to fix, revise, and reform. So here's your solution, and it's not a solution for the weak or the immature: Yes, you want to eventually ask Matthew for all of those things, but you have to also put all of them on the shelf and believe that the Creator is working to help you at the same time. I am not asking you to be blind to Matthew's negative tendencies, only have patience and compassion. He cannot change everything overnight. Please remember that the best environment for others to change is one of acceptance and approval. This is extremely difficult for you humans to grasp. Yes, hold in one hand the changes you would like to see, but in the other hand, give the other person ample time, space, and grace while they learn. No one learns well with a twelve-inch wooden ruler repeatedly spanking his hand. We will discuss what to do when there is much you want to change about your husband (see Chapter 23, "When There Are Many Things Your Husband Needs to Change"). However, for now, try to put his weaknesses on a shelf, believe the Creator is working, and deposit the Eight A's. Your lack of approval keeps Matthew from moving toward you. Being critical and constantly pointing out his mistakes and discussing how disappointed you are with him pushes his inadequacy button, and his subsequent shame makes him pull away from you, not move toward you."

This is all true. I hate to admit it, but I'm still chronically dissatisfied with Matthew. And I can see how I am pushing him away from me.

Genie's teachings are against my natural tendencies, though. It's sort of like my eating; I prefer a diet of chocolate cake and cheesecake, but it doesn't get me what I want. I'd like to let my words tumble out exactly as I feel them, uncensored, but as I've discovered, this sends Matthew's inadequacy radar into orbit. I am doing the very thing I don't want: pushing him away.

"Becoming a contented person is about accepting your lot from the Creator," Genie says. "You are fighting the Creator and the portion He gave you."

That sentence opens up another can of worms. Ugly, deformed, mean worms. Is he saying I need to deal with being a discontented person? Is that true? That is too unpleasant for me to deal with right now. I change the subject.

"I wish we'd hurry up with these A's," I say, "and get to how Matthew is supposed to meet *my* needs so I can experience the closeness that I crave."

By the expression on his face, I don't think Genie liked that comment too much. I guess he heard my remark as complaining. After all, he is a male and likes approval too. Maybe it made him feel inadequate. Is it possible that genies feel inadequate?

"And that concludes today's lesson on Approval," Genie says. "I am the current world champion of Magic Carpet Racing, and I don't want to be late for this year's race." And then he's gone.

Men do like to leave when women complain, no doubt about it.

I want to blame Matthew for our problems, and Genie keeps trying to force me to look at myself, at how *I'm* thinking, at what *I'm* doing. I'm confused and agitated.

Mrs. Serona's name appears on my iPhone. She is one of my calligraphy clients, the grandmother of the bride. What could she want?

"Jessica, I was checking on my invitations. I thought you were going to be through on the eighteenth."

I get my date book out and say, "Yes, they will be ready on November 18, Mrs. Serona." I am very careful to write down correct due dates.

"Oh, no, not November 18!" she squeals. "It was *October* 18. Oh, my! Oh, my! You haven't started?? What are we going to do?" She begins a true meltdown. I don't want to argue with this aged lady, but she did say *November* 18.

The wedding is only 150 invitations, so I can do that in around eight hours. I promise her I will have them finished in forty-eight hours. I move into overdrive and begin her invitations.

Matthew calls to tell me that a client gave him free tickets to Zoo Boo, a Halloween event at the Memphis Zoo. I tell him about Mrs. Serona and how I am occupied for the next two days. I suggest he take the boys by himself. He says, "Instead, it might be fun if I went with some friends from work."

Through the phone, I hear a familiar seductive female voice in the background say, "Go where? I want to go."

I am immediately frozen. *Think. Think quickly. Be wise with your words and don't unleash your hysteria.*

"Matthew, I know the boys will be terribly disappointed if you go with your office workers instead of them," I say. "The boys would enjoy that outing so much." I keep from screaming, but it is difficult.

"Okay," he says reluctantly. "I'll be home to pick them up after work."

That mischief-maker Indigo is too available. "I want to go," she says. Sick. I can hear her purring now. Ugh! Matthew wants to go with his coworkers instead of his boys? And I'm to give him approval, and this is how he treats his family?

Genie and I have covered six of the Eight A's, but I don't see how these last two A's are going to be helpful enough to change anything. Is there truly any hope for this marriage to become intimate?

I still doubt it. It's too big of a mountain to climb.

CHAPTER 8
Seventh A: The Affection Lesson

Tuesday, October 23

Chloe, Allison, and I are all meeting for coffee this morning. Allison called a sister meeting after a conversation she recently had with Dad. (Our Nashville sister, Jackie, reluctantly couldn't make it.)

Dad waited the appropriate few months to begin dating after Mom died in that car wreck three years ago and has been dating like a fraternity boy ever since. Most of his girlfriends are the same ages as Chloe, Allison, and me (Jackie is considerably younger.) This age thing of Dad's dates annoys all of us in a massive way.

"Dad says he's going to marry Rachel," Allison moaned.

"Rachel?" Chloe stammers. "She's younger than me!"

We all sit stunned as we think about Rachel. Rachel is a financially struggling, single mom with two little boys. Dad's nice portfolio might have something to do with Rachel's affection.

"Dad bought her a new BMW for an engagement present," Allison said.

No one says it, but we all three see our inheritance running through the young, smooth fingers of our dad's new wife.

"I don't even like her," Chloe says. "She squeaks when she talks."

I was thinking that, but I wasn't going to say it.

"Dad wants all of us to have dinner together," Allison says. "He would like us to eat together at someone's house because he says the conversation is better than at a restaurant. Who wants to volunteer to host this joyous event?"

Allison works almost full-time, and Chloe's house is too small. Therefore, I'm the lucky Martha Stewart.

After coffee, I call Matthew to tell him about Dad. "Matthew, can you please talk to Dad? How ridiculous it is for him to marry a woman young enough to be his daughter!"

"Jessica, I'm not getting into that one. If your dad finds some enjoyment in Rachel, I say let him go for it."

I'm repulsed by his comment. Go for it? We're all talking about sex here, right? Matthew wants Dad to go for it? Sick.

After I semi-recover from Matthew's abrasive comment, I realize that in general, however, I sense an increased softness in Matthew toward me. The eye contact, the lingering after dinner, and the conversation are all improved. Just when I want to give up the Genie program, Matthew moves toward me. After dinner last night, Matthew stayed at the dinner table thirty minutes after the boys had left and discussed some long-range financial planning with me. Those conversations soothe me. A man who is thinking of leaving doesn't talk to his wife about long-range financial planning. Or—I just think—maybe he's being extra nice to hide something with Indigo. Oh, my, I am a true head case.

I drive home and walk into the laundry room. Six piles of fresh laundry, all folded perfectly, like clothes stacked at J. Crew, await me. I am glad Genie hasn't given up on his whining student and returned to the Middle East. *I* would have given up on me.

I smile when I see him, always grateful for Genie's "happys."

"I also put two large casseroles of chicken spaghetti in your freezer," he says, "for your event with your father and Rachel."

That will take some stress off the day, having the entree already made.

"Let's get started," Genie says. "The Seventh A is Affection."

Affection? I might be good at this. I like to pat, touch, and hug people.

"Demonstrating affection to your husband would of course include being sweet, soft, girly, and flirty. It would also include demonstrating warmth, fun, cuteness, and a youthful, girlfriend-like quality."

I take that back. I'm definitely *not* good at this definition of expressing affection in a marriage.

"Affection has a brightness and softness. Smile, light up, kiss him hello. Do you understand what I mean by affection, Young Jessica?"

If he means, do I understand having affection for my children, the answer is a loud yes. But if he means, after a day of laundry, cooking, PTA responsibilities, addressing invitations, the kids' homework, my church obligations, and housework, do I feel like a girlfriend instead of a tired housewife, the answer is a huge NO.

"Yes, I understand," I say, fudging the truth.

"I hope you sincerely do understand because the affection of a wife toward her husband is considerably more important than most wives realize. After a few years of marriage, it is easy for wives to treat their husbands like business associates, making little eye contact and giving few smiles. Wives don't realize the need husbands have for the wife to be sweet and warm toward him."

Those last words—*sweet and warm*—cut me again. Why, I'm usually angry and cold, not sweet and warm.

"Women get a lot of affection from their girlfriends, but if a man doesn't receive affection from his wife, he goes without, and a part of his soul can dry up," Genie says. "I'm not blaming wives for husbands straying, but I have to tell you that not receiving affection from a wife puts a man in a position where he is more vulnerable to other women's expressions of affection. Men desperately need sweet and warm wives."

Hearing this need of men to have affectionate wives discourages me and at the same time escalates my fear when I think of the Mediterranean purring kitten at work. I have let my anger, discontentment, and disappointment with Matthew override my responsibility to be affectionate toward him.

"And an unaffectionate wife can never be a wife a husband adores," Genie says, continuing to drive the nail deeper into my already bruised heart. "Are you ready to proceed with the next aspect of affection? You seem a little ruffled from my last comments."

I'm not going to admit my massive failure in this area of affection. "No, I'm fine, Genie. You can go on." Soon, I'm going to deal with my little tendency to lie.

Genie eyes me as though he doesn't believe me, but when I sweetly smile, he continues. "Alright, then, we will focus on what most men feel is a very important part of affection, if not *the* most important part of affection, and that is sex."

Gulp. Sex? We're going to talk about … gulp again … *sex*?

"Don't worry; no specifics, no techniques," Genie says. "We will primarily discuss how a man views sex and how a woman views sex. I want you to see things from your husband's point of view."

Whew. I was afraid he was getting ready to make this Eight A's thing R-rated.

"Let me ask you a question, Young Jessica. Let's say it's your birthday or your anniversary. Your husband comes home with a present in a brown bag, unwrapped. He says to you, 'You know, it is a lot of effort to give you presents. And I'm expected to give them all the time. I really don't enjoy giving you presents, but I know it is part of being a husband. I wish I didn't have to do this, but oh well, here's your present. Hurry and open it so I can watch the game.' What would be your response?"

"My response?" I ask. "No response. I'd just Google divorce attorneys."

He chuckles. "A typical response from a wife, Young Jessica. Now think about what you say to your husband about sex. You know he wants to have it often and you don't. You give him an unwrapped, brown bag. You say, 'It's a lot of effort to give you sex. And I'm expected to give it to you all the time. I really don't enjoy giving you sex, but I know it is part of being a wife. I wish I didn't have to do this, but oh well, here's some sex. Hurry up and finish so I can watch *The Bachelor*.'"

I'm stunned. Stunned. Is that what it's like for Matthew? Like how I'd feel if he begrudgingly gave me birthday presents? Actually, he's not very good at the whole present thing, but that's another subject.

"Or here's another example, Young Jessica. Let's say you want to talk to Matthew tonight about the spat you had with your sister today. He says to you, 'I'm not in the mood tonight to listen. My head hurts a little. Maybe I can listen to you on Saturday night.' "

"Genie, that's not fair," I plead. "And it's not a good analogy."

"Oh, but it is, Young Jessica. Getting regular good sex is one of the major, if not *the* major reason a man marries," Genie says.

Well, finding someone to love me in a way that thrills me was my reason for marrying and that's not happening.

"The best analogy I have heard," Genie says, "is that sex is to a man what the welfare of the children is to a woman. It's in her bones. Sex is in *his* bones."

"Genie, you are overdoing it with that analogy for sure," I say. I mean I would swim the Atlantic for my boys.

"I am not exaggerating," he says. "Because women do not feel this way, they do not comprehend how men feel. But I promise you, sex is the highest spot on most men's priority list. You cannot separate a man and his feeling about his own masculinity and his sex life. Men are often plants with saggy, droopy leaves, longing for the refreshing waters of sexual release with their wives."

I had no idea what message I must be sending Matthew by my lack of interest in sex. I have always viewed Matthew as an oversexed creature who needed to deal with his insatiable appetite.

"You care about the kids and your house and your friends and your hair and your weight and your social life. Your husband cares about many interests too, but at the top of his and most other men's list, he wants a fulfilling sex life with his wife."

And why again aren't we talking about the top of *my* list? These self-centered thoughts keep bursting in.

"Women think they are good wives," he says, "because they are organized, good cooks, keep the laundry done, and are good mothers. But to a man, if a wife is not an engaged sexual partner, she's a disappointment. If sex is this huge to a man, and all he gets are a few scraps from the table, it is impossible for him to be thrilled with the woman he married."

Now this hurts. This hurts a lot.

"Women misunderstand men's sex drives," he says, "because women's sex drives are so different from men's. When she is stressed, the furthest thing from her mind is sex. When he is stressed, sex is one of the first things he wants to relieve himself of his anxiety."

Well, cheers for you, Genie, for understanding how much I don't want sex when I'm stressed.

"There's an old saying," Genie continues. " 'A little lovin' and some homemade biscuits perk up a marriage.' That saying incites fierce anger in women because that's a man's perspective; it's not at all what women want in marriage. Wives want emotional closeness and intimacy. Most husbands feel about emotional closeness and intimacy like many wives do about sex and that's this: 'Can we do that tomorrow?' "

I laugh. He's got this one right. Matthew's eyes glaze over when I want to have an intimate conversation.

"What you have to realize is that these minutes when a man is having sex with his wife may be the most important minutes in that man's week," he says. "Just because you have trouble biting off that truth doesn't make it less true. For many men, this is true. If sex is not the most important minutes in his week, it is close. Women are often disgusted by this. Women don't have this sexual appetite and have not studied men, so therefore they have not learned that men's sexual needs are usually front and center. Let's reverse this. What is the need you care most that Matthew fulfills?

"I have so many. Spending time with the family, giving me nonsexual affection, listening carefully to me, providing a good income ..."

"Try to pick one for now, Young Jessica."

"Okay, let's go with spending time with the family," I say.

"This is a great example because spending time with the family is not as important to Matthew as you," he says. "You want Matthew to *choose* to spend quality time with the family because it is the right thing, correct? You want him to curtail his other activities and make quality time with the family a high priority. You don't want to beg for it, either, right?"

I know where he is going with this.

"But with sex, which is a pressing and urgent drive that the Creator gave to men and that can only be satisfied in the confines of a monogamous marriage, you say to yourself, 'I don't feel that way, I don't understand it, and therefore, as far as I'm concerned, sex can be on the back burner.' "

If Genie is right on this subject, I have definitely not been informed.

"A wise woman will realize that although she doesn't possess this drive to the same extent, most likely her husband is semi-consumed with his sex drive if he is not getting adequate sex in his marriage," Genie says.

I can't go there. I can't get my mind around this. I don't *want* to get my mind around this because I don't want to face this and what it would mean. It's easier to think that his sexual needs are semi-repulsive and to semi-ignore them.

"Men have gargantuan appetites for sex," Genie says.

You've said that. Several times.

"Another truth that women have trouble accepting is that men are tempted with sexual desire whenever they see an attractive woman," he says. "Women are so ignorant about this. Many men are bursting at the seams with sexual desire all day long, and that your husband is sexually faithful is one of the greatest gifts he could ever give you. But not only do women *not* appreciate a husband's sexual faithfulness, they treat his sex drive like he's a dog in heat that needs to be tied up. A wife doesn't see that she is the only woman on earth who can legitimately meet this man's cry. Yet women are overscheduled, tired, and unresponsive to their husband's need."

I hate hearing this. Is he right? Is this need of Matthew's truly a gift from the Creator? Am I supposed to find out how to satisfy this? Puhllleeeeezzzze say it ain't so.

"This is a tremendous blind spot for women," he continues. "I wish women could live in their husband's body for one day and experience how many men wrestle with their sex drive all day long. When a woman understands this and makes the couple's sex life the priority the husband wants, she has entered the small percent of women who have an inside track to a man's heart."

I have believed Genie up until now, but this sex talk is over the line. Men can't be this ridiculous, can they?

"Let's talk about the difference in how often men want sex and how often women want sex," he says.

Matthew wants it every day, and I want it every month.

"Did you know that basic sexual desire is usually semi-set in a person before marriage? Just as I said before, people come into the marriage as a spender or a saver, a cleanie or a messy, and also with a basic amount of sex drive. Now, of course, there are many things that affect sex drive: health, self-esteem, etc., but in many ways, it is pre-set. In around 80 percent of my clients, the men want more sex, but surprisingly, in 20 percent of marriages, the women want more sex than their husbands do (see Chapter 32, "When You Want Sex More Than Your Husband Does"). I happen to know you are in the 80 percent with a husband with a stronger sex drive than you have."

That doesn't take a PhD to figure out, my friend.

"Therefore, as you well know," Genie says, "there's a problem when the husband wants sex five times a week and the wife wants sex every other week."

This guy's a regular genius.

"The solution is that a couple needs to negotiate and problem-solve, but few couples know how to do this. Couples can talk about the kid problems or money problems all day long, but they are uncomfortable talking about sex."

I'm uncomfortable talking about that I'm uncomfortable.

"So guess who gets to bring up sex to discuss it?" Genie asks.

"Not me," I say.

"Yes, you."

"I wouldn't know where to begin."

"You begin," he says, "with something like this: 'Matthew, I'd like to make you happy in our sex life, so I'd like to ask you some questions to see what you're thinking. If you could have sex as often as you wanted, how many times a week would that be?' "

"I don't want to know the answer to that question, Genie, and I'm certainly not going to comply with his animalistic sex drive."

"Young Jessica, how can you negotiate and problem solve this area if you're going to act like this problem doesn't exist? You need to address the issue. If he answers your question with something that upsets you, like 'five times a week' or 'every day,' don't scream, 'You beast!' Instead, say, 'Matthew, it's very manly that you have a strong sex drive. As you know, women often don't have as high of sex drive as men. So I thought we might discuss how to raise my sex drive and also find an amount of weekly sex that you'd be happy with."

Does anyone really talk like that? It sounds so contrived.

Genie continues. "Listen to whatever he says, and then make a compromise. For example, depending on his response, you could say, 'Matthew, what if we negotiate and try to have sex three times a week? And what if we scheduled it on certain nights so I could try to be rested on those nights? And maybe you could even get the boys in bed on those nights so I could take a bath and relax because it's way more fun for me to have sex if I'm rested and relaxed.' "

I've never heard of discussing sex like we were negotiating buying a used car.

"And men *agree* to that?"

"Of course, not all men will, but most men will because they want sex, and they aren't getting enough now. They see this as insurance. Their preference would be to have a wife on call for engaged sex 24/7, but most men have found out that this is not going to happen, so they are happy to schedule to insure a weekly amount.

"If Matthew wants to remain on a program where you have sex when the urge hits him, by all means, try to accommodate his preferences. But I've discovered that negotiating the number of times a week and scheduling which nights are the magic ones works well for many couples.

"And, Young Jessica, if for some reason you are prohibited from keeping the appointed magical days, realize how disappointed your husband will be. Be sure to immediately schedule a rain check date. Say something like, 'That family reunion and argument with your mother exhausted me. Could we possibly reschedule sex for in the morning or tomorrow night?' Only reschedule very occasionally. If at all possible, move heaven and earth to keep your appointed days."

"But what if I'm just tired on those days?" I ask.

"If your child comes in from basketball practice late, you fix him a nice plate of hot food. Then if he needs to turn a science project in, you research the project, make extra trips to the store, stay up late, do whatever you need to help him, and you do it *cheerfully.* That's how mothers care for their children. But if their husband wants sex, wives think, 'He is such a bother.' Wives have their children first in their hearts and need to put their husbands first."

He loves to dig that knife in and twist it around.

"Even if a man is hungry," Genie says, "a wife stops and fixes him some food. Or if the husband needs some pants for work, she will stop and iron his pants. But if he needs some sexual release, that is another category, and she is not interested in meeting that need."

But I don't mind cooking and ironing. Well, at least, I don't mind them compared to sex.

"Women come into marriage with the false romantic notion that if their husband really loved them, he would instinctively 'know' how to make her want sex. But the only marriage manual he gets is in her heart. Therefore, she is required to teach *him* how to please *her*. She must explain to him how much more in the mood she is after a bath, an intimate conversation with him, some time to relax, etc. She cannot expect him to know this."

The men in the movies know this.

"Men think that because sex calms them down when they are stressed," Genie says, "that women feel the same way. It is your responsibility to teach him that you feel opposite of that. But most wives expect men to already know that. Therefore, they see their husbands as selfish when in reality they are just not clued in."

Not clued in. Good description.

"Women have been creative," says Genie, "throughout the ages in figuring out how to make the husband happy in this area yet keep herself happy. Let me give you some examples."

Great. I hope the examples are only PG-13.

"One woman," he says, "has a husband with not only a higher drive than hers but also a higher interest in diversity, such as time, place, and apparel."

This sounds like he might be talking about Matthew.

"So this wife tries to keep things interesting. She calls him to meet her at the park for lunch and borrows a friend's van with dark-tinted windows you can't see through. The couple has sex and chicken for lunch."

This genie thinks he's Ben Stiller.

"Another woman meets her husband at the airport during the winter with nothing on but her overcoat and boots. That husband was excited on the drive home, to say the least."

I could never do that. I would be afraid the wind would blow open my coat.

"Another woman gives her children their breakfast, turns on *Sesame Street*, and tells the children she has to go to the bathroom. Then she and the husband lock the bathroom door and lean up against the sink. She's back in ten minutes."

TMI, Genie. T! M! I!

"Another couple has teenagers, and the wife likes sex better in the early evening, before she gets tired and turns into a pumpkin. Teenagers know something's up if the bedroom door is locked at six p.m. So this couple leaves their bedroom door open and unlocked and go into the walk-in closet, which you can only get to from inside their bathroom, and have pillows and blankets ready. The kids think the dad is taking a shower and the mom is talking to him."

"Doesn't sound comfortable," I say.

"Just ideas, Young Jessica. You'll have to come up with ideas that work for you and Matthew."

The only idea I have is to skip this A.

"All husbands are extremely sensitive when it comes to how their wives view them as sexual performers," Genie continues. "Therefore, it is crucial that you comment on anything positive when you and your husband are making love. Comments like 'you smell nice,' 'your muscles are big,' and 'that feels great when you do that' are extremely appreciated by the husband. If you think any positive thoughts, be sure and tell him. On the other hand, if you have any negative thoughts, especially don't express them during the intimate act. Instead of criticizing your husband, a better approach is to tell him what you want, not what you don't want."

But I have such a long list of what I don't want.

"Becoming more sexually compatible is not rocket science," he says. "There is a whole world of counselors, information, books, and DVD's available to help grow the sexual relationship. Knowing how important this area is to Matthew, it's worth your time to pursue this subject."

Yeah, like during my free time between two and four a.m.

"Young Jessica, you may not even know this, but your spiritual life and your sexual life with Matthew are very connected. When the two of you pray together and are connected spiritually, a woman feels safe and protected. This feeling of security makes her more open to sexual adventure, so it is an advantage to your sexual life to promote the spiritual life of your marriage."

Spiritual life and sexual life are connected in a marriage? Truly? I think this guy makes up half of this stuff.

"I have saved my most helpful piece of information about this subject for last," Genie says.

For last? Why doesn't he *start* with the helpful stuff?

"If the steps in the sex act are listed from beginning to end, what do you think the first step is?"

I stop and think. I've never thought about that before. The first step in sex?

"I guess it is being sexually excited or turned on, right?" I ask.

He laughs. "That's what most women think and because they are not 'excited or turned on' they don't want to have sex. But that's not the first step in sex. The first step in sex for many women is willingness."

I have to take that in. Being excited or turned on is not the first step; willingness is. I don't get it.

"Many women have to begin having sex before they are aroused," Genie says. "Do you see the gigantic significance of this truth? If a woman doesn't expect to be aroused until she 'begins' but is *willing* to 'begin,' she can therefore be turned on or excited, and then, well, you know the rest."

I am shocked. I was hugely unaware that willingness was the first step. Since I am not frequently aroused, I tell myself that Matthew is a bad lover and that he isn't doing the necessary things that I need to get aroused, like household help, helping with the children, or complimenting me. I never thought that it is natural and normal for many women to not be aroused until they "start." This is gigantic new information.

"I am not bashing wives with what I'm going to say, Young Jessica, but many wives are self-focused and think that how they feel is right and therefore do not realize that men feel entirely different. A man doesn't need emotional closeness to want to have sex. Women can be ridiculous about expecting their husbands to be like them. Instead, women are wise to see this creature as different, to go ahead and 'get started,' leave the problems in the marriage in another room, and enjoy the physical closeness the best she can. Women don't realize that men often require that their sexual needs are met before they are willing to work on other issues, such as emotional intimacy. What women say to themselves is, 'I need to be emotionally close before sex.' That may be the ideal scenario, but *wise* women say to themselves, 'He needs sex before he can be emotionally close.' These nuances in a woman's mind can change marriages."

Wow. All I can say is, Wow. And of course, I'm the lucky one who gets to go first, *again*. No surprise there.

We both sit without talking. I'm still stunned.

So Genie is saying that I can choose to be willing and then when I start, my arousal will happen. Genie loves to hit me with fire-hose thoughts. I've been hiding behind not being aroused and "Matthew doesn't deserve sex since he doesn't meet my intimacy needs" to deny him sex. But Genie is blasting away those excuses. He says it's *normal* for women to not be aroused until they "begin" and that men need sex before they can let down and be emotionally close.

"Because sex is ultra-important to men," Genie says, "it is a subject I ask my clients to please not ignore but to become experts in by exploring more resources. Great sex doesn't automatically happen in marriage as it does on the big screen. True, the best sex between the two of you is from a great relationship."

Previous lessons from Genie have been riveting, but none have rocked me like this one.

"If your sex life is upsetting to you, take heart," he says. "It can change so much that you won't believe you're the same two people."

I'll believe that when I see it.

"This was a difficult lesson, Young Jessica. I have left you another gift in the laundry room," and he was gone.

Try 'next-to-impossible' lesson. I'm still absorbing the idea that 'willingness' is the first step in sex. I also know that I have put Matthew on a scale where I measure if he deserves sex instead of realizing that, like the other A's, it is a deposit I give him to love him. My brain is going to explode.

I amble into the laundry room and find all my knee-deep ironing is done, even my Christmas tablecloths. Nice, Genie. Not enough to fully recover from today's lesson, but nice.

This A is going to take as much energy and thought as the previous six A's combined. Not only do I have to work on the "sweet and warm" aspect of affection, I have to get my mind around these new thoughts about men and sex.

Matthew calls to tell me that there's an added bowling practice tonight, and he's going to run home and get some clothes during lunch. I tell him I'll fix him a grilled cheese sandwich while he is home and he says he would appreciate that. I think I'll add a little *dessert* to that menu.

Matthew's coming home to a theme park with a roller coaster ride.

CHAPTER 9
Eighth A: The Authority Lesson

Wednesday, October 31

still chuckle—and blush—when I think about eight days ago when Matthew came home for lunch to get his bowling clothes. I said, "Want to take advantage of the boys being gone before I fix your grilled cheese sandwich?"

His astonished look was unforgettable. He was like a little puppy, hoping to get picked up and petted.

After our noonday rendezvous, Matthew said, "That was awesome, Jessica. I enjoyed that." We chatted and laughed during lunch and the closeness was apparent. I don't remember Matthew being that warm in months, if not years.

And last night—who can believe me?—I had my own Halloween party with Matthew. I bought an adult female costume at Party City to wear just for him. He did a double take when I came out in that short black costume and managed not to faint with shock. Again, his warmth and openness were apparent. That Seventh A is a lot more important to Matthew than I realized.

After our "marriage moment," I asked him about his preference on our sexual frequency, and he said ideally he would prefer three times a week but a consistent two would be great. We agreed to two times, since I'm more of a once-a-week girl. When I mentioned scheduling our marital-intimacy time, he balked at first, thinking it would take the spontaneity out of sex. However, when he realized how little sex he was getting on the spontaneity method, he softened toward the idea.

So we agreed to schedule sex! Wednesdays and Sundays are the enchanted days. And who can believe this? He's going to put the kids down while I take a bath and relax and get ready! That dance we did every night when he waited in bed and I took a long time getting ready for bed, hoping that he'd fall asleep, well, looks like that's over.

Whew. What a relief. That was exhausting. I don't know *why* I have been so reluctant to discuss sex with him.

I'm seeing a movement in Matthew, for sure. He asked me this morning if there was anything special I wanted to do this weekend. Imagine that! Usually I'm the one who begs and pleads for family time. Instead, he offered to take the family on a hike Saturday afternoon. This marriage is on a definite upswing.

My thoughts make me happy as I walk into the boys' school where I have a meeting with the principal and our PTA officer board. Sitting in the undecorated, needs-painting conference room are the other two PTA officers. The principal, Mrs. Smith, begins.

She asks if we, the PTA officer board, could manage an extra fundraiser in the spring because the school would like to purchase some new computers for the computer lab. I almost begin to explain that with my home calligraphy business, I will not be able to work on the fundraiser. However, the thought that this principal has been extra patient with Brandon's behavior issues because I am the new PTA president passes through my mind. Therefore, I agree to do the extra spring project, even though everything in me screams not to.

I call Matthew to tell him that I let the principal talk me into the fundraising task and why. "That's a mistake, Jessica. You can't spend that kind of time indirectly trying to protect Brandon. He has to learn to behave. I wish you had asked me before you accepted the job. You don't have time to do that and do your home business."

I don't like it when Matthew tries to tell me what I should do and shouldn't do.

Arriving back home, I walk into the kitchen and open the refrigerator to begin dinner. There's a lasagna in my own lasagna pan, with a note attached, "Bake at 350 degrees for 45 minutes." Lasagna is a favorite of Brandon and Josh.

Genie is sitting on the counter. Usually he begins by asking me how I've done with the A that he recently taught me. Today he had the modesty and graciousness to refrain from remarking about this last week's A, Affection. I appreciated that.

"Today is the last and the hardest of the Eight A's that we will discuss, Young Jessica. Let's take a walk in the nearby park. No one can hear or see me except you."

I still keep thinking I'm going to wake up from this dream. Taking a walk with Genie in the park? Ludicrous.

"The eighth A is Authority," he says, as we start walking toward the park. "Authority is the most misunderstood and most ignored genie principle of all."

I don't like the smell of the topic, but I politely listen. It couldn't be more alarming than that sex talk last week, could it?

"Governments must have leadership," Genie begins. "Businesses must have leadership, and churches must have leadership. Families are no different. It is not that the husband is more valuable or important than the wife; it's simply that groups must have leadership so there is order."

I knew I wasn't going to like this. I was right.

"In the past when I have talked to other young wives about the idea of authority, they have had many excuses why this subject does not apply to them. For example, some wives say that their husband is not as smart as they are, so why should they be under authority to him? Other wives point to his character flaws and again make the same assertion."

I don't think their reasoning is that hard to follow.

"Ugh, Genie! Matthew's going to start telling me what to do?"

"Slow down. We are going to discuss this. The Creator made the husband the head of the home," he says. "When you develop a gentle and quiet spirit and meet your husband's soul needs with the Eight A's, your husband will not want to go against your wise and kind counsel very often. When your husband sees that you are bent on doing him good, and that your very top goal in life is to make him happy, Matthew will then often bend to your influence. Maybe not always and maybe more as the years go on, but the genuine love you are learning to demonstrate to your husband through depositing the Eight A's will open his heart to your happiness, your needs, and your counsel. But regardless of whether these wonderful side benefits occur, you still must acknowledge your husband as the head of the marriage and respect him as the head because, otherwise, you are setting your home up for all kinds of discord and contention."

"What discord and contention?" I ask, not buying into this last A. If I'm going to consider this submissive stuff, I'm going to be sure that it's absolutely necessary.

"Children learn to follow authority as they watch their mother submit to their father. Otherwise, your children will develop rebellious hearts toward the Creator and toward other authority. You cannot avoid this truth: Your heart is the schoolroom for your children. When you are angry and rebellious toward your husband's authority, that is the lesson you teach your children—to be rebellious to their authorities."

My heart is the schoolroom for my children? That's a scary thought.

"However," he continues, "when you are meek, humble, and responsive to your husband's leadership, you teach your children to be responsive to authority. No child will ever be truly successful until they learn how to be submissive to the Creator. A mother's submissive and gentle heart may be the single most important quality she can have."

Why can't the single most important quality be shopping?

"The marriage is not to be a dictatorship," Genie says. "You are allowed to appeal to Matthew's decisions when, in your opinion, they are not in the best interests of the family. And as I said earlier, after your husband has lived with a wife who is meeting his Eight A's, you will be surprised by how much he will *want* to please you. The conflict between the two of you will die down immensely when his soul needs are met. But still you must reconcile that he is the ultimate head of the home and you must demonstrate this to him."

I feel the beginning of a major headache coming on.

"Genie, he's a bad leader. Really, he's terrible at leading," I plead.

"Only a few men are born with natural leadership abilities," Genie continues. "A woman will wait a lifetime for her husband to pick up the scepter and lead well; a smart woman hands her husband the scepter."

I'm not handing anyone anything.

We're in the park now, and I wave to a mother and her small children that I recognize from church. They have no idea I am accompanied by a genie.

"Even the strongest of men," he says, "will not continually fight a strong, quarrelsome woman. They eventually get tired and give up."

I guess Matthew has done that over the past few years to some extent. Like in the lawyer's office when I complained about the inheritance, he shook his head and went zombie on me. Now I understand why.

"Do not be upset that many men are passive and would rather wait and see what unfolds. Most have not been taught to lead. You can help your husband lead by asking him, 'What do you think? What is your opinion?' Tatoo those questions on your wrist."

I spent a lot of money getting a tattoo off my booty, and I'm not tattooing anything else anywhere.

"Seek his preferences," he continues, "and his thoughts. By the way, don't ask him how he feels; most men don't know how they feel. Ask him what he *thinks*. This, he will know."

Matthew eyes do glaze over when I ask him anything about how he feels.

"Men become especially passive," he says, "when they are in the presence of a strong, controlling woman. Instead of wanting to tame that lion, they just step back, let it growl, and roar. Then they try to escape."

Is the analogy of a roaring lion fair? Isn't he stretching all of this to make a point? I'm not a roaring lion, am I?

"How far does this go, Genie? I mean, does he get to tell me every little thing to do or not do?" I know this is a bad question, but I'm stalling. I don't think men understand how hard this issue is for women. I feel I'm going to lose my identity or lose my inner person. And I don't trust Matthew to make the right decisions; he's still such an imperfect husband.

"There is a legal term called *jurisdiction*," says Genie. "It means that a person in authority gives you the right to make decisions in a certain area. For example, you and Matthew can discuss if you have jurisdiction over the meals, if you have jurisdiction over the family's clothes, maybe over Christmas presents, etc. That's between the two of you to decide. Most husbands are happy to give wives jurisdiction, or the right to make decisions, over many areas. This is not a master/servant relationship I'm describing. This is two halves of one whole, working together."

Sounds like a bum deal to me.

"You are not to be a stool pigeon or doormat and simply say, 'Yes, Honey' or 'Whatever you say, Honey,' " Genie says. "You are to have a mind bathed in the Creator's Word so you can give your husband counsel from that source. The Creator didn't make a helpmeet to only do the laundry. If He did, He would have given the first man a slave. The Creator didn't make a person to only satisfy the man's physical needs; if He did, He would have given the first man a concubine. The woman, the wife, is bone of his bones, one with him, part of his very being. Her influence is not debatable. My *Wife School* shows you how to be the right kind of influence, to 'do him good.' "

I know I need to yield to Matthew, but I hate it. I absolutely hate it.

Genie is sensing my discomfort, but he forges ahead. "Let's discuss how to make proper appeals. Give me an example of a conversation where you and Matthew recently disagreed."

I have a great example. "Last week, Matthew said, 'I don't want the kids eating anything between meals. They need to learn self-control.' I was dumbfounded after he made that request. Matthew's father was in the military and ran their home like an army officer. To wake Matthew up when he was a kid, his father would march in, flip on the light, and demand that his bed be made with hospital corners before he could eat breakfast. Matthew said he didn't like his father's stern parenting style, but now I'm seeing army-sergeant tendencies in Matthew. And he doesn't realize how hungry the kids are when they get home from school. How do I handle a totally unrealistic expectation like that? I mean, he's not even home, and he's giving me orders how to feed the kids?" I can feel myself getting angry.

"To start with," Genie says, "a wise woman has self-control. She doesn't blurt out, 'How idiotic!'"

Those weren't my words, but they were close.

"A wise woman lets the heat of the moment die down," he says. "Then, when all the cortisol is out of everyone's bloodstream, usually the next day or at least a few hours, she sweetly fingertip-drops, "Honey, I was thinking about the kids not eating between meals. I like the way you are trying to build self-control in them. They will benefit greatly in the years to come with such a fine example of a father who is disciplined. I wanted to tell you, though, that they are extremely famished after school, and if I give them a little, healthy snack, it would help their attitudes during those three hours before dinner while they do their homework. If I keep it very small, they will not lose their appetites for dinner. Could we please try that?"

"That's so much work, Genie. Do I have to give all that praise and be so tippy-toe nice? Why can't we just hash it out, person-to-person? I thought it was healthy for people to communicate honestly and directly?"

"Of course it's important to communicate honestly and directly, but after watching marriages for thousands of years, I understand the preeminent importance of a wife communicating *respect* to a husband," he says. "When you're appealing to a judge in a courtroom, do you say whatever's on your mind, just letting any thoughts blast out? Can you imagine communicating honestly and directly with the judge by telling him you are annoyed that you had to wait on him for twenty minutes? Or if you're applying for a job, do you tell the potential employer that you think his hiring questions are juvenile? These examples are obvious. However, a woman addresses the most important relationship in her life, her husband, by letting any thoughts that come to her mind just tumble out of her mouth. I am not advocating that you be dishonest at all; I am simply telling you the benefits of carefully choosing respectful words."

I have this belief that Matthew should see the *real* me, ugly thoughts and all. I forget that instead I'm always called to have self-control over my tongue.

"If you are giving your children some medicinal herbs to heal a sickness," Genie says, "don't you add lemon and honey to sweeten the sour taste? Be sure to add lemon and honey in your appeals."

I haven't addressed Matthew with the utmost respect. My strong, oppositional style of relating is offensive to him, and I know it.

"I realize there is a fine line," Genie says, "between being manipulative and being wise with your words so you can influence. The real difference is your motive. Your heart must be right. I cannot fix your heart. Only in your relationship with the Creator can your heart be made pure."

Now we're going to talk about my heart? I thought we were working on marriage skills.

"Many women are tempted to use these principles of giving because they work, so they give to get. There is a very fine line in a woman's heart between whether she is giving to grow the family/ marriage culture or giving so that she will receive in a selfish manner. I cannot help you discern the difference; you will have to ask the Creator to tell you that. "

Truthfully, giving to get is not news to me.

Genie continues. "Life and death are in the power of the tongue, and a woman should do everything in her power to learn to use her tongue wisely. But what is down in the well of your heart will come up in the bucket of your tongue. It is your heart you need to examine."

I am a piece of work. A strong, controlling, manipulative piece of work.

"Back to your husband's comment on snacking," Genie says. "Of course, Matthew may stay adamant about his snacking decision and not want the kids to eat between meals. So you will have to consent. If the children are whiney and fussy or have other symptoms, you may appeal again but in a respectful manner. There is never a limit on respectful, gracious appeals with new information or ideas. Sometimes men need time to think about what you're trying to explain to them. And sometimes they need several appeals to see the situation correctly. Again, only you know whether the appeal is self-serving and manipulative or in the best interest of the family."

I guess badgering Matthew for more money in my clothes budget would not be in the best interest of the family.

"Carefully pick which topics you want to appeal," Genie says. "Women fuss over how the flowers are planted, how the pillows are tossed onto the sofa, or if they watch a certain football game or not. Seriously! They waste their appeals on nonsense topics. Pick five to eight things you deeply care about and save your 'appeal coupons' for those items. Common sense tells one that if you don't bark often, your bark will be heard."

I remember recently at a funeral my Aunt Sally barked at her husband, my uncle Stuart, "Sit down, Stuart. You're making me nervous by standing up." Uncle Stuart is a world-renowned cancer specialist and his wife is going to decide when he should sit or stand? I can see how *other* women's controlling remarks are unattractive, just not my own.

"Save your appeals," Genie says, "and ask for the things you truly care about: things concerning the children, your relationship with your husband, your family of origin, etc. You can't appeal everything. Use your appeal coupons wisely and sparingly. In fact, get out your Turquoise Journal and across the top of a page write, 'My Eight Top Concerns/When to Use My Appeal Coupons.'"

As I move to get my Turquoise Journal, I remember recently being mad at Matthew because some bathroom towels went on sale at such a great price and he didn't think we needed them. Bathroom towels! As if they are in my top eight concerns!

"Go ahead, Young Jessica. Write them down," Genie says.

So I do. I list one, our family's relationship with the Creator, two, the marriage, three, the children, four, our health, and five, church, six, my friends, seven, finances ..."

"The purpose of this exercise is to see that you don't want to use your appeal coupons on whether he uses a fork or tongs to turn the steaks on the grill."

I understand this concept of saving my appeal coupons. This makes sense. Why in the world do I have such a need to insist that Matthew take my driving directions so we save forty-five seconds?

Genie isn't through. "If a wife feels compelled to give her husband her advice, carefully and sweetly, she can say to her husband, 'Honey, I know you're getting ready to make a decision about the Smith account, but I wanted to give you some thoughts to consider while you're making that decision. Of course, I know you'll be making the final decision.' Most men can receive this counsel from their wives, if the wives are regularly depositing the Eight A's. Husbands need and want their wives' opinions. However, they want to retain the right to make the final decision, and you must give this to your husband."

This is hard to swallow. This morning, I told Matthew it was chilly and that he needed a scarf. He said that scarves get in his way and are a nuisance. I said, "You need to wear one or you'll get cold" as I marched into his closet and got his scarf. Was that really a hill to die on?

Grandma was right when she said I was the one who needed that wooden box.

"Although women are offended by the subject of authority, I want you to see the beauty of authority, Young Jessica."

Beauty? There's beauty in this confinement?

"In the beginning, there was a curse placed on man and on woman," he says. "Ironically, this curse can turn into a blessing. For example, originally the Creator cursed man with the burden of and the difficulty in making a living. Interestingly and ironically, one of the greatest satisfactions of a man is to learn how to conquer this assignment of making a living. Men achieve incredible fulfillment from a lifetime pursuit of their calling and career. Men may complain that the burden is enormous, but one of their most fulfilling satisfactions in life comes from their work."

Matthew complains about the pressure of work all the time.

"And, likewise, Young Jessica, most women hate the curse that their husbands will rule over them. But, alas, it is a means where women can be blessed. Older women who understand this will describe the benefits of a life lived under the protection of her husband, of being cared for, of being free to use her creativity and gifts in later life, of having a spouse who loves and trusts her, and who lets her influence him in important decisions."

I admit that sounds very nice.

"There are countless ways to honor your husband's authority, Young Jessica. Frequently seek his opinion and advice, tell the children to be quiet while Daddy is talking, direct the children to their father to get his opinion. He is the king of your home; treat him as if he wears the royal robe. Train your children to love and honor their father as the head of the home."

I'm quiet. I'm wrestling with how much I now realize I want to be in charge of the family and simultaneously how unwilling I am to give Matthew the scepter to lead. I don't trust Matthew to lead well. I'm afraid what would happen if I let him lead. I'm afraid, flat-out afraid. You don't have to be smarter than a fifth grader to understand a woman's fear and subsequent desire to lead.

As if Genie is reading my mind, he says, "Husbands will make mistakes. Do not be afraid of his mistakes. Your home will nevertheless flourish with a patriarch leadership."

I love the word *flourish*. I envision a lush garden with overflowing fruit and flowers. That is exactly the picture I want for our family.

Genie's last sentence helps me gain another perspective on male leadership. Although Matthew will make mistakes, a home set up with the husband/father as the head has so many benefits that I can relax and trust that we will be alright, even if he does make mistakes.

"Although the husband wants his wife's input, he does not want to feel like he has a leash around his neck," Genie says. "The husband needs to know he's the head of the home and the ultimate decision maker."

This truth is penetrating my heart. The other seven A's have been extremely helpful, but this A is life changing. We are going to change the government in our home to the husband leading instead of the wife. This is probably the most important decision I've made since I said, "I do."

I have been pressing Matthew to take us to New York for spring break. He says we don't have the money. I keep making plans and moving forward. Tonight, I will tell him I'm sorry, and that I don't even want to go unless he wants to go. I badger and push and manipulate. I do. I must stop. I can see how I always need to be right; I see how I disagree with Matthew strongly in front of the children, even slightly mocking him at times with my sarcasm; I see how I give suggestions on how to do everything better, claim to have more insight, know how to handle everything. Oh, no, I am that roaring lion!

"Rest comes from being under the proper authority, Young Jessica," Genie reminds me.

Yes, I know this and tell it to my children. However, I don't listen to my own advice.

Genie softens his tone. "I do not want you to be too hard on yourself as you realize how you've failed."

How did he know what I was thinking? This is creepin' me out.

"No doubt many women have admirable leadership qualities," Genie says. "But when the Creator made man and woman, He was making an earthly analogy of the relationship He wanted for himself and His creature. In that picture, He was the man and the creature was the woman. The man is to love and lead; the woman is to respect and obey."

I have never liked that O word.

"A wise woman builds her house with these principles, but with her own hands, a foolish one tears her house down. This A of Authority is where most women tear down their house."

I have usurped Matthew's authority on more occasions that I want to admit. And I have blamed Matthew for Joshua's disrespect at school. Joshua has watched me disrespect my authority, his father!

I see this tendency in my sisters and friends too. My friend Suzanna told her husband that she was getting a new house whether he agreed or not. My sister, Allison, demands that her husband buy certain stocks. My neighbor Brittany tells her husband how big a raise he needs to give his secretary.

"Continue to love Matthew with the Eight A's," says Genie. "Focus on your Turquoise Journal lists, and do this for five years."

"What?" I say in such a loud voice that the children playing nearby look over at us—I mean, at me. "Did you mean five *weeks*?"

Surely he meant five weeks. Or at the most five *months*.

"This program of the Eight A's that I'm teaching you is a five-year plan," says Genie. "No one wants to hear that. They want a plan that will work by the weekend. Think about the difference between a newborn and a five-year-old who is getting ready to start kindergarten. That is the difference in your husband in five years if you continue to deposit the Eight A's and you stop trying to fix, lead, and control him. Eventually, as I always say, your husband will open up and be interested in your desires."

My legs are tired. My brain is tired. I'm ready to go home and eat something to medicate all my guilt at being a roaring lion.

"Just remember that you'll never submit to your husband until you submit to the Creator first," Genie says. "This is hard to accept, Young Jessica, but the Creator made man first. Man needed a helpmeet, so the Creator created woman. The man was not created for the woman but woman for the man."

Before today, I saw submission as an antiquated, outdated idea. Today, I realize the family order was created for my benefit and protection.

"And with that we'll call it a day," Genie says.

"Genie, wait," I say. "That's all Eight A's. Are we finished?"

"Oh, no, Young Jessica," he laughs. "That's just Part I. The Eight A's are only the baseline. Now I will take you through Advanced Wife Training. We are only halfway there, if that. You have much yet to learn. Remember the chess analogy? I want you to be a chess champion."

I look around and blink twice. I'm on my bed in nap position with a beautiful Caesar salad with grilled chicken on a tray on the nightstand.

I remember Matthew telling me that he wished I hadn't take on the additional PTA responsibilities in the spring. I know now that I should have asked his opinion before I accepted the spring fundraiser job. He could have protected me from that responsibility that is now going to zap hours of my time. I think I'll tell him I'm sorry for not asking his opinion.

The phone rings, and it's the school principal, Mrs. Smith. She wants to know if we could have the fundraising carnival on April 5. She needs to know because her daughter is planning a late April wedding, and she wants to schedule all the other weekends in that time frame for wedding events. I reluctantly agree to the date. What a downer.

Later that night

Brandon is dressing up tonight like Spiderman for Halloween while Josh is going to be the Green Lantern.

I have philosophical problems with Halloween. I like the costume aspect of Halloween, but what mother likes her children going around and collecting disease-causing, sugared candy? I will ration out a piece or two in their lunches for the next few days, and then I'll throw the junk in the trash. I enjoy a little sugar as much as the next person, but a bag of trans fats and high fructose sugar is insane.

The boys get ready for bed, and I approach Matthew.

"Matthew, I wish I had talked to you before I agreed to do the extra fundraiser."

He continues to brush his teeth, but he is listening.

"I know you could have protected me from making that wrong decision," I say.

"Well, I appreciate that," he says. "I know you only want to help Brandon, but I think there are better ways to help him."

"I'll try to ask your opinion next time. Will you please forgive me?" I feel faint as I ask him. This is torture.

Matthew is not used to this.

"Of course I will, Jessica. Thank you for apologizing. You have certainly been trying to be a sweet wife lately."

Oh. My. Goodness. He is noticing! All has *not* been in vain. I'm a sweet wife? Whoopee!

Happily, I go up to read out loud to the boys and tuck them in bed. I hear Matthew's cell phone ring. He walks into the other room to take the call. I hear him laughing.

Fear and anger grip me, as I feel sure it's hot and spicy Indigo.

Genie said to not complain about her until I was repeatedly and faithfully depositing the Eight A's. He said that Matthew cannot hear me until I meet his needs. I am to trust the program, deposit the Eight A's, and then gently tell him that she bothers me but without the usual hysterical fit that I throw. I think I can check each of those prequalifying statements off the list, as it's time to *gently* tell him how I feel.

It's not just Indigo's looks that upset me. It's her coyness, her aloofness to me, and her smug confidence that she and Matthew share inside secrets about their accounts. I've thought it through. I have a plan. My tongue is in control. It's time to push "play."

"Matthew, was that Indigo?" I ask.

"Yeah," he said. "She needed to go over some info on the Hammerhead account."

"I don't expect you to understand this," I begin calmly, "but as a wife, I feel upset about a couple of things about Indigo. Honestly, Matthew, I think she is after you. Her eyes drip with seduction, and she seems to touch you every chance she gets."

"She touches everyone," he says. "That's just Indy."

Indy? *Indy*? A few seconds ago, I'm happy that I'm called a sweet wife, and now I am a volcano, getting ready to spew lava for miles. I need to take several deep breaths and calm down or table this discussion for later.

Genie's words wash over my mind: "A woman's hysteria and anger dismantle a man, much like stepping on a hidden grenade. When the urge to unhinge and fire threatens, calm down and think first."

How do I put a lid on this? How does any woman contain herself under this tsunami of emotions? I breathe deeply. I do it again. I can feel my blood pressure dropping back to normal. Okay, I've got control. Proceed, I tell myself.

"Matthew, I want to be the best wife in the world to you, and I will keep trying. I hope eventually you will be able to hear the ache in my heart about Indigo."

"The ache in your heart?" he asks. He stops and stares at me.

"Yes, Matthew, the ache. I know it is wrong to judge others, and it's impossible to truly read other people's motives, but there is a check in my spirit about Indigo. I wish she didn't work for you. It makes me unhappy that you are with her all day long."

He pauses. He pauses a long time. His expression is soft.

"I don't want you to be unhappy, Jessica, but I think she's harmless."

"I know you think she's harmless," I say. "However, as a woman and as your wife, I am telling you that there is an ache in my heart that she works with you."

He doesn't argue. He heard me. He is processing my request.

Somehow I keep quiet, gather myself, and go do another load of laundry.

"Stay with the program," I hear the Genie say in my mind. *"Keep depositing the Eight A's, stay calm, bury his mistakes in the cemetery in your backyard, and persevere."*

Genie is right; I need more training. The Eight A's have put our marriage back on track, but Advanced Wife Training is still needed. The marriage is better, no doubt about it. The marriage is *definitely* better.

PART II

Advanced Training for Wives

CHAPTER 10
What to Do When Your Husband Fails or Has Adversity

Wednesday, November 7

"Bye, Jessica," Matthew says as he gives me a kiss good-bye. "Tonight is Wednesday," he adds, winking.

I get a kick out of how perky Matthew is on Wednesdays and Sundays.

The phone rings. Who could be calling me this early? It's Rachel, Dad's new fiancée. "Hi, Rachel," I say. This is odd. She has never called me before.

She chats about various meaningless things for around five minutes. I ask her if I can call her back because I need to fix the boys' lunches for school.

"I just wanted to ask you if you would mind addressing the invitations to our wedding. There's going to be about two hundred of them. But we can chat when you call me back," she says.

Now I get it.

Number one, my dad has no business having a big wedding like that with this new young gold digger. And number two, I barely know her, and she has no business asking me for these huge favors. I mean, if Dad wants me to address the invitations, let him ask me or let me volunteer. This behavior of my younger, soon-to-be stepmother is probably a foreshadowing of what is to come with her in the family.

I stammer that I will have to see because I have so many other weddings I'm doing right now. I want to get Matthew's opinion on how to handle this.

After I say good-bye to the children as they leave for school, I begin my morning routine. As I throw in a load of laundry, I think how glad I am that *Wife School* is not over. Genie said he wanted me to be an eventual chess champion, and I barely know how the queens, rooks, and knights move in this marriage.

Opening the refrigerator, I find a beautiful baked chicken, green beans with sautéed almonds, and a romaine lettuce salad with goat cheese and strawberries—several gourmet notches up from my healthy but ordinary cuisine of regular vegetables and salad.

"Are you ready, Young Jessica, for Advanced Training for Wives?" the Genie says, appearing behind me. "Today, we are going to discuss how to treat a man when he experiences failure in a job, a goal, or any pursuit. Also, we will discuss your response when Matthew confronts hardship or adversity in his life."

A few months ago, Matthew's boss gave the huge Orion account to the new guy, Peters, in the office. Matthew had asked for it and was visibly upset when he was not selected to head up the account. I wonder how my reaction months ago to that failure will jibe with what Genie is getting ready to tell me.

Genie begins. "A wife's first response to any failure on her husband's part should be empathy. She should attempt to understand his pain from his perspective. If a wife feels condemning judgment toward her husband in her heart, again, she must reach for self-control. The worst thing a wife could say would be, 'Yes, I saw this coming. I was wondering when this was going to happen. It's because of the way you did so-and-so, you know.' "

I swear Genie listens in on my conversations.

"A man is frequently asking himself, whether consciously or unconsciously, the questions, 'Am I enough?' and 'Do I have what it takes to succeed as a man?' When he fails in any of his endeavors, his failure whispers the answer he dreads to hear."

Or his wife tells him.

"Because women are not wired to think in the same way as men, they often fail to realize that a man is processing the same situation from a very different perspective. When any of a man's goals to conquer or achieve are thwarted, he is immediately uncomfortable by his apparent deficiency. *Women must understand there is a hidden, fragile part of men that is easily broken and shattered when he faces any kind of failure.* Although his stern and stoic exterior may attempt to convince you that he is not upset by his unmet goals, it is a protective mechanism so you won't doubt his adequacy."

I've doubted Matthew's adequacy more times than the networks show the reruns of *Friends*.

He continues. "Your empathy should convey how hard it must be to encounter his huge trials and how you respect him for handling this adversity. Don't mother him, though. He doesn't want to sit in your lap and have his hair stroked like he did when he was four."

Little boys sitting in my lap is still pleasurable to me.

"A husband also doesn't want you roaring in with answers, giving advice, telling him what to do. I know women like to fix their husbands, but a wife's bossiness destroys a man's affection for his wife."

Mrs. Fix-it, that's me.

"A man needs a wife to be a sponge to absorb the pain or to be a pillow to soften the emotional fall, but instead, usually the wife becomes a highlighter, making sure her husband understands his mistake so he won't do it again."

Uh-oh. Memories of what I said to Matthew when he was not selected for the Orion account are coming back to me.

"What a man does want," Genie says, "is for you to restore his manly confidence. When your husband experiences failure, your goal is to express empathy and also a belief in his abilities."

Express empathy? Restore his confidence? Those goals have never been on my "to do" list.

"Another common reaction women have to their husband's failure is they give advice on how he could have avoided this adversity if he had done something differently."

Gulp. I remember asking Matthew if he had done anything to offend his boss.

"Genie, what does a wife say that is healing and helpful?" I say, trying to throw off the heaviness in my mind of my negative comments to Matthew.

"*This is a wife's moment,* Young Jessica. After a wife has listened carefully—without giving advice—she is now ready to respond with her healing words. When a husband is discouraged over failure or adversity, she must be quick to come to his side to express her faith in him and rebuild his confidence. That is her single goal for the moment. A wife must assure her husband that he will figure out how to handle this because she has such unwavering belief in his capabilities."

Uh-oh, bad memories are flooding again. I remember saying to Matthew, "I wonder if the boss will take away other accounts from you."

"Saying 'that must be hard' and 'I don't know how you handle so much pressure' are helpful sentences to say. Men need women who *believe in them, admire them, and encourage them by their unshakeable belief that he will figure it out.* Of course, your husband is going to make mistakes and, sadly, some pretty severe ones. But encouraging, forgiving, and accepting wives make molehill husbands into mountainous ones."

I wonder if I am going to flunk all the Advanced Training for Wives lessons like I'm flunking this one.

"A man longs for a woman who trusts him even though he makes human mistakes. But he does not want to tell you this. He wants you to instinctively know it."

To be fair, there's a ton of stuff I wish Matthew instinctively knew too. I could use a little empathy myself from him. No need moaning about that now to Genie. He will only say that he is going to teach me to ask for what I want from Matthew after he first teaches me to properly respond to him.

Genie continues. "He does not want you to give him a three-point plan to fix things. Instead, convey to him that he has the strength to endure or the know-how to solve the dilemma."

I usually give Matthew five-point plans with sub-points. One time, I created a Power Point presentation on my iPad about what I thought he should do on a certain account. No joking, I really did.

"Genie, when he shares his failures with me, my brain lights up and solutions start popping up everywhere in my brain. So my inclination is to give him ideas to fix his problems. Doesn't he want my great ideas?"

"Eventually, he will want your great ideas," Genie says. "But it isn't the time to bring them up immediately. Wait until the raw wound is healed a little and then bring up your brilliant ideas later in a non-offensive manner (see Chapter 13, "How to Explain Anything to Your Husband.") Even if the answer to the problem is overtly obvious to you, you still need to offer compassion versus moving into your instinctive advice-giving mode. When a husband allows you to see into his hurt, it is not the time to give unsolicited advice; it is the time to boost his confidence and ego."

Men's egos. I forget how large their ego tanks are and about the hole in the bottom of their tanks that drain nightly.

"When a man trusts a woman enough to be vulnerable with his failures, she must come through for him and have an unfaltering belief that he is man enough for the problem. This vote of confidence and belief in him will pour concrete and creativity into his veins. If a man's wife believes in and trusts him to figure things out and succeed, he will often feel he is enough to handle the ordeal."

Instead, I make Matthew feel like he's a dope.

"When Matthew feels he's failed, his ego is like an egg tied to a shoe, and you are the shoe, Young Jessica. That means that every word you speak, every step you take, must be soft and careful. No stomping around, or the egg will break. Instead, bring out the padding, the cushions, and the gentleness."

I bring out a hammer.

Genie continues. "A man's failure in his job hurts him like a woman's failure to conceive or a having a miscarriage hurts her. The pain is deep and pervasive. A wise wife will realize that how she handles this moment, this shining moment, will determine whether she restores and rebuilds her husband's confidence or destroys it."

Fly swatter is an accurate description of my prior techniques.

"Affection escalates in a husband for his wife when she knows how to treat him when he is down," Genie adds.

I love affection. I *adore* affection.

"Young Jessica, now I am going to tell you something that will seem absolutely ridiculous to you. Are you ready? Be prepared to be stunned at this advice."

As if being stunned at Genie's advice is something new.

"When your husband experiences any failure, the best way you can tell him that you still believe in him and are not bothered by his failure is to desire him, to want him sexually. This is a language men can hear, a perfume they can smell. All your words are helpful, but your desire for him tells him that he's still a man, that he can figure this out, and that he has what it takes."

"Ludicrous, Genie. The last thing in the world I want to do when I'm upset is have sex. Are you sure you're right about this?"

"I'm absolutely right, if he's in the 80 percent of men," he says. "You must continually realize this other person, this husband, is repeatedly, wildly different from you." (Read Chapter 32, "When a Woman Wants Sex More Than Her Husband Does" if you are in the 20 percent of women.)

" 'Wildly different' is underestimating it, Genie. If it weren't for your thousands of years of experience, I'd doubt you on this. Especially this sex stuff that you say can help heal a man's bruised ego. It's sort of pitiful to me."

"I know women tend to think like that, Young Jessica. Since it's not how women feel or how they process hurt, they tend to call it 'pitiful.' You must keep remembering that the Creator took two creatures, male and female, to express His single nature. You are only half of that combination, and you naturally only understand one perspective."

Humpf. Sex for healing a bruised ego? Doesn't make sense to me, but maybe he's right. Maybe I'm demanding that Matthew process life and think like a woman. Maybe I get this male psyche thing even less than I thought I did.

"Don't be discouraged," Genie says. "You have made giant strides in understanding your husband. You are learning how to love and respect him in a mode that he hears. Do not be discouraged that you do not understand it all yet."

Nice of Genie to offer a little empathy himself. Empathy does feel calming.

"So when my husband fails," I say, "you want me to be sympathetic, have empathy, be sensitive, not give advice, boost his ego, and have sex with him? Do you want me to climb Mount Kilimanjaro too?"

He smiles. "Love gives what is needed, not what it wants to give or what is easy to give."

That is certainly how I love my children.

"I think I will watch today's sunset from Mount Kilimanjaro," Genie says. "Good suggestion." And with that, he vanishes.

Allison's name is appearing on my caller ID. We have been talking a lot lately because she is worried that her husband, Zach, might lose his job.

"It happened, Jessica. They let Zach go. It's final, really final. How are we going to pay our house note? My stupid little job won't begin to pay the bills around here." She breaks down in tears. Allison has worked so they could have extras, and extras they certainly have. Nice, new cars, a big suburban house that is beautifully decorated, the newest technology, etc.

I've been coaching both of my married sisters in the Eight A's as Genie has been coaching me. Today's advice will be perfect for Allison. I am sad for her and Zach but, at the same time, relieved that I have something helpful to say to her.

I begin my long conversation with Allison as I leave to pick up the boys from school and take them to their haircut appointments.

Explaining the principles to Allison of what to say and do when a husband experiences failure solidifies them in my mind. The best way to learn anything is to teach it. Allison seems open to my suggestions.

After Allison and I hang up, Matthew calls to tell me that Mr. Hammerhead, one of his biggest clients, has offered to let our family use his condo in Santa Rosa Beach for a long weekend this spring.

"That is so exciting, Matthew!" I think of the A of Admiration and go for it. "I don't think most clients offer their personal condos to their advertising executives. I have a feeling that you're over-the-top great at this job or Mr. Hammerhead wouldn't be so generous." These moments of admiring Matthew are becoming more and more a daily habit.

"Well, I don't know about that," he says, modestly. "But I'm very complimented that he wants to give me a weekend at his condo. The days he offered are April 4 through April 7."

My heart sinks. April 5 is the Saturday of the fundraising carnival! Mrs. Smith nailed down the date last week so she could let her daughter have the other surrounding weekends for wedding activities.

"Matthew, is there any way we can ask for another weekend? That's the carnival fundraising weekend."

"No," he says, trying to hide his disappointment. "He offered those specific dates. It would be rude to ask for other dates."

"Let me call Mrs. Smith and see if we can change the carnival date," I say.

We hang up, and a feeling of disappointment washes over me. My independent living of prior months is coming back to bite me. I can't believe all the mistakes I've made in the past. Before I fall down into the hole of regret, I remind myself that I can't be perfect overnight. I must forgive myself, determine to keep living the Eight A's, and not focus on prior mistakes.

I call Mrs. Smith to see if we can reschedule.

CHAPTER 11
How to View Your Husband's Work from His Perspective

Monday, November 12

've been on the phone all morning trying to get Matthew's family organized for Thanksgiving. Looks like ours is the lucky house again to host the event. Matthew only has brothers who aren't married, so there aren't any sisters-in-law to help with the food. Matthew's mother, Daisy, will bring her unhealthy white flour rolls, Aunt Dena will bring her usual relish tray, and Aunt Bobette will bring her delicious pumpkin pies, but otherwise, I'm the sole cook.

I called Mrs. Smith, the principal, last Wednesday after Mr. Hammerhead offered us his condo during the April 5 carnival weekend. Mrs. Smith was afraid to schedule the event for March because of the weather, and yes, her daughter has showers, luncheons, etc. every other Saturday in April. She thought May was too late to schedule a carnival and acted like April 5 was the only date in the century available. I told her about our condo offer in hope that she would let me out of my agreement to spearhead the carnival, but she didn't. I'm starting to not like her very much.

Chloe calls to tell me that Rachel called her and asked if she could borrow a dress that she saw Chloe wear at an event recently. This woman has chutzpah!

"Why don't you open your freezer, Young Jessica?" a deep voice asks, startling me a little.

I smile at my welcome visitor and open the freezer to find eight huge casseroles, all wrapped in freezer paper and marked Sweet Potato Casserole, Broccoli and Rice Casserole, and Cornbread Dressing. There's even a frozen cooked turkey! I am almost through with my cooking for Thanksgiving! Tra-la-la-BOOM-de-ay!

"Nice work, Genie," I say, as the stress over Thanksgiving oozes out of my body.

He smiles. "Today we are going to discuss how essential a man's job is to how he feels about himself."

I didn't see a green bean casserole. I hope there's one in there.

Genie jumps right in as usual. "A man will often define himself by what he does for a living. Is he a painter? A researcher? A mechanic? Contrary to this, women primarily define themselves by their relationships. For example, although a woman might be an interior designer or a nurse by trade, what is most important to her is that she is a wife or a mother."

I have noticed the intensity of the job/career thing with men. Yes, I know I have gifts and want to use them, but they are not as important to me as my relationships.

"That's why birthdays are monumental to women," he says. "Birthdays are when a woman measures how satisfying her relationships are by how others treat her on her birthday."

I don't want much from Matthew on my birthday, only a present (wrapped), a card (preferably mushy), a cake (with candles), to be taken out to dinner (at a *nice* restaurant), and a parade.

"A man defines himself mainly by his work, by what he *does*. Jobs define men in their minds. What he does is who he is."

Genie pauses as if he is not sure about what he is going to say next. "This is a strong analogy, but it is fair to say that a woman's grief over a miscarriage is similar to a man's grief (which he would often hide) over losing a job."

I protest. "Genie, surely not. That analogy is stretching it." I think I have a genie that is prone to exaggeration.

"See?" he asks. "You can't even conceive that the pain you would feel over a miscarriage would be similar to a man's pain over losing a job. That is why we need to discuss his work. Women often do not comprehend the enormity of how a man feels about his calling and career."

"Okay, Genie. Let's assume that Matthew's job is ultra-important to him in a way I don't grasp. What will that mean to me?"

"For one thing, once a woman understands the importance of a man's work," he says, "it will change how she listens to him. Often women hear their husband's repetitive work stories and think, 'Ho hum, heard this a million times. Why can't he talk about something I'm interested in?' "

I do get tired of hearing about Matthew's different advertising accounts.

"A woman is wise to learn as much as she can about her husband's occupation. This area alone affords vast opportunities for her to admire and appreciate him. Also, it's hard for a man to feel close to a woman when she doesn't enter into this area of his life where he is enormously invested. Only a foolish woman would choose to be uninterested in her husband's work."

I only want to hear about selected topics regarding work. For example, that scamp, Indigo.

"When young, new guys come into the agency with better ideas and more enthusiasm," Genie says, "Matthew's security will be threatened. A wife who is smart will understand the competition her husband feels with these other men and will be his biggest fan."

Men are so ridiculous in their competition with each other.

"There are a few men out there who are internally driven," Genie says. "They will succeed in their work without any support from a woman. But the vast majority of men will need a woman at home who believes in them and fills their tanks with praise and confidence to thrive at a high level. What affection a man has for a woman who has unshakable confidence in his abilities! Men conquer achievements they would not otherwise accomplish when there is an affirming woman at home."

Obviously, I'm not on the Marriage Honor Roll yet.

"A woman can't give a man what he derives from his calling," Genie continues. "Therefore, the more she understands the importance of his work, the more she endears herself to him."

So much to learn.

"Men especially enjoy having their wives appreciate their Goliath efforts at work. An example of such a comment would be, 'Matthew, I realize we enjoy this nice home, healthy food, and many nice extras because you work very hard and are generous with us. I know your paycheck doesn't automatically come in the mail, but you use blood and sweat to get that paycheck. I really appreciate it.' "

"No one ever thanks me for the laundry," I say. "Or the trips to the grocery or all the vacuuming. It's simply expected and taken for granted." I feel a little pity party coming on.

"You are right, Young Jessica. But remember, a wise woman builds her home. She gets air blown into her balloon from the Creator, and then she has air to blow into the balloons of her family. She is content with the Creator's favor. *Her husband's appreciation is a bonus.* Don't begrudge giving. Self-focus makes your soul small and ugly.

"Got to go," he says. "There's a sale on flying carpets in Turkey."

That last comment about a small and ugly soul was alarming. I hate that I sometimes have a selfish heart. My mind begins to berate me because I have multiple weaknesses to work on. I have to stop and remember that I am forgiven by the Creator, and so I must forgive myself. Onward and upward!

I do know, however, that I'll never listen to Matthew's work stories in the same manner again. I am changing at the speed of ... well, at the speed of a flying carpet!

I call Allison to see how things are going with Zach since he is now unemployed. She answers the phone in tears. I think she is upset over Zach's unemployment, but I'm wrong.

"Dad has been in an accident, Jessica. He's at Baptist Hospital in the emergency room. Can you meet me there in twenty minutes?"

Thoughts of the same scenario three years ago when my mother was killed in a car accident flood my mind. I grab my keys and jump into the car.

I call Matthew on the way, and he shows up at the hospital the same time I do. I burst into tears as he puts his arm around me.

Rachel walks in around the same time as Matthew and me. "My pedicure got all messed up because it wasn't dry yet when I got the call." Oh, puhllleeeezzzzze tell me she didn't say that.

We sit for hours as they do multiple tests. Finally, we find out that Dad is going to be okay, as he has only a broken leg and some heavy bruises. I am relieved beyond measure.

Walking into his room, I see a nurse fluffing up his pillow. "Harry is going to be alright," she says. The trim nurse is around Dad's age, and I notice she has no ring on her left hand.

"His name is Harold, not Harry," I say, being polite but wanting her to know Dad's real name.

"I know," she says. "But I told him that I am going to call him Harry because no man should have hair like that at his age. He has hair like a twenty-year-old."

Dad beams, broken bones and all. Why can't he find a nice lady like this nurse to marry?

Rachel then walks in with an obvious grumpy attitude. She isn't very warm to Dad, I notice. How can we free him from this net that is about to descend upon him?

CHAPTER 12
How to Correct Your Husband

Wednesday, November 21

The drama has not stopped since Dad was in the hospital.

Chloe overheard Rachel talking on the phone to someone where she said, "He looks so gross and old in that hospital bed."

We three sisters couldn't agree on what to do or say about it. We don't want to hurt Dad, but we also feel obligated to let him know what kind of viper he is about to become entangled with.

Finally, we decided that we would meet with Dad and tell him the truth. So we did. Then Dad confronted Rachel, she denied it, and now she says she's doesn't want anything to do with the three of us again. Dad is understandably upset. Crazy-making at its finest.

Tomorrow is Thanksgiving, and I'm stressed, even though Genie did most of the cooking. I sit down to make a list of what still needs to be done. "Iron tablecloths. Polish silver. Set tables. Make flower arrangements."

"Can I help you with that list, Young Jessica?" Ahh, the soothing sound of that gorgeous *abracadabra* voice.

My stress dissolves as we walk through the house, and with a flip of Genie's wrist, I have a gorgeously decorated Thanksgiving table with a starched tablecloth, polished silver, pilgrim figurines, and fresh flowers. *Better Homes and Gardens* should drop by to photograph my table.

"Genie, you're a lifesaver," I say, which I mean in more ways than just helping me with Thanksgiving. I physically feel all my stress knots untie as I tear up the list I previously made. I move to get my Turquoise Journal to take notes.

"We have a difficult topic today, Young Jessica. I have been around for centuries and whatever culture I am in or whatever century it is, I have noticed that women are wired to correct their husbands. This will be the subject of our discussion today."

I've noticed this, too, among my sisters and friends and, ah, well, yes, in myself. Wives understandably don't like their husbands' manners, clothes, social skills, work habits, time with their hobbies, or any number of a zillion things. It seems to me and to all the women that I know that it is a woman's birthright to fix her husband. We see a leaky faucet, we fix a leaky faucet.

"Interestingly, as I've said before, a wife is extraordinarily sweet and accommodating during courtship in order to win the man. He thinks she is going to remain that easy and accepting. He thinks he is acquiring a new cook, a consistently engaged sexual partner, and a round-the-clock admirer. So imagine his surprise when she begins Operation: Transform-the-Flunkee after the wedding."

Well, Matthew's clothes *were* ridiculous. And it is still absurd how much time he spends bowling.

"Men hate, and I emphasize the word *hate*, a discussion of their faults and weaknesses. Whenever a man is criticized or corrected, you must remember that his 'failure alarm' is set off, which is excruciatingly painful to him. Therefore, figure out the top five to eight things you care about and try to ask for only those things. Don't casually throw out, 'That's not the way I wanted the garage cleaned,' 'That's not the peanut butter I wanted you to buy,' or 'That's not what I would have said to your boss.' You wear a man out with so much criticism, and then he loses affection for you."

You've told me that before. Can we just get on with it?

"The information that I'm going to give you today," Genie begins, "would prevent many divorces if women knew these relationship strategies. Now we will proceed to today's topic: how to correct a husband."

Yippee. I've been waiting for this topic. Matthew has a looonnnng list of things to correct.

"Because correction is so agonizing to a man," Genie says, "you must realize that you can only rarely correct him. I like to tell wives that they need sixty-seven positive deposits into a man's tank for every criticism or correction. This is how severe negative judgments are to him."

"Where do you get these statistics, Genie? Do you make them up?" I ask.

"Actually I do, but after centuries of trying to repair marriages, I have seen what works and what doesn't. Sixty-seven is not a scientific number, but it is large to show you the vast difference between positive comments and negative comments. If your whole relationship is characterized by the positive Eight A's, your relationship can handle an occasional—and I emphasize the word *occasional*—negative remark. Even then, with this huge ratio, you have to be soft and think carefully about the best way to tell him something without offending him."

Ugh. Another sermon on using kid gloves and tippy-toeing around.

"I'd like to also remind you," Genie says, "that it is never best to correct Matthew when you are angry. Try to hold your tongue and later think of what to say to him. Wait until you are no longer irritated when you begin. Humans tend to cut and stab one another when they are angry and later regret their harsh words."

I don't need any examples of letting angry words fly and the subsequent damages.

"Also remember," he says, "we're on the five-year plan. Matthew is going to have weaknesses that need addressing, but not all at once. In fact, pick one thing to tell him and don't flood him with several requests. A man literally can't take it. He will retreat into himself, leave the house, or find some way to distance himself from you. I have yet to see a husband whose affection for his wife increases from her abrasive correction. Even though he needs it, it will rob you of his affection."

"Genie, this sounds like we're talking about eight-year-olds."

"Eight or eighty," he says, "men hate correction. Therefore, you must learn the art of *telling your husband what he needs to hear without offending him.*"

More discipline for me: don't eat too much, don't spend too much, don't directly confront the husband about all his junk. Exhausting.

"The first thing you'll want to figure out," Genie says, "is what exactly is the most important thing he needs to hear. Again, you can't address six things at once. *One* issue and, again, it must be bolstered by sixty-seven positive deposits."

Does any woman really do this?

"The best way to correct a man is to not correct him at all, but instead, catch him doing the specific situation right and praise him."

Huh?

"For example, let's say that a husband doesn't work hard to be friendly and outgoing at parties, with friends, with the kids' teachers, etc. Instead of putting forth any effort to engage others, he is quiet and barely talks. Rather than hitting him over the head with his lack of social skills, the best way to address this flaw is to wait until he is vivacious and then tell him, "I love it when you are outgoing like that. Did you see how much that store clerk enjoyed you? I was so proud of you. How delightful you were in that situation! And that was so clever what you said. I enjoyed it so much."

This is like rewarding laboratory monkeys in a social science experiment.

"Genie, what if he never gets it right, so there's no opportunity to praise him?"

"Then we move to the second strategy," Genie says. "And that is to frame the request right. Give me an example of something that upsets you about Matthew."

Oh, baby, what do I choose?

"I don't like that he bowls so much. I wouldn't mind him bowling a little, but I think it's selfish how much he is away from the boys and me."

"Instead of using words like *selfish*, reframe the situation," Genie says. "For example, what you want to communicate is that you love his influence on the children, you enjoy his company, and that you can tell that peacefulness and happiness in the home are greater when he's around. You want to assure him that you enjoy him having a hobby, and that you want him to bowl, but could he please discuss or negotiate how much time he's away from the family? He will be much more receptive to the idea that he's wanted, needed, and appreciated rather than a head-bashing session where you scold him for ignoring his proper responsibilities to be at home with you and the children."

I know Genie has a webcam hidden somewhere in this house.

"Young Jessica, by now it goes without saying that before you attempt to talk to Matthew about a weakness or fault, you must consistently be depositing all Eight A's. It is virtually a miracle how those Eight A's open a man to your influence. I repeat this often because you, like the women I have taught in previous centuries, tend to forget this vital point."

It's easy to forget stuff that is hard to do.

"The third strategy I want to discuss in regard to when a wife needs to correct a husband," he says, "is to use the 'sandwich' technique. First, the wife figures out what correction she specifically wants to tell the husband. Then, she begins with a compliment, gives the correction, and finishes with a compliment."

Work. Work. Work.

"For example, suppose a wife wants to tell a man that he repeatedly forgets to take the trash can down to the edge of the street for the garbage man to pick up. She ends up doing it most weeks, even though it is one of 'his' jobs."

Matthew remembers his household chores. I need to write that down in the Turquoise Journal on the list of "Things Other Husbands Do Wrong."

"Here is an example of how she would use the sandwich technique. 'Honey, I appreciate how you help me around the house. That was great how you cleaned the grill on Saturday (bread). By the way, would you please remember to take the garbage down to the street this morning (meat)? Oh, and thank you for planting those pansies for me. It makes me happy the way you help me around the house (bread).'

"Do you see the sandwich pattern? Compliment, friendly request/correction, and another compliment."

It sure would be easier to yell, "Don't forget the trash, Bozo."

"If Matthew hears you and does what you ask," Genie says, "remember to praise him for doing it. If he forgets again, don't unload the artillery. Simply say, 'I bet you'll remember next time' and drop it without a long speech."

How does he know I give long speeches?

"And now we get to the best technique of all for communicating something negative to your husband," Genie says.

This guy makes the Energizer Bunny look lazy.

"The last technique is called 'word pictures.' I will discuss it next time when we are going to talk about *How to Explain Anything to Your Husband*. But I've got to run because there is a sale on sapphires in Syria, and I am looking for one for my turban."

Genie's gone, and I'm glad, for that was enough for today. My brain runs out of room easily with these teachings.

Awww, look! There are napkin rings made of autumn leaves and berries on my dining room table to complement the harvest theme.

My Thanksgiving stress now completely dissolved, I decide to do a few errands before the boys get home from school. Since Matthew's office is near our house, I decide to leave a sweet note on the dashboard of his car. I pause in the parking lot to write the note and see a yellow Chevy Camaro pull in. I am aware that the Mediterranean scalawag drives that sexy car. I dip down in my seat so she can't see me. Oh. My. Gosh. Can you wear a skirt that short to work? And a sweater that tight? This isn't the photo shoot for the Victoria Secret's catalog, girlie. Dang it, and dang it again.

CHAPTER 13
How to Explain Anything to Your Husband

Friday, December 7

t's 6:30 a.m., and the phone rings. Who can that be?

"Good morning, Jessica," says Hallie, one of my brides. What could she want at this hour?

"I thought my wedding planner said the wedding invitations would go out four weeks before the wedding," she said. "But I misunderstood her. The invitations are go out *six* weeks before the wedding."

I'm barely awake, but I can feel my adrenaline and annoyance mounting. I groggily do the revised math calculations in my mind. Originally, I was to have her invitations finished by December 24. But if she wants them two weeks earlier, they need to be finished by December 10. In three days!

"Hallie, you have 275 invitations, and you are telling me you want them in three days?"

"Yes, this Monday," she says, oblivious to my inconvenience and to the early hour.

These Bridezillas can wear you out. They forget the rest of us have a life.

"I'm afraid that's impossible, Hallie. I have a full weekend planned. I can try to move up the date, but I can only get them to you a week early."

She bursts into tears. Really, do I make enough money in this calligraphy business to put up with this insanity?

I tell her I will try to get the invitations to her by next Wednesday even though that will be severely pushing it.

After the boys leave for school, I throw the breakfast dishes into the sink because I want to be one of the first in line at the electronics store when they open this morning at ten. They are selling iPads for only ninety-nine dollars to the first ten customers. That price is crazy! I grab my purse and head for the door, afraid that I am already too late.

There's a knock on the front door. Who can that be? I see that it's my neighbor Cammey, whose husband, Peyton, works with Matthew. Actually, to be accurate, he's a bit over Matthew in seniority and authority. Cammey and Peyton have an only child, Charlie, who is in Brandon's class. Brandon doesn't like Charlie, but I instruct him to be nice, especially since he is a neighbor and the son of one of Matthew's coworkers. To be honest, I don't like Cammey much, either. Her whole world revolves around Charlie and his happiness. Her incessant chatter about him is annoying. I mean, hello? I have children too. I wish I could pretend I wasn't home, but Cammey might see my car leave since she can see my house from hers.

"Cammey, good morning. Is everything okay?" I don't want to act too friendly because I'm hoping she wants to borrow a quick cup of sugar and won't stay to talk.

"Do you have time to talk a little bit?" she says and then continues to walk into my house without waiting for an answer. "It seems that the boys at school are leaving my Charlie out, and Charlie says that your Brandon won't let him sit at the popular-boy lunch table."

Cammey looks like she's going to cry. This is the perfect example of her trying to blaze any easy path for Charlie.

"Cammey, I'm so sorry. Of course we need to talk about this. Would you mind if I called you back to discuss this later today? I was headed out the door and—"

"I knew it, I knew it," she says, backing up and starting to leave. "I knew you wouldn't be helpful. Your Brandon is one of the popular kids, so you don't have any idea what it's like to be on the outside. I thought that maybe since we were neighbors and our husbands worked together—oh, never mind." Her eyes are now actually wet as she's walking away.

"Cammey, I'm sorry about Charlie, and of course, I want to talk about it and see if we can fix things. Only I'm late leaving and—."

Cammey is already halfway down my driveway.

Brandon has told me that Charlie goes around pinching everyone, and that the guys don't like him. What am I supposed to do about this? I hope Matthew has some advice. And what do I say to Brandon about being nice to Charlie? I look at my phone to check the time and am pretty sure I've missed any discount iPads. Cammey's explosion takes the air right out of me.

I call Matthew as I gather my coat and purse to leave. He is greatly annoyed with Brandon. "Jessica, we will deal with Brandon tonight. He can't leave Charlie out. I have to go."

Again, I don't get what I want from Matthew. And now I'm worried that he won't handle this situation with Brandon the way I want him to.

"Do you like to wrap your Christmas presents in paper or have them in bags?" asks Genie. I didn't expect him this morning. This is my second unexpected visitor.

"Genie, I don't mean to be rude, but—"

In his hand is a new iPad. This genie beats Santa Claus any day.

I put down my purse and coat and try to simmer down from the unexpected confrontation from Cammey. Genie and I momentarily discuss Cammey and Charlie, but he is ready to begin today's lesson. I try to switch gears from the Brandon-Charlie issue to wife mode. My emotions feel ragged.

"Today we will talk about how to masterfully explain anything to Matthew," Genie begins. "This includes your opinions, thoughts, and feelings. However, there are a few important principles to cover before we get started."

Thinking of the short skirt that Indigo was wearing two weeks ago when I saw her in the parking lot, I realize I need to explain to Matthew that he needs to enforce a dress code at work. Honestly, there are a number of things I need to explain to Matthew.

"Although a man can have a heroic nature," the Genie begins, "and will risk life and limb to protect others or to fulfill his duty, he usually has a rather simple emotional nature and can be baffled by the complexity of a woman's inner life. Men are not trying to hurt or ignore women; they truly think completely different from you. This technique to communicate something to your husband that I will teach you today gets under his radar and enables him to understand your point of view."

"Genie, I thought that when I found my soul mate, he would instinctively know my feelings and needs. Or at least he would work hard to figure out what I'm feeling or thinking." My sisters have also felt the same way.

He laughs. "You and most other wives go into marriage believing this. What a damaging lie. Wives think if their husbands loved them enough, they would be able to read their minds. Or at least, as you say, if the husbands tried harder, they could understand them."

Matthew doesn't try hard at all to know what I want or how I feel. I mean, for Pete's sake, just ask me!

"Men do not come naturally wired to understand a woman's complex emotional makeup, Young Jessica. They want to please their wives, but they have no idea how to do it. You have to teach them."

I teach my children; I didn't expect to have to teach a husband.

"And men do not possess your feelings, so naturally they do not understand them," Genie says. "You must learn how to appropriately teach them to him."

I wish I could download this information to a Kindle in Matthew's head and be done with it.

"I need to remind you that teaching your husband never involves criticizing him," Genie says. "The number one way women try to teach men is to criticize them by saying things like, 'Oh, you do that wrong. Here is the right way to do it.' A man can be a giant oak tree with strength and leaves for shelter and shade, but if you criticize him, it is like taking away the sunlight. Eventually, this man will die on the inside. Therefore, you have to find a way to teach him without criticizing him. *It takes great skill to explain how you feel to a man without making him feel inadequate or that he is being criticized.*"

There he goes, talking about a man's ego again. His fragile, easily cracked ego.

"Another point we need to bring up before we get into the meat of today's lesson," Genie says, "is the problem women have with 'flooding' their husbands. The moment women get married, there are one million things the new husband needs to learn. And the wife wants him to learn them overnight. Pick one thing at a time that you want to teach your husband. You can't fuss that his mother comes over unannounced, that he doesn't pick up after himself, that he doesn't call when he's late, that he needs to stop wiping his nose on his sleeve, that you don't want him to watch sports all night, and that you want him to ask you about your day. Flooding the poor guy is not effective."

What's a poor woman to do when there's so much to address? Short skirts in the office, lack of understanding my feelings, impatience with the children—.

"The last introductory comment I want to make before we begin today's lesson is that sometimes husbands are reluctant to give you something you want, and if you are capable, you should take care of it yourself. For example, if your husband doesn't want to read out loud to the children at night, you do it. If he doesn't want to keep a good checkbook, you do it. Try to fix what you can without pulling on him."

Matthew doesn't care about decorating for Christmas and is frequently whiney when he is asked to help. Maybe I could let that go since I have so many other important issues. "Today's lesson is how to explain anything to your husband. For centuries, great teachers have used analogies and illustrations to teach their subject matter to others. Today, we will learn about word pictures, which is an advanced form of these techniques."

Yay! I get to tell Matthew what I want him to change! I'm diggin' this lesson.

"For example," Genie says, "what is something you want to explain to Matthew that he does not understand?"

Of course, several possible examples wrestle in my brain to be picked as the topic, so it is hard to decide on one. I pick one that Genie and I have not discussed before. "Genie, sometimes when Matthew and I are scheduled to go out on a date, he forgets. Even when he doesn't forget, he often gets involved in a project at work and comes home an hour late. Then I'm upset before the night even begins. He thinks his work trumps everything, and that I should understand."

"I like this example," Genie says. "First, find something in Matthew's world that he cares about, that he is emotionally attached to."

"His bowling," I say.

"Good choice," he says. "So you might say something like this: 'Matthew, suppose you had a special night of bowling planned and you were to meet your friends at seven o'clock at the lanes, but your bowling buddies didn't show up until eight o'clock and didn't contact you. How would you feel?' "

"Go on," I say.

"After Matthew has made that *emotional* connection with how he would feel, you say, 'That's how disappointed I am when you come home late when we have a date.' "

This is interesting, but I'll never be able to come up with these word pictures.

"I need another example, Genie."

"Alright," he says. "Give me another situation in which you would like to explain something to Matthew."

If he had given me a little notice, I could have prepared a list of twenty.

"When Matthew is upset about something at work, he will often take his anger out on me. For example, one evening he was especially upset over an incident at work. We had an evening scheduled to go to another couple's house for dinner, so I took her a scented candle as a housewarming gift. On the way to their house, Matthew shocked me by saying, 'How do you know what scent she likes? You can't give people scented candles if you don't know what scent they like. I bet we have lost friends because you are not careful about gifts.' Genie, I know he was upset about something at work, and none of that conversation was really about the candle, but it was hurtful to be treated like that."

Genie raised his eyebrows. I can see this example has stumped him.

"All humans have weaknesses," he says. "But most can be taught, if done in an intelligent way. The average woman would explode at this outrageous accusation and insult her husband right back, thereby perpetuating the dysfunctional cycle that Matthew began. A wise wife, on the other hand, would merely say, 'Matthew, I know you are upset from work, but I don't like what you said to me. We'll discuss it later.' Then she would table it and think of a great word picture to later tell her husband."

What woman has that kind of self-control? I'd want to blast the guy, right there, right then.

"Here's a word picture you could use, Young Jessica, at a later date when the intensity of the moment has died down. 'Matthew, suppose you are at work, and your boss has lost the biggest account of the firm and also his teenager was expelled from school. You know how upset he is over these issues, but when you walk into his office, he says, "Matthew, I think we lost that account because you took them to eat Mexican food. You don't know if they even like Mexican food, and they probably thought we are a bad firm because of that." ' "

I can see where he's going.

"That's good, Genie. I like it. And Matthew would emotionally feel how unfair that accusation was by his boss."

"Correct, Young Jessica. Then you would tell Matthew you knew he was upset over whatever happened at the office the other night when he accused you of losing friends because of innocent acts like bringing people candles without knowing their scent preference. However, you still felt it was unfair, and it hurt your feelings. Matthew will now hear this."

I like this. I can see that this will be effective.

"How will I ever think of these examples, Genie?"

"You will need to take some time and be creative. Use your Turquoise Journal to brainstorm some ideas," he says. "*Can you imagine the long-term difference in a marriage if a wise, mature wife did not return evil-for-evil and instead changed the normal relationship pattern of 'dishing it right back' to taking time to think of wise word pictures?*"

"I won't be able to do this," I say. "I get too upset and heated in the moment."

"I think you have more self-control than you give yourself credit for," Genie says. "Once you have a plan and a strategy, more and more you will be able to hold your tongue. This Advanced Training for Wives is to make you a marriage champion, not training so you get by with an average marriage but rather an astonishing, breathtaking marriage."

I do want that. I do. But the thought hits me again that I am the one trying to grow the marriage, learning all these techniques, while Matthew doesn't put forth much effort in the marriage.

"Why again do I have to work so hard to do these complicated word pictures while Matthew doesn't work very hard on our marriage?" I ask.

"We can have that conversation again, if you like, about what's fair or what works," Genie says.

What's fair or what works? I don't seem to remember that those two things are different.

These teachings wear me out. *They are opposite my natural inclinations*, which are to spill out all the poison I am thinking and feeling. It's going to take some practice and time to master the skill of giving "word pictures."

And it's going to take some determination to continue with the whole *Wife School* thing. I probably need to accept that women are usually the ones who care more about growing the marriage relationship than their husbands, so they are the lucky ones who get to do most of the work.

"By the way, you can use word pictures to talk to kids too. Come up with a story in which Brandon feels left out by the other boys, and then tell him that's how Charlie feels. Alright—enough for today," Genie says. "And there's a surprise in your living room."

There sits a Christmas tree, all set up with my own ornaments and decorations. That's three hours of time that Genie saved me. Now I've got a little time to think of a couple word pictures to tell Brandon about how Charlie feels left out and also to tell Matthew about how upset I am that he works with Ms. Skank USA.

I jot down a few ideas, and then Dad calls. "Rachel broke the engagement," he says.

I wait, gearing myself up to handle his meltdown while simultaneously feeling calm and relief wash over me.

"Remember that nurse in the ER? The one who calls me Harry because of my thick hair? I ran into her at Walgreens this morning and asked her out. We're going out this weekend."

Well, what about that? No Rachel, no meltdown, and a new date! This indeed is good news!

I'm excited to tell Allison and Chloe that we are rid of Rachel. I call Chloe first, and she is ecstatic. Then I call Allison. Allison is too upset about Zach not having a job and there being no money to buy her children Christmas presents to be very concerned about anything else. She talks for thirty minutes about all the troubles in her life.

Is everybody else's life as messy as mine or is it just me?

CHAPTER 14

What to Do When Your Husband Mistreats You

Friday, December 21

Matthew has left for work, and the boys are sleeping in since it is Christmas break.

As I walk out to get the morning paper on the driveway, I see Cammey across the street and wave. She acts like she didn't see me. This issue with Brandon and Charlie is far from being over. Matthew and I have tried to talk to Brandon about being nice to Pinching Charlie, but even if he is nice to Charlie, he says he can't make the other boys like him.

Cammey was also rude to me last night at Matthew's office Christmas party. But that was the least of my concerns because Intriguing Indigo was there in a short, skin-tight, leopard-print dress with a plunging neckline. Every man there was salivating, including Matthew.

Even though I had on a new outfit, I still felt frumpy. And invisible.

When I came out of the restroom, Indigo was laughing and grabbing Matthew's arm. "That is MY husband!" I wanted to scream. Matthew moved away from her when he saw me. This Indigo issue is *not* over. I am still extremely upset over it. Indigo and Matthew have even been to lunch alone twice in the last two weeks, supposedly on business.

On the way home, however, I did not go into my usual hysterical meltdown but rather again calmly let him know I was upset by Indigo. He still does not see my view-point at all, claiming again that she is harmless. I am very discouraged this morning.

Tonight, I am hosting the Christmas get-together for my side of the family. I have little Christmas spirit and even less energy to get ready to entertain.

"How's your party looking?" asks Genie.

"Oh my goodness, Genie," I say. "What are you doing here? My boys are asleep upstairs!"

"They can't hear or see me, so no worries," he says.

Sometimes I talk out loud to myself anyway, so it's not a big deal if the boys hear me talking to the air.

I trust Genie and begin unloading on him. "I'm extremely frustrated about Matthew not seeing my viewpoint about Indigo. And on top of that huge irritation, I like the house to shine when I'm having guests and I still need to do more cooking."

Yes, I am hinting, and yes, I feel a little guilty for doing so.

"I like preparing for parties," Genie says. He flips his wrist into the air and the house immediately has that party-ready shine. There are meatballs, chicken wings, and all sorts of delights on the counter in my most beautiful dishes. "Let me put these goodies in the refrigerator, and then we can discuss our lesson for today. It is another difficult lesson."

Maybe it was rude to hint, but wow, what a spread!

"The topic today is what to do when your husband mistreats you," Genie says.

"Very apropos topic," I say.

"There is no marriage in which spouses do not occasionally offend each other," he says. "I have taught you how to treat your husband so that less and less you offend him and instead meet his needs. Now it is time to talk about how to respond when he mistreats you."

If I was on Facebook, I'd click "Like."

"There are three levels of offenses in a marriage and therefore three different strategies for dealing with each level of offense. Let's begin with strategy number one, which is used for the lowest kind of offense. It is called 'overlooking.' "

Well, I'm not overlooking Ms. 36D Indigo.

"Overlooking is a skill," Genie continues, "that only mature humans seem to master. It is more than being annoyed and not saying anything, which, by the way, actually builds resentment. Overlooking is the ability to *not* be offended."

I'm extremely offended by Indigo. Offended to the max.

" 'Overlooking' is not counting an offense," he says. "It is like being steam and letting the offense pass through the vapor instead of being a brick of ice and feeling the offense hit the hard surface. It's *not* being unconscious to the offense. No, you are aware of the offense, but you let it pass through. You don't record it. You overlook it. You let it go."

Click "Unlike."

"Humans make many relational mistakes, Young Jessica. Most of these mistakes are not meant to be personal. People are simply into their own worlds and concerned with their own issues. Therefore they speak words and choose actions without weighing or evaluating their impact on others. Keep a standing rule in your mind that most of the time you will choose not to be offended. This is extremely healthy human functioning."

"Like this morning," I say, "I was offended when Matthew told me he likes Thursdays because he and Charlie, a friend from work, go to Chili's to eat lunch. Since I make his lunch most days, doesn't he know that comment was offensive?"

"This is a perfect example of a level one offense," he said. "My hunch is that Matthew was not criticizing your lunches. He was probably only saying that he enjoys doing something different. I would recommend your overlooking this remark."

Making lunches is a lot of work, so if Matthew doesn't like mine, maybe he wants to make them himself.

"Let's look at a strategy for a level two offense, 'speaking the truth in love.' Do you have another more potent example when Matthew offended you recently by his words or actions?"

"This morning Matthew told me that he will be bowling in a tournament next Saturday," I say. "I know he loves bowling, and we've agreed that he can bowl two Saturdays a month. But this will be the *third* Saturday this month. He didn't even mention that it was his third Saturday! He knew he was cheating on the agreement."

"This is a perfect example of a level two offense," Genie says. "The first thing to remember is to not throw a hissy fit but to gain control of your emotions and tongue. Level two offenses are annoying but not evil. They should be handled by speaking the truth in love. Your first task is to see if there is additional information that Matthew has that would be helpful for you to understand his choice. An example would be to calmly say, 'Matthew, I thought we agreed on your bowling on Saturdays twice a month. Since this is the third Saturday, you must be thinking something different. Could you please tell me what it is?' "

That's giving him the benefit of the doubt. Not in my arsenal.

"Do you see the calmness?" Genie asks. "Did you notice the non-accusatory question? The wife is simply asking for his thoughts, believing that there is a probable reason. There is no hysteria, no sarcasm, no criticism. Just a request to understand."

I guess I don't win any prize with what I let rip, which was, "I guess you don't have to play by the rules, huh, Matthew?" I grimace at the memory. I don't think I'll confess my little sarcasm to Genie.

"Explore what Matthew is thinking," he says. "Listen carefully before you tell him your perspective. If he doesn't have a good reason and you feel upset, get hold of yourself before you begin. Lower your tone. Add some sweetness to your voice. Then calmly say, 'I thought we made an agreement. Please treat me with the same courtesy you'd like to be treated with, Matthew. You wouldn't like for me to break an agreement without consulting you.' "

Does any woman really act this calmly when she's been mistreated? No woman in Tennessee that I've ever known acts like that.

"No fit. No crazed woman," Genie continues. "Just a reasonable, sane female, speaking the truth in love. It's a very effective yet rare way for emotional wives to communicate with logical husbands. Men appreciate this direct, soft, non-hysterical confrontation."

To speak with that composure and to forfeit my sarcastic accusations would indeed be a modern-day walking-on-water.

"Now we will discuss the third strategy to use with a level three offense," Genie says, "which is called The Big Guns. Matthew is not allowed to mistreat you. Can you think of something very serious he did lately that would be in this category?"

The example explodes in my brain.

"Genie, you've heard me talk about his coworker, Indigo. In the past two weeks, Matthew and Indigo have been to lunch alone twice to discuss their advertising accounts. I've been furious about it. When I spoke to him about it, he said I was acting like a jealous little kid."

Genie shook his head. "Men are often very misinformed in this area, and I know this hurts you deeply, Young Jessica. That example would definitely be mistreating you. Even though Matthew may only be working, it is disrespectful to you for him to go to lunch alone with a woman. Sometimes a man can't help it, and he will find himself alone with a woman once, but certainly not two times, such as this. This issue needs to be addressed."

I'm actually relieved. You never know what Genie will say, and for once, he's on *my* side.

"Matthew keeps insisting it is only business," I say. I feel certain that vampy, puffy-lipped villain Indigo is not "only business."

"I am reluctant," Genie says, "to teach this third strategy to most women because until a woman is consistently giving her husband the Eight A's, she is not ready for this advice and teaching. Do you think you're ready, Young Jessica?"

I bet I'm not. But what the heck.

"Sure I am, Genie," I say.

"Here is a test: Does Matthew feel like you put him first in your life? Does Matthew feel your lack of resentment, your true affection for him, and does he know that your desire is to do him good? Does he feel that one of your top goals in life is to make him happy?"

"Those are impossible standards, Genie," I gripe. Those standards are somewhere over the rainbow.

"Yes, they are," he laughs. "But are those the goals in your heart, and does Matthew sense that are you moving toward them?"

"Matthew knows I've done a 180-degree turn around," I say. "I'm not perfect by any means, but Matthew knows that something is wildly different in the last few weeks. I am trying to daily fill his tank with the Eight A's. I know he feels I am seriously trying to make him happy." I could do a lot better, but my change has been elephantine.

"No wife is ever perfect," Genie said. "But that kind of effort on your part qualifies you to hear this. But one more thing before I tell you how to approach him if he's seriously mistreated you, Young Jessica."

The suspense is killing me.

"You cannot use this technique very often," Genie says. "Use it very rarely. Use it only when the issue is of paramount importance. Pick only situations that are extremely hurtful to you, not casual slights by your husband."

"I'm about to flip out over these lunches with the Victoria Secret coworker, Genie," I say.

"I agree that this is the right time to play your joker card," he says. "What you want to composedly say to Matthew is something like this: 'Matthew, making you happy as a husband is at the top of my list. I know I don't do that perfectly, but I am trying every day to make that come true. Do you feel that?'"

I could say that. It's a little braggy, but I could say it.

"By saying that," Genie says, "you're establishing with Matthew your right to ask for something big. This strategy has to be *earned* before you can use it."

I feel like I'm getting in on a trillion-dollar secret. "I'm trackin' with ya, Genie."

"After Matthew acknowledges your efforts to love him in a language he can hear, you say, 'I want you to know I am extremely hurt that you are taking Indigo to lunch by yourself. Even though you insist that it's innocent, and maybe it is, I am distraught over it. I want to love you and make you feel special, and I don't feel you are treating me with the same respect. Even if you don't understand my feelings, I am asking you to abide by my wishes just because I'm asking. I'm not asking you to understand. I'm simply asking you to not be alone with her just because you love me and because I'm asking.' "

I'm surprised at Genie. Usually his teaching is about giving, sacrificing, and persevering. Now, he's telling me to brag on myself a little about being a good wife and to ask for something. I like it. I like it a lot.

"A husband can't adore a woman he can mistreat," he says. "You must not let him mistreat you. A woman must be strong enough to not be needy but, at the same time, smart enough to know when it is wise to tell her husband she is hurt. It's a delicate balance."

It's a balance I don't get yet.

Genie's teaching has been about meeting Matthew's needs, about overlooking, and about giving up my rights. There's a fullness I feel with this teaching, like oxygen rushing into *my* lungs instead of always blowing oxygen into *his* lungs.

"I want to warn you, Young Jessica, how most husbands will respond to this. It's almost comical that you can predict this. When you tell them how hurt you are about something they've done, they will try to convince you that they did not mean to hurt you, that you read the situation wrong, and that they are not guilty. Really, don't laugh when he does this."

Genie has been to this rodeo before.

"What do I do when he tries to wiggle out of it, Genie?"

"What do you think most wives do when the husband tries to wiggle out of it?"

"They get mad?" I ask.

"Correct," he says. "Wives get angry, and then all of their previous good communication goes down the drain. When you get angry, you lose. The other person feels they do not have to listen to you because they think, 'She's an angry, insane, and unstable woman, so I don't have to pay attention to what she says.' "

I have felt insane and unstable, so this makes sense.

"Continue to speak calmly," Genie says. "An example would be, 'Maybe you are innocent, Matthew, and I'm not saying that you're not, but all I know is that I feel extremely hurt and want you to stop being alone with her.' "

I can't imagine getting through all that without being angry.

"A husband can't argue with the fact that you're hurt," Genie says. "He can argue with whether you *should* feel hurt but not *if* you're hurt. So don't try to give him a bunch of reasons why your hurt is justified. Just tell him that you are. If you are trying to live the Eight A's, he will hear you. He may not say much or give you any real sign that he's heard you, but he has heard you."

"Genie, what if after all this monumental strategy, he goes to lunch with her again?"

"It's important for you to continue to deposit the eight A's during this time," he says. "But if Matthew doesn't stop the lunches, you can add consequences. If you usually watch Sunday afternoon football with him, you could say, 'I am upset because I don't feel you are respecting me, as you continue to have lunch alone with Indigo. I am going to the mall to air my brain and see if I can restore myself.' "

"The obvious consequence to me," I say, "is to lock the bedroom door."

"I don't normally recommend women refusing the sexual relationship just because she is offended or upset," Genie says. "However, if there are ultra-serious issues in the marriage, such as adultery, alcohol addiction, or abuse, this *Wife School* program is not recommended. You will need to get human advisors and counselors."

Whoa—glad I'm not dealing with *those* issues. At least not yet.

"Let's review the principles we have learned today," Genie says. "Number one, overlook any offense whenever you can. Number two, calmly and rationally speak the truth in love. Number three, bring out The Big Guns when you have been severely mistreated."

This "Big Gun" strategy is quite different from the "Big Gun" strategy I usually use. I typically come in with my combat boots and machine gun and annihilate everything in sight.

"This is a complicated topic," Genie continues. "If a woman can take a five-year approach, can fill up the husband's tank with the Eight A's, and will use self-control in her speech to her husband, miracles truly occur in husbands. The miracles are not overnight. But with these principles, I have seen thousands of immature men be transformed into world-class husbands."

"I do need to explain one more principle I don't like to teach until women are giving their husbands the Eight A's, though," he says.

More?

"You are his queen, not his doormat. Therefore, when he mistreats you, do as you would do in the childhood game of Mother, May I? and take one giant step back. Emotionally, that is."

What?

"Women's natural tendency when their husbands mistreat them," he says, "is to pursue the husband with questions and demands and smothering remarks. All he wants to do is get away from this oppression. The wise response to a husband who mistreats you is to step back emotionally, give him more space, and remove yourself physically and emotionally. One wise woman whose husband had mistreated her said to him, 'I know you're going out of town for three days. Please don't call me during that time. I want to think about things.' That was a Mother, May I? giant step back to give the husband some breathing room. The husband's tendency when a wife does this is again comical. He begins pursuing her, the very thing she wants."

Relationships on Earth could not be any more complicated.

"As much as men like to feel needed," Genie says, "there is a paradoxical attraction to a wife who doesn't need him. In other words, she's happy without him. He is not needed to complete her as a person. She is whole in her relationship with the Creator. She is not a doormat, a whiney, needy, sappy thing. She is a regal queen, a woman who gives. However, a woman who respects herself does not allow her husband to mistreat her."

"Can you give me an example?" I ask.

"One Christmas in France a hundred years ago, a wife had repeatedly deposited the Eight A's in her husband's tank. But he had withdrawn emotionally. He was sulky, mysterious, and non-affirming. He was in the kitchen, acting cold and aloof. Realizing that she had done nothing wrong, and that this man was disengaging from her for no reason, she put on her happy, independent personality. She began singing and swishing around the kitchen, doing her chores. Then she said, 'I am going to town to buy a Christmas tree, and I'll be back.'

" 'What?' the husband asked. 'We always do that together.'

" 'I know,' the wife said. 'But I want to go by myself this time.' And in her happy, independent mood, she left."

My eyes are big. Come on, Genie. What happened next?

"When this wife got home with the Christmas tree, she was singing and as happy as she could be. Something switched in the husband's brain, and he didn't even know it. All of a sudden, he was friendly and offered to help her decorate the tree."

"Now here's the smart thing the wife did next: She didn't discuss the issue with him. She didn't ask, 'Are you ready to be nice?' She didn't say, 'Well, glad you are out of that mood.' She dropped the issue. Men can fall into moods and mistreat their wives, but when they do, women are to play Mother, May I? and take one giant emotional step backward."

Genie knows what works in marriages. He doesn't recommend what's easy, nor does he recommend what's popular; he recommends what works. It's extremely rare to see a wife respond to her husband with this kind of finesse. Usually, the wife hounds and badgers the husband about his inadequate relationship skills. The marriages I see around me are certainly not winning any blue ribbons at the fair.

"A woman carries a mystery and regality about her when she doesn't allow herself to be mistreated," Genie says. "As I've said, I'm reluctant to teach this, as women can abuse this topic and use it selfishly and manipulatively. A woman who is faithfully depositing the Eight A's will be focusing on her husband's needs, but alas, there is balance and some boundaries."

I am certainly glad for this teaching today. I've been waiting for this "balance" for months. I needed to hear this. All of Genie's previous lessons have been about giving. This lesson might be my favorite teaching of all.

"I must go now," he says. "I have ironed your outfit for tonight, and your front porch is swept. Also, I want you to know that I left multiple gifts for Allison's kids anonymously on her front porch. She's been so upset that her children weren't getting their usual Christmas since Zach is out of work. Don't act like you know anything about it. Have a nice time at your party." And he disappears.

I have a moment of true Christmas cheer as I think about how jubilant Allison will be over the anonymous gifts.

But my moment of bliss is interrupted by a text message from Matthew, telling me that he will be thirty minutes late coming home. He knows I'm having a party, and that I like him home early on those occasions. I wonder what came up. With The Big Guns confrontation about Indigo looming, I think I will overlook this offense of his being late.

I decide that after everyone goes home tonight, I will have that Big Guns talk with Matthew about that curvy Mediterranean fairy in his office. I think I will write out my ideas in my Turquoise Journal to get prepared.

Later that night

Dad brought his new girlfriend, Debbie, to the Christmas party. She is extremely attentive to him. How refreshing to have someone genuine in his life who seems to truly care about him. A new puppy is always the best medicine for a lost one. Our family doesn't drink alcohol, but I could smell a little alcohol on her breath. Oh well, a glass of wine before she came over is not the end of the world.

Allison couldn't stop talking about the anonymous gifts on her doorstep. Bikes! New clothes for the kids in the right styles and sizes! Legos! Playmobile! Books! Barbie

Collector Holiday Dolls! That was over-the-top extravagant of Genie. Allison was sure that Chloe and I had left the presents, but we convinced her that we didn't. Nice work, Genie.

Matthew is getting ready for bed, and I am gearing up for the Big Guns talk. After I change into my nightgown, I carefully say almost word-for-word what Genie suggested earlier today. I finish with, "Even if you don't understand my feelings, Matthew, I am asking you to abide by my wishes and not go to lunch with her alone, just because I'm asking. I'm not asking you to understand. I'm simply asking you to not be alone with her just because you love me and because I'm asking."

I am ready for him to buck. I am ready for his arguments.

Matthew takes a deep breath and says, "Alright, Jessica. You've been so sweet lately, and if this is hurting you this much, I will take steps to try to not be alone with her."

What? What? No arguments? No resistance? What is this?

I hug him, and since I am in my thin nightgown, he gets excited. I'm not in the mood, and it's not Wednesday or Sunday. So I remind myself, *Get started. Willingness is the first step.*

I comply. Sometimes I give my husband a drink of water just because he's thirsty. And *wha-wha-boom,* he heard my Big Guns!

CHAPTER 15
What to Do When You Disagree about Parenting

Thursday, December 27

What a great Christmas we had. With Matthew's agreement to not be alone with Indigo, I noticed I had especially positive feelings for him. The new affection in our marriage seemed to radiate throughout the whole house. The warmth was like fairy dust sprinkled not only over the marriage but also over the boys. I have been a fool to not realize how the affection in my marriage translates to security for our boys.

I'm afraid it's back to real life this morning, though. No fairy dust anywhere to be found.

Matthew has gone to work, and the boys are playing outside. I stomp around the kitchen, throw open the dishwasher, and bang the dishes loudly as I put them into the cupboard.

"My, my," Genie says. "We've lost our Christmas cheer, haven't we?"

Even the sight of my good friend Genie doesn't put me in a good mood.

"Two steps forward, one step back, Genie. Matthew infuriated me again this morning. First, Joshua spilled his juice and Matthew chewed him out for it, even though it was an accident. Then Matthew told Brandon he was grounded all weekend and off all his electronics for not putting his dirty clothes in the hamper. In addition, he told both boys last night that because they left their new skateboards in the middle of the garage, they were off their skateboards for a month. I think he's too strict and rough with the boys. He's gone a lot of the time, and when he's home, he's a drill sergeant. I know he was stressed about an account at work, but still, I hate it when he's an ogre at home."

I think about all the effort over Christmas I made to pour those stupid Eight A's into Matthew's tank, and then, on my most important concern in the world, the boys, he disappoints me! Yes, he has made some progress in agreeing to not be alone with Indigo, but why can't he be more patient and understanding with the boys?

"Now, now, let's slow down and discuss this," Genie says. "Is Matthew abusive to the boys?"

"No, he's not abusive. But he's certainly no Bill Cosby. He has a short fuse with the boys, always yelping about discipline. I want him to be *relational* with the boys."

Mess with me, but don't mess with my children.

"I know you're frustrated," Genie says. "And I'm sorry. Disagreements about parenting comprise one of the most common sources of conflict in marriage. Let me ask you another question: Do the children like Matthew?"

That's a strange question.

"Even though they complain about him to me," I say, "I know they love him and want his attention and approval."

"You will not want to hear this," he says, "but even though Matthew doesn't parent exactly the way you want, he is not the shrew you accuse him to be. He's not abusive; he spends some time with the boys, even though it's not as much and in the manner you specifically want. Matthew can't be perfect."

That was not the sympathy I was looking for.

"When you criticize Matthew about his fathering skills," Genie says, "it only makes him want to pull back and let you handle the boys all by yourself. You don't want that."

Sometimes I think I do.

"Let's back up and lay some groundwork for thinking about parenting," he says. "Children need to respect and have affection for their father to turn out well emotionally, spiritually, and psychologically. A woman cannot give children everything they need; they need a father. Therefore, it is imperative to the children's welfare that they are close with their dad. When there is tension in the marriage, many women pull the children to themselves in order to punish the husband. But she does not realize that it is the *children* she is punishing. She is denying them something they basically need, and that's a close relationship with their father."

I would never on purpose deny my children anything they needed.

"Also, you must realize that men do not have the same nesting instincts and hormones that you have as a woman. While your children and you are inseparable in your mind, men do not have this connection. Therefore, a wise woman builds the relationship between the husband and the children."

"Genie, he doesn't care."

"Not like you want him to maybe," he says. "But he cares. That is why I am going to give you a strategy to help him care more. Wise women for centuries have promoted the relationship between their husbands and children because they realize how important it is to the development of the children."

I would fight a dragon for my children.

"Let me give you a few basic ideas to help build the relationship between Matthew and your boys," Genie says. "For one thing, teach your boys to love and respect their father. Tell them wonderful things about Matthew behind his back and in front of him. Never criticize him to your children. How selfish it is of a woman to rob her children by lowering their respect for their father by criticizing him!"

I wonder if he can see the guilt on my face.

"Another basic idea that women fail to grasp is that if you want Matthew to want to spend time with the boys and with all of you as a family, he's going to have to enjoy it. Praise him for every effort you see him make toward the boys. Say things like, 'I saw Brandon's happiness when you tousled his hair.' 'I'm impressed that you handled that incident without anger.' 'I appreciate your time at the park. I know you have a lot on your plate, but you still chose to spend time with our family.' "

I guess it would be ridiculous for me to bring up that I'd like a little praise myself.

"Other ideas to say would be, 'I appreciate your reading to the children at night. I can tell they feel secure and happy when you are around.' 'Thank you for praying with the kids. You are pointing them in the right direction in life.' 'The kids love your being their coach. I can tell how proud they are that you are their father.' 'Thank you for the wise conversation you had with Josh. How awesome to have a dad with such wisdom.' 'I heard Brandon bragging on you to his friends.' "

Yeah, well, who wouldn't like to be washed in that sea of compliments?

"Women can be rather stupid," Genie says. "What they want is for their husbands to want to be home and be involved, yet they criticize him for every little thing he does. Who would want to be around that? Who wouldn't want to play two rounds of golf on Saturday to escape that?"

Or bowl six games.

"Common sense teaches women that men want to be where they are praised, attended to, and treated like a king," Genie says.

How about the queen? Is everybody forgetting the queen?

"I frequently discuss this next idea in *Wife School*, but I want to reiterate first that you cannot ask your husband for everything at one time. If parenting is at the top of your 'want' list, ask Matthew to go to parenting seminars with you or to listen to a CD series. But remember, he cannot renovate the house, go to graduate school, volunteer heavily at church, work fifty hours, and still have time for the kids. Be wise and intentional in what you ask for."

I know I get tired, but I forget that Matthew is finite too.

"Encourage Matthew to be around other men who love the Creator and are also good fathers," Genie says. "This is one of the best things you can do to help Matthew grow in his parenting skills."

Great idea. Matthew likes to hang around that creep Jordan who likes to marathon bowl and ditch his family.

"You are wise to be concerned about this area in your marriage, Young Jessica. It is tremendously important that you and Matthew get on the same page about parenting. There is terrific parenting material out there to assist you. Some of the best resources I've come across are put out by the Love and Logic Institute. They have parenting information for each stage of childhood and teens."

I haven't heard of them. I'll Google them when we are finished.

"Don't think I am taking a very complicated subject like parenting and acting like there are easy answers. I want you to see that you must be a learner in this extremely important subject. I want you to be able to influence Matthew to want to take that journey of learning with you. Therefore, it might be wise to review some of our recent topics, such as How to Correct a Husband (Chapter 12) and How to Explain Anything to a Husband (Chapter 13)."

I need a Genie School for parenting. I need a Genie School for everything.

"If you and Matthew have conflict about parenting, it is necessary that you resolve the issues and get on the same page. The children will suffer otherwise."

I'm not about to let my children suffer if I can help it.

"Don't be upset that Matthew is not as focused on parenting as you are. Nest building and caring for the young are two of a woman's natural strengths, not a man's. Use your wise skills to influence Matthew in this most important area."

I continue to have expectations of Matthew to be perfect in every area. Why won't I lay this down?

"I am going to a White Elephant party for genies tonight," Genie says. "Would you mind if I took that plastic purple vase that your Aunt Helen gave you for Christmas?"

"Be my guest," I laugh. "I didn't know which closet to stick it in." Or which garbage can.

"By the way, today was closet day," he says. "Look in all the closets in your house." He takes the purple vase and disappears.

I open the sports equipment closet. I open the storage closet. I walk around the house and find every closet in the entire house perfectly organized. I take a deep breath and enjoy the beauty of the order inside the closets.

I also think about how I am going to make Matthew enjoy being home with us. Then I will ask him if he would be willing to attend a parenting seminar or to listen to CD's together. What was the name of that group Genie suggested?

I get out my computer and Google "Love and Logic." Ah, there it is, the Love and Logic Institute. LoveandLogic.com. I order two sets of CD's.

Josh runs inside, crying, with blood streaming down his face. The gash on his forehead is deep and needs stitches. The boys were playing hockey without their helmets, but this is not a good time to get upset over that. I load them into the car and head for the emergency room. I call Matthew to join us.

I hate emergency rooms. They remind me of when I lost my mother.

CHAPTER 16
What to Do When Your Husband Has a Bad Idea

Tuesday, January 1

Josh needed seven stitches last Thursday. Emergency rooms do bring back painful memories, but with two rambunctious boys, I need to get more used to stitches and broken bones. Matthew was at lunch when I called him to meet us at the ER. Yes, Indigo was there too because they were working on a campaign, but so was another coworker, Adam. Again, that's progress, definite progress. I made sure Matthew knew I was pleased that he had included Adam. Of course, what I'd really like is for Indigo to leave the firm, but one step at a time. One step at a time.

Not only has Matthew agreed to not be alone with Ms. Plunge-Neck, he is coming through for me in other areas associated with her. Today is New Year's Day, and Indigo invited several coworkers and their spouses over to her cozy apartment to watch some football Bowl games. Matthew knew I wouldn't want to go, so he declined for us before he even asked me. I need to tell him again how much I appreciate that.

Since Matthew is off work, he took the boys to the park to fly their new remote control airplanes they got for Christmas. Matthew drove my SUV so the airplanes would fit in the large back compartment.

"I detailed the interior of Matthew's car for you to give to him as a thank-you for taking Adam to lunch along with Indigo," Genie says, appearing in my kitchen as Matthew drives out of sight. "That husband of yours is doing great in *Wife School*."

I walk into the garage to look at Matthew's car, and it is immaculate. Matthew will love it.

"The lesson can't be too long today because your family won't fly planes long in these freezing temperatures," Genie says. "The topic today is what to do when your husband gives you a bad idea."

I'm pretty sure I need a little coaching in this area. Matthew suggested last week that we take Daisy, his mother, on vacation with us this summer. Matthew thought she could help us watch the kids. To say I went ballistic would be underestimating my response. Matthew can't see how his mother treats me and how it affects me.

"Husbands are notorious for having, in the wife's opinion, lots of ridiculous ideas," Genie says. "Actually, their adventuresome ideas are often brilliant, like my buddy Ben Franklin's, who flew a kite in a thunderstorm."

His buddy Ben Franklin?

"However, at other times," he says, "men can have ideas that neither help him nor anyone else."

Like the idea of taking Daisy on vacation.

"A couple of centuries ago," Genie says, "a husband who was a farmer was obsessed with rebuilding an intricate and detailed birdhouse in his backyard when his barn and fences were falling down. This drove the farmer's wife berserk."

A birdhouse? The poor woman.

"Then, in the 1960s, another husband, an Elvis follower, wanted to buy some fourteen-karat gold chains to wear around his neck with his leisure suit when the wife, who had been hanging up the clothes on the line in the backyard, wanted a clothes dryer."

Do men like this exist? They wouldn't be sleeping in *my* bed.

"Suppose a husband goes on and on," Genie says, "about what a great idea he has for an outlandish and extraordinarily expensive trip. He wants to take off two months from work and sail around the world. Your car is about to die, the air conditioning system needs to be replaced, and the children have outgrown their clothes. Even though there are not sufficient savings, the husband keeps talking about his fantasy trip."

I'd go ahead and pour cold water on that trip idea right up front, kind of like stepping on a match in a wooded area before it started a forest fire.

"Resist the urge to be negative," Genie says. "Instead, praise his motive and offer to consider their idea. For example, say, 'Honey, I think it's great how you have a zest for life. Let's sit down and look at our money together.'

"Then, when you sit down and calmly look at the money, most men will come to their senses and realize their idea was unrealistic. Usually, you never have to say a word. And by the way, after he comes to his senses and his ideas do sizzle out, puhllleeeeze refrain from commenting, 'I never thought that would actually work anyway.' "

I don't like this guy recording my actual statements and playing them back.

"The examples go on and on of men who have had bad ideas," Genie says. "Let's talk about the husband who wanted to take his wife to a tracker pull for their anniversary. Of course, the wife had absolutely zero interest in this tobacco-chewer's event and felt terribly misunderstood that her husband would even suggest this activity for their anniversary."

I need to write this down on the "Things Other Husbands Do Wrong" list. Sometimes Matthew looks like a saint.

"The wife's first inclination is usually not the best, as her first inclination is to let him know exactly how ridiculous she thinks his ideas are."

Letting my thoughts rip like a parachute cord—that's little ole me.

"Self-control is always the first strategy to reach for," Genie says with a smile. "And the next strategy is to find something, anything, nice to say about the husband's suggestion. An example would be, 'Honey, that's so nice you want to be with me.' "

"Does any woman naturally have this self-control?" I ask, incredulous.

"Hardly any," he replies. "Usually, it must be learned and acquired."

It's good to know I'm in the majority.

"If you're flabbergasted by his idea, feel shell-shocked, and can't think, stall so you can think of something to say later."

"Stall? And how do I do that?" I'm seriously interested because I feel like I frequently get cold water thrown in my face in the form of bad ideas and have no idea how to respond.

"You say, 'Let me think about that for a little bit and see if that would work.' "

"Isn't that a little deceitful?" I ask. "I mean, I know I don't want to go, so shouldn't I just tell him that?"

"It takes practice and maturity to find the balance between truth and graciousness. If you stall for some time, you can think of how to respond truthfully and graciously. If you spit your answer right back, you're only being truthful."

All this self-restraint stuff wears the stew out of me.

"Alright, time has passed, so now what do I say?" I ask.

"You could say, 'Honey, I've been thinking about going to the tracker pull for our anniversary. I am really grateful you want to take me out for our anniversary. Do you think there will be enough money to buy those tickets and that new washer and dryer we've been talking about?"

I laugh. "What if he says, 'Sure, that will be fine'?"

"Then," Genie answers, "you stall again. That didn't work, so you need to go to your corner of the ring and think some more before you come out again with another brilliant try."

I laugh. "Okay, so what's my next move?"

"To be honest, by now," Genie says, "he's a little aware that you are not 100 percent in, so he's ready for your next move. You could say, 'I'm still thinking about the tracker pull, and I wish we could sit down and look at the money. I like to do all the things you want, but I also want to be sure we can purchase things we need for our family.'

"You have basically told him that you're not truly interested in the tracker pull, but you have done so with grace. If there's enough money for the tracker pull and the washer-dryer, you could sweetly say, 'Honey, we can go to the tracker pull if it is important to you, but for our anniversary, I was hoping we could do something that we were both interested in.'

"You are going to have hard conversations in your marriage, Young Jessica, but know that *how you say things makes all the difference in the world*. I am not proposing that you must get your way at all. I am simply instructing you how to handle the moments when you are suddenly faced with a negative situation or a bad idea. Most women fly off with the mouth when they should use self-control and kindness. By doing this, wives would prevent what is equal to nuclear damage in a marriage."

Over and over again, Genie says to use restraint in how I talk to Matthew. He says death and life are in the power of the tongue. I'm starting to see the power. I didn't want to get up in the middle of the night when our boys were babies, but of course, I made myself. And now, I don't want to modulate and bridle my tongue, but I can make myself. A wonderful marriage is not going to appear until I get control of my tongue.

Genie disappears, and I'm glad I have a few moments to lie down and rest before Matthew and the boys come home. I feel more tired than usual. My period is late, which is probably why I feel so bad, but I'm sure I'll start tomorrow.

I lie down on the sofa, but immediately I hear the text message ringtone of Matthew's phone. I guess he forgot to take his phone. I get up to see who the text is from. It's from that hooligan, Indigo. "Wish you were here. The gang is not the same without you." Doesn't she know he's married? Where does she get that kind of nerve? That text is definitely crossing the line.

I hear the garage door go up. Are they home already?

"Wow, Jessica," says Matthew, "my car looks amazing. I can't believe you detailed the interior of my car!"

I am almost ready to launch my torpedo and rail about Indigo, but he cuts me off.

"I thought of a great idea while we were flying the remote-control planes," Matthew says. "What if I take the boys camping next weekend in this below-freezing weather? My father always said that activities like that makes men out of boys."

Oh, dear. The boys are eight and six years old, hardly time to start making men out of them. I've got to deal with his bad idea *and* his rogue assistant's redundant pursuits. Watch your tongue, I tell myself. Watch your tongue.

And to top everything else, I feel rather nauseated.

CHAPTER 17

How You Contribute To or Diminish Your Husband's Reputation

Friday, January 4

didn't immediately say anything to Matthew about Indigo's text last Tuesday. Happily, he brought it up to me.

"Listen to this," he said and then read me the text. I think he is beginning to see that her motives are a little shady. Again, I told him, with graciousness, gentleness, and honesty, about the hurt in my heart because she works closely with him every day. He didn't argue with me or try to talk me out of my feelings.

I also used the information from my last lesson when Matthew suggested that he take the boys camping in this sub-zero weather. Instead of going this weekend, our family now has a camping trip planned for spring break when the weather will be in the fifties and sixties. Kudos to you, Genie. Two possible mine explosions were averted.

The boys went back to school today. I saw Cammey standing at the bus stop and waved. She barely waved back and then turned abruptly around. That drama with Pinching Charlie is not over. I honestly don't know what to do to amend things with her. I gave Brandon a word picture, describing how he would feel if he were left out, and I'm hoping he will extend some kindness to Pinching Charlie.

Now I am faced with taking down the Christmas tree and putting away the Christmas decorations. I have zero energy to do this. What I really want to do is take a nap, but it is only morning.

Walking into the den, I notice that Genie is sitting on the sofa with a cup of peppermint tea. "Your decorations are in the attic, young Jessica. And the tree is by the curb, so the garbage men will get it."

How will I ever go back to living like a normal human after this?

"Young Jessica, today we discuss how you contribute to or diminish your husband's reputation." Genie is all business, as usual.

Hey, he swept up all the pine needles too. Sweet.

"Women are not aware how much influence they have over their husband's reputation. What the wife says about and how she treats him in public influences what other people think about him."

I have talked about Matthew's weaknesses too much to my sisters, I'm sure.

"A wise wife can elevate a husband's reputation substantially," he says, "and a foolish wife can cast a dark cloud over it with her words and even her insinuations."

"What do you mean, Genie?" I ask.

"For example, what do you automatically think about a man who is married to a woman who makes statements like 'Men are lazy bums' or 'I had no idea that marriage would be like this.' "

I raise my eyebrows but say nothing.

"What do you think of a man who is married to a woman who says, 'My husband will never work hard enough so I don't have to work' or 'We needed money for our son's braces, but my husband bought himself a bass boat instead.' "

I hear these statements all the time when I'm with friends or other groups of women. I may have even dropped a few comments myself.

"Now, let's take the wise wife," Genie says. "What do you think of a man whose wife makes statements like 'When my husband says it, I know it's the truth' or 'If a neighbor needs help, my husband is the first one there.' "

"I understand this," I say. "I've never even met my hairdresser's husband, but I think he must be a Greek god. She tells me how he does the dishes, takes care of the cars, volunteers at homeless shelters regularly ..."

I remember yesterday in the grocery when I saw an old friend and asked about her husband, Blake. Her reply was, "You know Blake, getting by and playing golf." I couldn't help but think that Blake was lazy.

One day for a joke a few years ago, Allison, Chloe, and I had an uproariously fun time going through the alphabet, listing a weakness of our husbands' for each letter of the alphabet: A, Annoying, B, Bumbler in bed, C, Complainer. How hurt Matthew would be to know I did that.

"What a wise woman does," Genie says, "is make her husband a hero to others, in front of him and behind his back. A critical wife damages her husband's reputation in a great way, whereas a wife who praises her husband in public builds his reputation. A wife and a husband are one. When she hurts his reputation, she is hurting herself."

I'm hurting myself? I haven't seen it in that light before.

I do get this. I have a friend who volunteers in the lunchroom with me at school. Her husband has quite a winning way about him, and after the Christmas fundraiser at school, Matthew was thinking about asking him to join his bowling league. Earlier, my girlfriend had confided to me that her husband had cheated on his income taxes, and I told Matthew, of course. Matthew then didn't invite him to bowl. Nor did we invite them to our Fourth of July cookout.

Genie interrupts my thoughts. "Brag on your husband to the kids, your family, the neighbors, his friends. Make him out to be a hero. How sad it is when wives criticize their husbands to the children, hoping to win the children's affection for themselves. Wives love to drop little mean remarks about the father to the children when wives have resentment toward the husband. Mothers say, 'You know your dad can't hold onto a dollar or you'd have that bike.' How selfish of mothers to rob and steal from their children like this! Don't they know that children need to love, respect, and be close to their fathers so that they can psychologically and emotionally develop well? Women are ridiculously guilty of trying to keep the children from being close to the father to punish the father. They don't realize that they are punishing the children."

Brandon was imitating his father a few months ago by mimicking how Matthew searches his hair for gray hairs. We laughed behind Matthew's back, and I casually dropped, "Don't be vain when you grow up." Honestly, I am embarrassed about my behavior.

"Don't waste time with regrets or past mistakes," says Genie. "Start fresh today. Talk about your husband in a complimentary way to your children, to your friends, to your acquaintances. Handle his rough issues with a counselor or a trusted older woman. Remember, your husband's habits are annoying, not evil. Even though I repeat myself often when I say this, *Wife School* is not for wives with husbands who are abusive, are alcoholics, or who have affairs. Wives must, of course, get human counseling and additional help with those problems."

Grateful that I am not struggling with those issues, I think of my Turquoise Journal and realize it has been collecting a little dust. I need to get it out and review all of Matthew's many positive qualities again.

"There's a big snow coming in, and your kids will be off school for a few days," Genie says. "There are a couple of new sleds in the garage for your boys." And he's gone.

I look out the window. Snow flurries are beginning to fall.

I don't think I'll ever talk about Matthew in public again in the same way.

I feel nauseated again and still haven't started my period. Matthew and I use protection, so, of course, I'm not pregnant, but I decide to run to the pharmacy just the same to get a pregnancy kit to put my mind at ease.

Dad calls while I'm in the car. "Honey," he says. "I'm in love. I think I want to marry Debbie."

What is it with this guy? What is his deal? Can't he date a woman a few months before he runs to the altar? Time to call a Combat Sister Meeting to combine mental forces. I call Chloe and then Allison. We three generals are meeting tomorrow at one o'clock to create a battle plan.

I can't stop thinking about Dad. I do the pregnancy test while I'm on the phone with Chloe. As I'm ranting about Dad wanting to get married, the little plus sign lights up on the test strip.

Oh. My. Gosh. Are. You. Serious?

CHAPTER 18

When Your Husband Doesn't Reciprocate or Try to Meet Your Needs

Monday, January 28

It's been over three weeks since I took the pregnancy test and found out it was positive.

Discovering I was pregnant was shocking, but the real shock was how thrilled I was. Pregnant. With a new baby inside of me. A baby I was going to love like I love Brandon and Josh. Matthew and I decided years ago that since we had two healthy boys, we were finished having children. But honestly, my heart never really felt completely at peace with that decision. I was pregnant, and I sensed it was a baby girl. *Elizabeth is a pretty name*, I had thought.

However, ten days later, I started bleeding and lost the baby. Even though I knew I was pregnant for only ten days, I got very attached and have been grieving the loss of the baby I was carrying. Now my heart is tugging to talk to Matthew about getting pregnant again. No wonder men have so much trouble understanding women. I have trouble understanding myself.

Matthew was a disappointment during the miscarriage. He couldn't understand why I was so devastated since I hadn't specifically wanted to get pregnant. He kept saying, "You only knew you were pregnant ten days." One night he even said, "Do we have to talk about losing that baby again? Can't we ever talk about anything else?" I am still wounded from that comment. I mean, I kill myself to deposit the Eight A's into this guy's tank, and truly, sometimes I get back rubbish and sewage. The sadness I feel is towering and oversized. My low mood feels sticky and impossible to escape.

My iPhone rings, and I pull myself together before I answer it. It's another one of my neighbors, Maggie. I finished the wedding invitations for her daughter yesterday and dropped them off. She hasn't paid me, so maybe she wants to drop off the check. Or maybe she wants to gush over the beautiful calligraphy.

"Hey, Maggie."

"Jessica, you won't believe this," Maggie begins. "Yesterday after you dropped off the invitations, I started stuffing them. After I had stuffed and sealed around 150 of them, my daughter Carlie dropped by and noticed that the printer got the date wrong. How could I not have noticed? I have already sealed 150 of your envelopes. I tried to open them so we could save them, but they tear when I try to open them. The printer has an emergency re-do on the invitations, but the problem is, now I need you to re-do 150 of the outer envelopes."

How does this happen? Seriously, how? I'm about to give up my calligraphy business because of the drama of these women. The mothers are as bad as the brides. Is Maggie going to pay me for the first ones as well as the re-do envelopes? Being a neighbor, the situation is touchy.

"What do you think about my paying you for the invitations you originally did and give you fifty dollars extra for the second time around?" Maggie says.

Uh, hello? The 150 re-do invitations would be around two hundred dollars, not counting the rush job, and she wants to give me a measly fifty dollars? Do these people think I do their invitations because it's what I like to do in my free time? I tell her I'll think about it and will call her back.

Before we hang up, Maggie says, "Isn't that fun that Cammey and Peyton are having a potluck Valentine's Day party for the couples in the neighborhood? I think that is so cute of her. I'm bringing a vegetable dish. What are you bringing?"

Cammey, of course, is the mom of Pinching Charlie. Brandon had asked Charlie to sit at his table, but the other guys didn't want Pincher around. Brandon says he is not in charge of where people sit at lunch, and he tried. He did tell Charlie, though, that he thinks the other guys might like him more if he would stop pinching everyone. I was pretty proud of Brandon for saying that. Anyhow, Cammey is having a Valentine's Day party for the neighborhood and is leaving us out. I admit, it stings a little. Okay, maybe a lot. I politely tell Maggie we're not invited and can tell she is surprised.

Quickly, I call Matthew to tell him. "Jessica, I hate those parties. I'm glad we're not invited." Such a man's response. Direct. To the point. It's over.

"I don't really want to go either, but at least I want to be invited," I say. Matthew has to abruptly get off the phone, and I feel dissatisfied—again—with Matthew's response. I wasn't finished discussing my feelings.

I mosey back into the kitchen for my second cup of coffee. Or is it my third? I need to be careful how much I drink if I'm thinking again about the P-word.

On the kitchen counter, there is a beautiful barbeque brisket with brown rice and grilled zucchini. I have missed my satin-panted friend. "I'm glad to see you again, Genie."

I guess he stayed away on purpose while I worked through my grief over the baby. Having emotional turbulence seems to be the norm, not the exception, with me.

"Today's topic will be what to do when your husband doesn't reciprocate giving you the Eight A's," begins Genie.

It's eerie how he matches the topic to what is going on in my brain. I could certainly use some A's from Matthew to fill up my own empty tank right now.

"This is primarily a review lesson," he says "But after centuries of teaching this subject, I realize women need to be repeatedly reminded of some basic tenets of *Wife School*. You will be familiar with much of today's subject matter."

I often wonder if and when Matthew is going to be seriously interested in meeting my emotional needs. It's as if he is glad I am meeting *his* needs and that I'm off his back, but there is no concerted effort by him to try to be tender, romantic, understanding, or intimate. He is doing better in some ways, I guess, but he's still such a typical man, interested in work, sports, and sex. It's frustrating to keep depositing these Eight A's and feel like I'm never going to get the love and care I want and need. Sometimes, like now, I really get sick of it.

"I understand how difficult *Wife School* can be for women, Young Jessica. Women have learned how to meet their husband's needs, yet the men have not yet learned how to meet their wives needs. I am quite familiar with the disappointment you feel. I have seen this countless times. After all your efforts, you are frustrated that you are not getting what you want from your spouse."

Well, hopefully, Genie has a remedy in his back pocket—if those silly, silky pants even have pockets.

"One of the reasons, as I've said before, that your husband is not going hard after your needs is because he doesn't know they exist."

"That's not true," I abruptly disagree. "I have told him a million times."

"Yes," he says, "but remember that it is difficult to explain blue to a color-blind person. Men don't understand women because they are vastly different. Men are simple creatures and are basically happy in a marriage if there is enough sex and not too much drama. You, on the other hand, are complicated creature. A husband is like a single button sewn on a piece of cloth. You, in contrast, are more like an intricate wedding gown with hand-stitched pearls and embroidery. Since he is not like you, he doesn't understand you. Deaf people can't hear Chris Tomlin."

He overdoes these analogies, but I do like Chris Tomlin.

"Marriage is only supposed to fill around 25 to 50 percent of your relationship plate," Genie says. "The other 50 to 75 percent is to be filled with other relationships. When you expect Matthew to fill 90 percent of your relationship plate, the result will be unmet expectations and disappointments, as we discussed last September when we discussed the A of Acceptance."

Last September? That was eons ago.

"Another common pattern that women fall into," he says, "is that they put all of their focus on the WM, the What's Missing that the husband doesn't bring to the marriage. Often, the WM for women is emotional intimacy and connection. But regardless of what the WM is, the wife focuses exclusively on it and ignores the enormous gifts the husband *does* bring to the marriage. This is remedied by reading and rereading your Turquoise Journal entries."

I still haven't picked that Turquoise Journal up, even though I thought about it.

"One can't plant an apple seed in May and expect apples in June," he says. "Things take time. You are sowing, but it is not time for the reaping. You must be patient. Many women start out with my program but grow weary in giving. Do not succumb to that."

Weary. Dog tired. Burned out.

"Remember to reinforce any positive attempt Matthew makes to meet your needs," Genie says. "Wait until you see a little bud of effort from him bursting through the soil. Water it with praise. For example, let's say he admires you in a way that delights you. An example would be if he tells you how pretty you look in your yellow snow jacket."

I do have a yellow snow jacket. The only thing Matthew said was, "How much did that cost?"

"After your husband gives you a hint of meeting any need," he says, "you remind him the next day how good it felt when he said or did whatever it was. *You train him with your attention and your delight when he does something you enjoy.* Bring up your enjoyment of his comment a couple of times. He will eventually learn that he gets rewarded for those behaviors."

Sounds more like training a dog. "Here, Fido. Here's a doggie bone for rolling over."

"As you continually deposit the Eight A's, his affection for you will grow," Genie says. "Thus his expression of affection will eventually grow also. It's the Law of the Harvest, Young Jessica. If you plant apple seeds, you get back apple trees. When you plant the Eight A's, you will eventually reap more A's. Farming takes patience, my dear."

Patience? I can't even wait for the coffee to finish brewing before I have to pour myself a cup.

"I know you want attention, affection, appreciation, and admiration," he says. "You are a dry, wilted plant, and you need watering. The key to this dilemma is for you to get restored by the Creator. The ideal is that you overflow from that encounter and become a fountain that refreshes others. In due time, you will reap because there is a cosmic law that states whatever you sow, you shall reap. Stop looking at what you're not getting, and focus on Matthew's positive lists in your Turquoise Journal. When you least expect it, Matthew will water you. You must trust me on this."

Give and love and trust and wait. These instructions are getting rather annoying.

"All beautiful works of art take time," Genie says. "And your marriage is a fifty-year, beautiful work of art. Tell yourself that you will continue to build your marriage by depositing the Eight A's and by taking responsibility for the beauty of the marriage. Miracles happen when a woman applies her multiple talents and intuition to building a magnificent marriage. Choosing to continue with these *Wife School* principles when your husband does not reciprocate will eventually break down his boulders."

I guess my sledgehammer method hasn't worked.

"I also want to mention one more possible reason," Genie says, "that Matthew is not reciprocating in trying to meet your needs. It is sometimes possible that a wife violates the *Wife School* principles and is not even aware of it. Sometimes, unbeknownst to her, she makes the husband feel inferior."

Inferior? What is he talking about now?

"Many women have a blind spot," he says, "in that they don't understand how sensitive male pride is. Even little things, like contradicting Matthew's stories, will make him feel unsupported. If he says he likes Irish Spring soap, don't argue that you think Dial soap smells better. If he says he ran up six flights of stairs, don't correct him that it was only five."

But he gets the details wrong in his stories.

"Also, your teasing may make him feel that you are not supporting him," Genie says. "Making small jokes about his pudgy stomach will feel to him as if you are siding against him instead of supporting him."

Oh, so Genie overheard that remark I made to Matthew? That's called "creeping," Mr. Chiseled.

"One man told me," he says, "that he heard his children making fun of how overly concerned he was about his height. They were laughing that he only wore shoes with a certain sole so he would appear taller. The wife joined in, laughing too. He felt betrayed by her, and that she should have defended him to the children instead of joining in their laughter at his obsession over his height."

"Genie, that man's ego is ridiculous."

"In a perfect world of perfect humans," he says, "men would not be sensitive to the slightest hint of criticism or teasing. But in the real world, men are sensitive to criticism and having their faults and weaknesses discussed. You would be wise to remember this."

Handling a man's ego is similar to handling a contact lens.

"In order for a man to reciprocate, he needs to feel safe with you," Genie says. "A husband needs to know you will not take that little jab at him and make fun of his personal idiosyncrasies. When a woman lives the entire *Wife School* principles, she will eventually win his trust."

"So are you saying it's *my* fault that Matthew doesn't reciprocate?" I ask.

"I didn't say that," he says. "I am only telling you that you should be careful to guard against these subtle behaviors that many women think are fine because a man with a sensitive nature will react and withdraw his affection."

And they talk about women being difficult when they're having their periods.

"To finish, Young Jessica, we will discuss when a man does not reciprocate and you have *not* violated the *Wife School* principles."

Obviously, Genie doesn't think this applies to me. But fine, I'll listen.

"It cannot always be summer in the marriage," he says. "There are not always reasons why men fail to reciprocate and try to meet your needs. Sometimes there's nothing you can do but wait it out and play your hand of Eight A's. It's natural to have negative feelings toward your spouse when he does this. You are giving, and he is cold. You will naturally feel rejected, and that feels hurtful. *Remember, this is the man you were given to love.* If you are not careful to wait it out and let this cloudy weather pass but instead begin unleashing your feelings, you will make matters worse. Hard times and negative feelings are part of any close relationship. Try to take care of yourself during those times. Get a babysitter, and do things that restore you. Take the pressure off Matthew to meet your needs and to validate you. Read your Turquoise

Journal. Continue the Eight A's. He will move toward you eventually. Give him some time, space, and heavy doses of the Eight A's."

Sure. Of course. Right back to the regular advice: Keep giving the magical Eight A's.

"*Focus on what you give and how you love, not on what you're given or how you're loved.* It is a thousand-year-old recipe for success in marriage. If you persevere, you will see that I am right. Learning to not be offended is one of the most difficult skills you human beings ever master."

I don't like persevering. I don't like waiting. I don't want to overlook offenses. I want brownies or an unlimited shopping spree at Nordstroms.

"Ask the Creator for a heart that is not offended and does not demand its rights. You are not to be mistreated (see Chapter 14, "What to Do When Your Husband Mistreats You"), but husbands are messy and will have offensive behaviors. Bury your husband's weaknesses and transgressions in the cemetery in your backyard and focus on what he does right in the marriage."

I really don't get this. Matthew doesn't fill me, but I'm to keep filling him. Oh sure, that's fair.

"A humble and meek wife can choose to give and love, even when her husband is wrong and when he is difficult. *This is how wise women build their houses.* Admittedly, your culture doesn't live like this. Don't try to get instructions for marriage from a culture that doesn't walk with the Creator. Get your instructions from the Creator's Word."

Wife School is tough today. Life in general feels tough today. Maybe I need a manicure and a pedicure to cheer me up.

"One more thing I would like to say is that you can ask for what you want from Matthew or make your desires known as long as you do it graciously, respectfully, and not too much at one time. Again, I want to remind you that until you are depositing the Eight A's and until you have gotten control over your tongue, you should not ask for things. I can't stress enough how important it is to not ask for too much at once. And know that although Matthew may deny your requests, as long as you are living the *Wife School* principles, your husband's heart is being softened and plowed. *Men naturally want to please their wives when wives repeatedly meet their soul needs.*"

Genie disappears without a good-bye.

Here we are again, back to me. I'm to be humble and meek. I'm to have a gentle and quiet spirit. I'm to lay down being offended and to realize this is the man I was given to love. Meekness is the opposite of my anger and annoyance. Oh, isn't there an herbal supplement I could swallow to fix this?

It is comforting, however, to know that when Matthew is reluctant to meet my needs, it's probably because he is blind to them. Yes, sometimes Matthew is plain selfish, but who isn't? That's the plight of human beings. You can't be in relationship with any human being if you are going to demand they not have a lower nature. I certainly have one. Forgiveness is necessary to all relationships on the planet.

I can recommit to focusing on depositing the Eight A's instead of bemoaning how empty and needy I am. I can take responsibility for getting my needs met by the Creator instead of begging and draining Matthew to meet my needs. And I need to remember, there is nothing wrong with graciously, respectfully asking for what I want. I need to reread my notes from the lesson on using word pictures (Chapter 13, How to Explain Anything to Your Husband).

I write in my Turquoise Journal, "Don't be mad he's a young apple tree and not ready to bear fruit. Be patient. You're on the fifty-year plan." My mood feels a little lighter.

Allison calls, crying again. Zach still hasn't found work, and he told Allison that they are going to have to give their house back to the bank. I hurt for her.

"Can you believe that Zach is letting this happen? What kind of husband lets his house be repossessed?"

Oh, my. I am beginning to have a new awareness of other women's tendencies to blame and badmouth their husbands. What Zach needs right now is a cheerleader, not a disgruntled coach. It's a lot easier to see other women's mistakes instead of my own.

Dad calls to relay some friendly information he heard about a childhood friend of mine and mentions that Debbie wasn't feeling well and missed work today. He also casually mentions that he and Debbie were talking about a wedding in Vegas. Dad!! I beg him to slow down.

CHAPTER 19
What to Do When the In-Laws Are a Problem

Friday, February 1

"Jessssss-i-ca! Jessssss-i-ca!"

I'm stunned as I hear that voice in my kitchen. I would recognize that high-pitched, whiney voice anywhere. It's my mother-in-law.

"Daisy?" I ask, bewildered and angry that she would show up at my house unannounced and walk in without knocking.

"I'm having my bridge club over on Monday," she begins, "and I wanted to borrow your punch bowl."

I'm so upset I'm nearly out of my mind. Of course she's welcome to my punch bowl, but how inconsiderate to walk into my house unannounced. I feel violated and am sizzling with annoyance. I've got to start locking the door.

"Daisy," I say, "I'm on my way out. Why didn't you call? I could have left it on the porch for you?"

My irritation is not concealed, and the look across her face shows she sees it. "I didn't realize you were busy," she says in her pitiful, squeaky, hurt voice. "I'll take it and leave."

I'm only going to the cleaners and to the bank, and admittedly, those errands aren't important, but heavens! The nerve of her! My own mother would have called first!

I have had issues with Daisy since the day I married Matthew. I remember her coming over the day after Joshua was born, and the first thing she said was, "Didn't have time to put on any makeup?" After I bought some new bar stools for my kitchen counter, she commented, "Does Matthew like you spending all his hard-earned money on decorating?" Her advice has been endless and the compliments have been non-existent. The rumor is that Matthew's father repeatedly cheated on her during their marriage.

Daisy has had a sad life, in my opinion. She has been overweight, struggled financially, and has had trouble keeping girlfriends. I feel sorry for her, but enough is enough.

After she left, I get in my car and dial Matthew. "What is the deal with your mother?" I ask. "She shows up unannounced and walks in without knocking?"

I do not receive the sympathy I'm looking for.

"Can we talk about this when I get home?" he asks. "I'm in a meeting." His annoyance at me was apparent too.

I want to scream, "Can't you fix your mother? She's driving me crazy!" But he has already hung up.

I get the dry cleaning and make my ATM stop. **As I drive up our driveway, there's Genie, washing my windows.** Now that's a sight that makes me chuckle, ole Mr. Satin Pants with rubber gloves and a hose. It's thirty-four degrees outside, yet he acts like he's in the Bahamas.

He waves, and as I approach, he mists my car with the hose.

"I thought you might need a little cooling off after that confrontation with your mother-in-law this morning."

He now lives in my walls and hears everything?

"Can you believe her, Genie? She drives me stark raving crazy."

We both sit briefly on the porch steps in the beautiful, cold February sunlight and drink the hot apple cider that he had prepared. But even with the cider, I'm too cold, so we go inside.

"Today our lesson is about in-laws, and it's rather involved," Genie says.

"Why are you giving me a lesson about in-laws?" I ask. "I thought you were teaching me about marriage?"

"Even though Matthew's mother upsets him frequently with her outlandish behavior, he loves her very much and wants the two of you to get along," he says. "One way to love Matthew is to honor his parents."

Did anyone ever think that maybe Daisy should honor me and call before she shows up?

Genie continues. "Even with the best mother-in-laws, there can be tension. Older women have reared their sons and don't easily relinquish them to the new daughter-in-law. Both women feel they have ownership rights to this same man, and women can get competitive."

"I know Daisy is Matthew's mother," I say, "and I understand her desire to still be involved in his life. But what do I do with this woman who criticizes my housekeeping, lets my children watch TV that is way too risqué for their young eyes, and tells me right after I have a baby that Matthew always liked skinny girls?!"

"Handling in-laws can seem to be a little overwhelming," he says. "But once you get some principles in place, the knots seem to untie. These are the principles we are going to discuss. How does the Creator feel about in-laws? What does honoring in-laws look like? Why does it matter if you honor your in-laws? And lastly, we will discuss how to set healthy boundaries by speaking assertively but kindly."

I am more than willing to set boundaries. How about "Call us once a year—on Christmas"?

"First we will discuss how the Creator feels about in-laws. The Creator requests that children honor their parents. When you married Matthew and became one with him, Matthew's parents became your parents too."

My parents now? Matthew's parents are now *my* parents? I might have rethought the whole marriage if I had known *that*.

"The Creator asks that you honor them, not love them," Genie says. "Honor is a choice about how you treat their position. This is freeing to you. You do not have to be best friends with Daisy or even shopping buddies, but you need to determine how to honor her. You cannot ignore this counsel, as your children are watching how you treat your parents and in-laws and will follow your cues as to how to treat you later."

Egads. Really? This is news. My boys are learning how to treat me in my old age by watching how I treat Daisy? I can't ignore this subject like I wish I could.

"Let's begin by looking at what it means to honor Daisy," Genie continues. "Even if you feel she is not worthy to be honored, you are required to 'salute the uniform.' That means, even though you don't have affection for her, you are required to treat her with respect because of her position as Matthew's parent."

"She overruns me. She shows up without calling, she's rude, she's annoying—"

"We will get to setting healthy boundaries, Young Jessica. But for now, you must accept that honoring her is your duty. Once you can swallow that principle, the rest will be easier."

Nothing is easy yet. I don't want to swallow anything; I want to puke.

"The most helpful advice I can give you, Young Jessica, is to realize that her behavior is not evil, just annoying. That will help you accept her."

Now that is an interesting concept. I am angry at her behavior as if it were evil, but Genie is right. She's not evil, only annoying. That does help reframe things.

"A hard thought to digest," Genie says, "is that the things about her that bother you are probably things about yourself you don't admire. When you are upset over the weaknesses and wrongs of another, realize that you probably have the same tendencies. "

Whoooaaa. Is this true? Am I inconsiderate like Daisy? Rude? Pushy? Critical? I'll have to think on that.

"When you see the connection between her aggravating behavior and a similarity in you, it allows you to forgive her and focus on changing the one you can change—yourself."

How did we get around to fixing me again? Can't we fix someone else for a change?

"Genie, if I could do things the way I really wanted, I'd see her once a year," I say. "But I know that wouldn't be fair to the grandchildren or to Matthew. How do I reconcile my lack of desire to be with her and my duty to honor her?"

"Talk with Matthew," he says. "See what he thinks about how much you should be involved with her. After all, this is a way to love Matthew, to treat his family respectfully. Even if *he* has issues with his family, he wants you to be kind to them. Together you two decide how often you get together with Daisy, how often you call her, and how often you let her have access to the children. You two are in charge, not Daisy."

I hadn't thought this through. We're in charge of how much we see her? We can say no if we want to her invitations and ideas? This is empowering.

"Couples vary in how much they communicate with or visit their parents," he says. "Some couples may decide that they will call every day or every week or so. Other couples may decide to have the in-laws over for one meal a week or maybe only plan on having them over for the holidays. And some couples decide to visit the in-laws three times a week, or once a week, or once a month. The point is that the couple decides what it looks like for them to honor the parents, and then the couple sets boundaries. They are in charge of setting the boundaries, not the parents or the in-laws."

I need a cigarette, but I don't smoke.

"Give me an example," Genie says, "of something Daisy does to upset you."

"Let's take this morning," I say. "She shows up at my house unannounced and walks in without knocking."

"I really liked how you handled that," he says. "You gladly gave her the punch bowl, asked her why she didn't call, and stated your plans. If she does this again, you are free to politely say, 'Daisy, I get shaken up when people arrive at my house unannounced. Would you please call me first next time?' She won't like it, but being assertive and kind is necessary with people like Daisy."

I hate conflict. Why can't people just act right?

"Another healing thing you can do with your mother-in-law," says Genie, "is to ask her advice. Now, I know you don't want her advice on parenting or marriage, but ask her advice about cooking a recipe or on some topic that is not emotionally charged. Older women love to give their advice and feel needed when asked. Find subjects that are not tension-filled and ask her advice. She probably knows some information that you would like."

I would rather *give* her some advice—shut up and go away.

"Another tip and then I'm off for the day, Young Jessica. Always have her over on her birthday. This one act on your part is surprisingly healing. Birthdays are huge to women, and if you can show up strong on her birthday, it will be a large deposit on your part."

I like birthdays. I could do that.

"The best advice for you to remember is that you are training your children how to treat you by how you treat your in-laws and parents. Give love, overlook an offense, and forgive. Isn't this how you want your children to treat you?"

I know I will be in the mother-in-law role someday. Now is when I train my boys how to honor me in the future by how I treat Daisy.

"Remember, your husband will love you for your kindness to his family," he says, "even though he himself might struggle with them. When you honor your in-laws, you win in many ways."

And he's gone.

This was a lot to swallow. I look out the window at the bare winter trees and feel the cold barrenness in my heart toward Daisy. This is an area that will never be easy, but at least I have a game plan and strategy for handling her. Matthew and I will discuss it tonight.

The doorbell rings, and it is the furniture deliveryman. I'm so excited! I've been waiting for this sofa to arrive for weeks!

The men bring in the sofa and set it down in the living room. That's strange. The fabric looks like it has a green cast instead of the caramel color I picked out. I think the furniture store got the wrong fabric on my sofa! I run into my bedroom to retrieve the original color swatch. Oh, no! It's the same!

I call the lady at the furniture store who helped me pick out the fabric. "The sofa looks green instead of the soft cream color I thought I was picking out."

"Mmmm, well, I'm sorry to hear that. Different lighting has a tendency to bring out different shades in fabrics. There's nothing I can do about that. "

Now she tells me? This is a twelve-hundred-dollar sofa, and *now* she tells me about the lighting?

Dad is beeping in on the other line. His airline tickets for Vegas are for this weekend. I decide I had better take his call.

"I have a little problem, Jessica," he says. "Debbie got a DUI. It seems she has a drinking problem she's been hiding from me."

CHAPTER 20

How to Wisely Handle Conflict with Your Husband

Wednesday, February 13

Talking Dad out of canceling the wedding was not difficult. Maybe he is realizing that he can't meet women and then marry them the next month.

Mrs. Smith, the principal at school, is calling me. She probably wants to know what progress I've made in planning the carnival. Actually, I've done nothing. I wonder if there is any way I can still beg out of it, as I have zero interest in that event.

"Hello, Mrs. Smith," I say.

"Jessica," she says, "I have a little boy in the office with me who was found cheating because he wrote the answers to a test on his hand."

My heart drops. Oh, no. Oh, no. I feel like I am being kicked in the stomach.

"Brandon wants to talk to you," she says.

Mrs. Smith hands the phone to Brandon, but he can't talk because he's sobbing. This parenting cap I wear can drain the life right out of me.

Mrs. Smith sends Brandon back to class and makes an appointment for Matthew and me to come in to discuss the matter with her. Before we hang up, she says, "And how is the carnival coming?"

I decide not to try to beg off. "Fine," I lie.

We hang up, and I stare out the window. Cheating? My boys may be boisterous and fidgety, but cheating? The helplessness I feel to do life well hits me pretty hard today. I'd like to conquer life and have it all fit neatly in a box with a bow, but truly, life can never be conquered, only managed. Family may be the most wonderful gift of the Creator, but today, I feel like it is the most draining.

Tomorrow, both boys have Valentine Day parties at school. I have volunteered to make cookies for Josh's class, but the cheating episode has drained any vestige of energy I had. However, it looks like a barefoot chef has come to the rescue as far as the cookies are concerned, for on my kitchen table are various kinds of cookies of dinosaurs dressed in red- and pink-icing clothes and holding hearts. *Good Housekeeping,* eat your heart out.

"Children will be children," Genie says. "Cheating in third grade does not mean that Brandon has a life of crime ahead."

Listening to my Love and Logic CD's has thankfully changed my perspective and has increased my knowledge on parenting. I am distressed over Brandon's cheating but not destroyed. I will listen to the CD again on childhood cheating and stealing. I think I can now refocus and listen to Genie.

"Today we will explore how wise women handle conflict with their husbands," begins Genie.

This is a perfect topic because I know Matthew is going to explode over Brandon's indiscretion and is going to want to over-discipline him.

"A couple of thoughts before we start," Genie says. "Every unresolved conflict in a marriage is like adding a brick to a wall between the two of you. At first, the brick wall is low and can easily be scaled. After time, though, the wall gets higher and the barrier between the two of you becomes thicker."

Unresolved conflict is cumulative? Kind of like excess calories.

"Many of you humans have this mistaken idea," he says, "that if a couple loved each other the way they do in romantic comedies and romance novels, there wouldn't be conflict. Nothing could be further from the truth. *Working through and resolving conflict is necessary to achieving true intimacy and mature commitment.* The problem is that couples have not been trained to properly work through conflict."

What? Working through conflict is necessary to achieve intimacy? That foreign thought slaps me. I thought conflict meant that we were incompatible, that there was something seriously wrong in our marital relationship.

Genie has these mind-blowing thoughts. Conflict is necessary? Necessary to achieve that beautiful word, *intimacy*? Why, that's a new perspective on conflict. Instead of running from conflict, I need to focus on learning how to have appropriate and intimacy-building conflict.

"Growing up, my father swept all his feelings under the rug, trying to hide them," I say. "And my mother was constantly picking at my dad to do more, be more, nag, nag. I thought conflict meant that people shouldn't be together."

"You already understand that there are two major methods people use to inappropriately handle conflict," Genie says. "The first is the aggressive mode. People get upset, yell, blame, raise their voice, criticize, bully, are disrespectful, sarcastic, or they belittle others to make their point."

Check for Mom's style.

"The other method of inappropriately handling conflict," Genie continues, "is to be passive, withdraw, and not communicate one's feelings. Individuals with this approach choose to stuff negative feelings and thoughts."

Check for Dad's style. I'm not sure I received a graduate-level course in conflict management while I was growing up.

"Now we will discuss the healthy way to have conflict," Genie said, "and thus, increase intimacy."

I can't help it. Every time he says "increase intimacy," I get excited.

"Would you please give me an example of a conflict that you and Matthew recently have had?" he asks.

The example that comes to mind seems small and inconsequential now compared to this cheating episode, but I offer it anyhow because it caused an argument. "Genie, the boys are the only ones at school without designer tennis shoes. Matthew doesn't understand how important these shoes are to boys in elementary school, so he refuses to buy them for the boys."

"Good example," Genie says. "Let's begin our discussion with a premise that is the most frequently ignored when there is conflict. The premise is to first understand the other person's viewpoint."

I have heard that before, but I certainly don't ever do it.

"Before you rush in with your opinion and all the facts that support your opinion," he says, "listen *without interrupting* to your husband's perspective. Let him get it all out. Repeat his thoughts back to him so that he feels *completely heard*. What was Matthew's perspective on buying the tennis shoes?"

"He said he was working like a dog to pay the mortgage and the electricity bill, and we needed to fund our IRA's, not buy some ridiculously overpriced tennis shoes," I said.

"So then what did you say?" he asked.

Oh, dear. I hate to admit it.

"Well, Genie, I said, uh, I said that, uh, I thought it was selfish of him to not let the boys have what all the other kids have." I am ashamed as I hear myself out loud.

Genie was unmoved. "That's okay," he said. "It's typical of how many couples respond to each other when they don't get their way. Can you think of a response that would have shown Matthew you were truly listening and seeking to understand his perspective?"

This is hard. I have trouble thinking of something.

"Uh … I could have said, 'Matthew, you do work very hard for our money, and you want to be sure we spend it wisely, correct?' "

"Excellent, Young Jessica!"

Yeah, well, I botched it in the actual conversation, though.

Genie continues. "Then when Matthew agreed, you could have said, 'Matthew, I appreciate how hard you work. I also like how careful you are with our money and how you want to save for our retirement. I respect that. Is there anything else you want to tell me?'

"That last question is so valuable," he explains, "because most wives are overanxious to get to their point and therefore don't ask that question. This is where you can learn about your husband and explore his values. Don't overlook this last question."

I'm a midget on the NBA team of mature marriage.

"After and *only* after you listen to and mirror back his thoughts are you to then ask, 'May I please now tell you my perspective on the shoes'?"

What a difference that would have made if I had treated Matthew with respect. I am miles away from getting to the other side of this large, dense forest of marriage harmony.

"Until the other person feels understood," Genie says, "they are reluctant to listen carefully to your viewpoint."

Why don't they teach conflict management in school instead of who discovered the Navaho River?

"Another premise to keep in mind," Genie says, "is that no matter what Matthew says, you are going to bridle your tongue. No sarcasm, no contempt, no raising your voice, no name-calling, no emotional outbursts. The moment you become hyperemotional or hysterical, the husband stops listening. A calm voice is respected in a discussion; an emotional outburst is often disregarded, as it is assumed it is spoken from one who is mentally unstable."

I may be a little dingy, but I'm not mentally unstable.

"And if you do err and raise your voice, or if your tone communicates disrespect," he says, "remember it is imperative to ask for forgiveness. All spouses err in marriage, but asking for forgiveness when you make mistakes helps to rebuild and restore the relationship."

I now remember saying, "Matthew, you don't 'get' our kids!" Not exactly a textbook response. And I never asked him to forgive me. Sometimes I feel like a failure in *Wife School.*

"Listening well to a husband's viewpoint and mirroring back his thoughts opens a husband to hear your opinion," Genie says. "Then in a calm voice you can give your perspective. Wise women know that if they get hysterical and angry, they lose. Never stoop to that. Never attack him with your words. If you do, you are virtually insuring that he will lose his affection for you, even if you win the argument and get your way."

I want affection from Matthew, but I also want my way.

"When you are angry, the temptation to be disrespectful is enormous," he says. "Watch yourself carefully, as these are the moments in which spouses communicate rudeness and contempt. Marriages are destroyed by nothing greater than rudeness and contempt."

Weakness pervades my entire being as I think of situation after situation where I have communicated not only disrespect but also contempt. But Matthew has done the same thing.

"Genie, tell me what to say if Matthew is rude to *me* during a conflict. He told me I was immature and materialistic to try to keep up with all the rich people on our street." Matthew had dished it out just like I did.

"If Matthew is rude and you are being respectful, you say, 'Matthew, I want to please you, but I get upset when you call me names like "immature" and "materialistic." Could you please talk to me respectfully?' If he continues to be disrespectful, say, 'I'll be back later, and we can resume this discussion. Maybe you can treat me with respect then.'"

I like that idea. I treat him with respect; he treats me with respect.

"Wise women never allow their husbands to be disrespectful to them," Genie says. "But don't retaliate with anger; instead, respond with a wise, controlled, calm response. It will increase his esteem for you and increase your ability to influence him."

"Genie, what if Matthew begins to make ridiculous or sarcastic accusations? For example, he said that because I wanted the boys to have the expensive shoes, I was probably going to insist they have new BMWs when they turn sixteen."

I was annoyed and a half by his comment. Such sarcasm.

"If Matthew is critical or negative, your natural response is to be offended. However, an extremely wise response would be for you to humble yourself and ask yourself, 'Is there a partial truth in this message for me?' If you can choose to not be offended, you can grow personally as well as grow in respect to your marriage. This teaching, however, is only for the very mature and advanced students."

I must not be mature and advanced because I'm pretty sure I won't be digging around to find any partial truths in Matthew's criticism.

"It's fine," Genie adds, "if you and Matthew both feel differently. In fact, it's normal and healthy. All spouses have different points of view. As I've said before, if you are wise and respectful in communication, secret elves go to work in his brain to show him your perspective. You have a built-in advantage in that husbands want to please their wives, especially if the wives are consistently depositing the Eight A's."

I love that built-in advantage.

"Matthew will often give you what you want because he longs for a happy wife," he says. "Be sure you do not misuse this feature and manipulate your husband; it will only come back to haunt you. Matthew does not want to be played."

And I admit I have a manipulative streak in me.

"The next step we are going to discuss is negotiating and contributing creative solutions," Genie says. "Most couples somewhat instinctively do this. Negotiating is imperative in marriage. For example, maybe the boys could do some work to help Matthew. Maybe you could use some of your clothes budget to help with the price of the shoes. There are multiple ideas that might make both of you happy."

No one's touching my clothes budget.

"Genie, what if Matthew and I have conflict over a large issue, such as he wants to transfer to another city to live?" Matthew has mentioned this, but he would have to drag me by the hair to leave my sisters.

"The principles in handling conflict are the same whether the issue is about shoes, moving, or how to discipline a third grader who cheats at school. Eliminate any negative behavior, such as sarcasm, anger, disrespect, and name-calling. Listen deeply, mirror back Matthew's viewpoint, be extremely respectful, praise any good points he makes, table the issue for a break if there's an impasse, and offer multiple creative solutions. These are important principles, no matter the conflict."

Well, I'm not moving to another city, no matter what.

"I want to mention something one more time because it is extremely crucial in a marriage relationship," Genie says. "If you see that you made a mistake, were disrespectful, or were just plain wrong, learn to say, 'I was wrong. Will you please forgive me?' I have been repeatedly surprised over the centuries how few people use these healing sentences. Admitting you were wrong and asking for forgiveness is level one in my relationship teaching. Nevertheless, these techniques are rarely used."

The hardest three words to say in the English language are *I was wrong.*

"I am going to give you another helpful statement to say during conflict," Genie says.

More? No, not any more. This is too much already.

"In the middle of the conflict when there is an impasse or much anger, try saying, 'Matthew, I know this conflict is difficult for both of us. But I love you, and I'm committed to our relationship. This issue is important to me, and I'd like to finish working through it, but I know it's unpleasant right now for both of us. All relationships have to work through conflict. We can do this."

"You say that in the middle of the conflict?" I ask, surprised.

"Yes, because you humans get so fearful during conflict—fearful that the other one is wanting out or has lost affection or commitment. These comforting statements about the security of the relationship will defuse fear in the other spouse."

Of course, no one is defusing my fear. I'm the lucky one who gets to worry about Matthew's fear. Typical. Obviously, I'm still not that mature wife who focuses on giving and loving.

"I have already told you this today, but I am going to repeat it because it is where so many women hit a snag. Remember, when Matthew throws you a curve ball as far as an idea, situation, or viewpoint, and you immediately feel upset and sense an ensuing conflict, reach for self-control. Literally say to yourself, 'I'm upset; find some self-control. Don't let this anger spew out in ugly streams.'

"If you feel yourself accelerating into anger, memorize and have this sentence ready, 'Matthew, this idea (occurrence, situation, conflict) surprises and upsets me. Let me think about it before we talk about it. I always want to honor you, and when I get upset, I am not as respectful as you deserve.' "

I've got to remember that Matthew deserves respect because he wears the uniform of husband, not necessarily because he is always virtuous.

"Young Jessica, you do not have to be ready with an immediate comeback. Difficult communication is inevitable in marriage, but what is not inevitable is your throwing verbal hot water in his face with your emotional escalations. These moments in a marriage when a wife lets loose are very difficult for men to recover from. Men's feelings are truly lessened for any woman who treats him with such disdain. Don't believe the lie that your marriage can take verbal whippings and not be negatively affected. Do everything you can to stop these tsunamis before they begin."

Genie says the same thing over and over again, but it's a different song, a different stanza. The grooves in my brain where we hash it out are deep. Knowing how damaging these artillery war games are is not new information. But I must listen, as I have not mastered this important teaching. I don't want to lessen Matthew's affection for me. On the contrary, I'm trying to *grow* it! Gosh, even after all these months, I've got *scads* to learn.

"One last comment and then it's time for Genie Shuffleboard in Yemen. Look again at your notes from the Eighth A, Authority. When there is an impasse after much debate and negotiation, it is helpful if the wife remembers who is the ultimate CEO of the family." And then Genie disappears.

Pretty rude of Genie to drop that bomb and cut out. Admittedly, though, I am still struggling with that A. If I were Genie, I would also rather play shuffleboard instead of listening to a bunch of bellyaching from me.

I forgot to thank Genie for the Valentine cookies. Wouldn't the hosts on the *Food Network* be envious of these?

I decide to get started on that horrendous carnival that I'm in charge of. I again have to push Brandon's upsetting cheating episode out of my mind. Matthew texts me to remind me we are meeting tonight to sign papers to refinance the mortgage on the house. He received the papers at work but brought them home for me to keep. I begin to look in my hot spots, but after thirty minutes of looking, I call Matthew.

"I've looked everywhere for those refinance papers, and I can't find them anywhere."

"We're meeting at six tonight to sign the papers, Jessica," he says in a tone I don't like. "You *have* to find them."

I hear some talking in the background that I can't distinguish. Then Matthew says to someone, "Way to go. Thanks so much."

"Oh, never mind," Matthew says to me. "Indigo scanned the papers into the computer when I got them here at the office, so we can just reprint a set. See you at six."

Not only do I not tell him about Brandon's cheating, but Mesmerizing Indigo is showing me up with her ultraefficiency.

Also, tonight is Cammey and Peyton's Valentine party to which most of the neighborhood was invited—except us. I wonder how I could apply Genie's teachings on conflict to healing the problem between Cammey and myself?

Sometimes I would like to run away and hide. I remember when life got tangled and difficult in the von Trapp household in *The Sound of Music*, and Maria went back to the abbey where she could disappear from life. But hiding and disappearing, as Julie Andrews' character discovered in the movie, doesn't solve problems.

Maybe instead of going to an abbey, I'll make a run to T.J.Maxx.

CHAPTER 21
How to Be Attractive to Your Husband

Tuesday, February 26

Matthew and I have gone around and around about how to handle Brandon's cheating incident. It was almost two weeks ago, and we still can't agree. The conflict makes me anxious.

Last night was Matthew's mom's birthday. My heart begins to race from even more anxiety as I replay in my mind our conversation from last night.

Daisy was originally happy that I had invited her over to celebrate her birthday. From the kitchen, I could hear her talking to Matthew in the living room.

"Matthew, I don't understand why you won't set me up with Harold," she complained. "We're about the same age."

Jolted like I had received an electric shock, I realized Daisy was trying to get Matthew to set her up with my father! Does she think that the suave Hairy Harold would possibly be interested in her? Why, my dad can almost have his pick of women. I swear she's demented.

After that, Daisy came into the kitchen where I was sautéing garlic in butter for my Shrimp Spaghetti recipe. "Oh my, real butter," she said. "That's so fattening. I don't know if I saved enough calories for all that butter."

Since when do I have to check with you about what I'm serving for dinner? I thought but, of course, didn't say.

"Have you tried Pilates, Jessica? I've heard it's great at taking off tummy fat, even if it's been there for years. You should try it. I think Matthew would enjoy your losing a few pounds."

Uh, excuuuuuuuuse me? Is this Punked? *Or maybe* Candid Camera? *I mean, does anyone in real life act like this?* I was completely flabbergasted.

I looked at Daisy to see if she was kidding. She wasn't. She really wasn't. I have six to eight pounds to lose compared to her forty, and *she* was talking to *me* about losing weight? She has Marilyn Monroe-yellow hair with one-inch black roots, and she was giving *me* advice on how to be attractive. Absolutely unbelievable.

Then Matthew came in the kitchen. "What's that smell? Is something burning?"

I was so befuddled by Daisy's remarks that I had forgotten that butter burns easily, so instead of sautéing the garlic, I scorched it.

I was having a terrible, horrible, no good, very bad day.

I literally shake my head, as I realize that replaying last night in my mind is unproductive. I need to get started on the five hundred Wilson wedding invitations. With my home business soaring, I raised my calligraphy rate to two dollars for a set of inner and outer envelopes. That's one thousand bucks coming in. I *love* having a little mad money. And to top that off, Matthew lets me spend it however I want. I should write that down on one of his lists in my Turquoise Journal.

I walk to get my calligraphy supplies and, *presto*, all five hundred invitations are finished in my handwriting, organized, and ready to give back to Mrs. Wilson.

"After the tirade you endured last night," Genie says, "I thought you might enjoy a big 'happy' today."

Try a *huge* "happy." This gift from Genie was comparable to twenty-five hours of time. Genie, let me count the ways I love thee.

"That will free up some time so you can begin working on that carnival," he slyly suggests.

I'm filled with dread as I think about my procrastination in organizing that event, which is only two months away.

"Let's take a walk while we talk today," Genie suggests. "Remember, no one can see me but you."

I bundle up in my Patagonia jacket, a scarf, gloves, and two pairs of socks. I hate being cold. Genie adds a scarf and ear muffs to his ensemble of satin pants and sleeveless vest, which exposes his chest. He looks hilarious. Today I have a Jack Black Genie.

We walk by Cammey's house, and the thought of the unresolved conflict with her pricks me. I still need to deal with that. Always something.

"Our topic today is being attractive to your spouse," says Genie.

Actually, I think about being attractive quite a bit. Wouldn't it be great to be naturally beautiful and skinny? However, I'm afraid I didn't get the best genes for that.

I wonder what this Mideastern leprechaun is going to say about my being attractive to Matthew.

"You can have confidence that all men like two principles of attractiveness: freshness and femininity," he says. "I've never met a man yet who liked slovenly clothes, thick, greasy makeup, or dirty hair. Also, men repeatedly favor a soft, feminine look as opposed to a hard, masculine style."

My wardrobe is replete with tailored grays, browns, and blacks. Especially black.

"Men differ, of course, in how much makeup they like and in which styles they prefer," Genie says. "A husband's preferences are for the wise wife to discover. Most women dress to please themselves and their friends, not their husbands."

Now that I think about it, when I'm in the dressing room at J. Crew, I imagine how I will appear to my friends at the PTF, not how Matthew will view me.

"Women try hard before marriage to look their best because they know that appearances matter to a man. But after the marriage, they 'let down' or 'let go,' thinking the husband should accept and love them the way they are."

Perfuming and pampering myself was standard protocol when Matthew and I were dating. Now, it's more of a "what's comfortable" look, I admit.

"Men care. They do," Genie said. "Men want an attractive spouse. They want a spouse that's pleasing for them to look at."

Yeah, but here we go again. That takes effort!

"The best way to truly know what Matthew's preferences are is to ask," he says. "Wear something soft and colorful, and then ask his opinion. And don't get offended, no matter what he says. Women get offended when anyone discusses their looks in a corrective fashion. They think their looks are completely their own business, and that their husband should be happy with however they look. This is not the case, and the wise woman will realize that for thousands of years men have cared a great deal about their wife's appearance."

Matthew likes me to dress young and somewhat hip. However, I prefer to dress more tailored, so, obviously, Ann Taylor wins.

I have always thought that if Matthew really loved me, he would be happy with however I look. Now Genie is telling me I have been misinformed, and that my looks matter to Matthew.

"When a husband comes home from work," he says, "he likes to be met with a happy, fresh-looking wife. Not necessarily a beauty pageant queen but certainly not a slovenly mess. Most men understand a few pounds after a baby's birth, but a fit figure and a little work on the hair, makeup, and clothes show respect for him. You will have to search hard for men who don't agree with this."

I guess I sort of knew this deep down but hated to face it. You know, more for me to change.

"If you are having company, you freshen up by putting on clean clothes and tidying up your hair and makeup. Or if you go out, you remember to dress up and fix your makeup. But at home, the husband often gets your leftovers from your busy day. What you must remember is that it gives the husband pleasure to look at his attractive wife."

It's true, I use my best efforts to look nice for others, not Matthew.

"The best way to solicit Matthew's opinion is to give him choices," Genie says. "For example, say, 'Matthew, do you prefer me to wear dresses or pants?' 'Matthew, do you like my hair short or long?' 'Matthew, do you like me to wear a little makeup or do you like more?' He will tell you the truth if he thinks it's safe and that you truly want to know."

Matthew has been afraid to be honest in the past because the Wicked Witch of the West appeared if he said anything to upset me.

"The uncomfortable topic for most women is their weight," Genie says. "Staying in shape takes a lot of work. Establishing a daily walk is a great starter. A brisk, twenty-minute walk every day is at least ten pounds a year. And the difference of a daily walk over two years is even more.. But getting a twenty-minute walk in every day is a challenge for most moms. Forming this habit will take substantial effort."

I already have too much to do. Walking *every* day? Gosh, isn't there another way?

"Sugar is one of a woman's worst enemies as are simple carbs, such as white flour. This is not a course on weight loss, but women can learn to increase exercise, decrease sugar and simple carbs, and transform their bodies. Most men are very proud of his wife's slim figure."

I've got a shelf full of exercise DVDs that are rarely used. I know I could track my food, too, and that would be helpful. I want to be slim, but my fitness program seems to be at the bottom of my list of priorities. Maybe I could start with ten minutes of exercise a day to see if I could form a habit.

Genie is right about one thing: I'm touchy about my weight. And there's my dear sister Jackie who significantly struggles with her weight. Becoming skinny is another subject that could use an entire *Genie School*, sort of like the one I'm getting on marriage.

"To balance this subject," Genie says, "I want to remind you of the preeminence of inner beauty to a man. Some of the world's most beautiful women are left by their husbands."

I know this too. The most beautiful girl in my college sorority was married to a man who cheated on her and then moved out.

"I don't want to blame wives for their husband's indiscretions, but in many situations, women who are extremely beautiful are spoiled and do not make the Eight A deposits into their husband's tanks. They incorrectly think their beauty can keep a husband. No outward beauty on Earth can replace the Eight A's."

I think of my shopping trip to Macy's yesterday. I was rummaging through the textured hoses, trying to find a pattern and size that worked, and this beautiful, red-haired goddess appeared. Her skin was flawless, her clothes were pressed and coordinated, and her figure was tiny. Without so much as a glance in my direction, she states in a matter-of-fact voice, "I need to get in there and look at those hose," like she was shooing away an annoying fly. She reminded me of the White Witch in *The Lion, the Witch, and the Wardrobe.*

Quickly, this woman's ravishing beauty diminished into a bag of bones with some makeup and perfume. She became a mannequin to me, void of any true beauty and life, painted up but with no nurturing life within.

I can see exactly how men would initially be attracted to this bombshell but would soon realize the tree was hollow, a home to maggots and vermin.

"A woman's goodness, sweetness, and kindness make her the most beautiful," Genie says. "The outside is important but not nearly as important as the inside. Women throughout the ages have sought how to be rapturously gorgeous, but alas, nothing is as beautiful as a lovely heart. A lovely heart is a source of nourishment and a refuge for the burdens of others. Estée Lauder will never be able to sell this ultimate beauty."

I think of the money I have spent on creams and lotions to stay young and beautiful while often dismissing the prerequisite step of having a lovely heart.

Genie is gone, and I take off all my outer layers. I feel better after a brisk walk, no doubt about it. I know the benefits of exercise are too numerous to count. I guess I need to preplan my food, log it, and get serious about losing these pounds because I know it's important to Matthew. And it's important to me.

I get out my laptop and start planning my new eating program. I know it's time for a new hairdo too.

And lastly, but most importantly, I get out the Creator's Word. I have neglected this inner beautifier for too long.

Now it is time to do a little more work on the dreaded carnival coming up in five weeks. Phone calls, e-mails, and more phone calls.

Allison is on the other line. I put her on hold while I finish talking to another friend, Sylvia, who is going to assist me with the carnival. When I return to Allison's call, she asks me if she can stop by for a minute. The Sister Rule trumps being busy.

Allison is here in five minutes and immediately bursts into tears. Zach got a job in Nevada, she says, and they are moving in three weeks. I call Chloe, and she stops what she is doing and hurries over. We all three sit in my den, whimpering together. One of the Three Memphis Musketeers is moving!

CHAPTER 22

How to Help Your Husband Be a Spiritual Leader

Monday, March 3

've got a long "to do" list today, and it's already noon. First, I have to make and take dinner to my friend Abigail who recently had a baby. After that, I have to go to the printer to get some items printed for the upcoming carnival. Then I've got to pick up the boys from school and take them to the dentist. After that—I'm worn out even listing all of this—the boys are each going to separate baseball practices while I go to Allison's and help her pack.

Thinking of baseball takes my mood down a notch. I'm concerned about Brandon's bad attitude regarding baseball season since he's not getting to pitch. The coach wants him in the outfield, and frankly, it's embarrassing the way Brandon has responded to the coach.

Mathew ended up grounding Brandon for a month for the cheating incident. I wish Matthew would address the boys' character weaknesses more. These boys need the direction of a father as well as their mother. We all need more direction and leadership from Matthew.

"I hope Abigail likes my beef tenderloin," a friendly voice says. "I've gotten rave reviews on this recipe for centuries."

I never know whether he's kidding or not with these "century" remarks.

"And of course, here's a beef tenderloin along with some green beans and mashed potatoes for my favorite client," Genie says.

"I'm your *only current* client," I say.

"Oh, that's right, you are," he says as we both smile.

With cooking off my "to do" list, I can relax and listen to today's topic.

"Today, we will discuss how to help your husband be a spiritual leader in your home," Genie says.

It is ridiculous how this wizard reads my mind.

"The best starting point for you is to begin to ask Matthew his opinion about various subjects," he says. "But be careful and intentional about the topics in which you ask his opinion. For heaven's sakes, don't bring up a topic so you get a chance to give your opinion and set him straight."

Uhhhh, I wonder if Genie is thinking about when I asked Matthew his view on how much parents should volunteer at school so I could tell him how I wanted him to volunteer to run the concession stand?

"When you ask Matthew for his opinion, listen deeply, and praise his ideas and thoughts," Genie says. "Resist the urge to correct him if you disagree. Of course, you are entitled to give your opinion, but remember to offer it as *your* opinion, not as the positively, absolutely, *only* way to look at things."

That's how I often feel. My opinions *are* positively, absolutely, the only way.

As I listen to Genie, I realize many women in the twenty-first century would shudder at Genie's advice. Liberated women want to go man-to-man in hashing out issues. I have learned from Genie that I never win Matthew's affection when I'm too strong, opinionated, unmoving, and forceful. Men are not attracted to wives who bark like army sergeants.

"Ask Matthew about the subjects in which he is a master, not the subjects in which you are knowledgeable. Ask his opinion about the NBA lockout, about the best cars to buy, and about the best movies of the nineties. He has multiple opinions and would love to have an eager audience. Of course, you will discuss topics in which you are both interested, but women forget how sexy and attractive it is to ask a man his opinion and to be an impressed audience of one."

"Sexy?" I ask.

"Yes, it's very sexy to a man for a woman to want his opinion," Genie says.

What is my problem that I'm such a know-it-all instead of asking my husband's opinion? I bet Flaming Indigo wants his opinion all the time.

I hate it when Genie discusses an area in which I know I'm weak. I am extremely opinionated. Sometimes I forget appropriate boundaries and become argumentative.

"This is an aside, but affairs often start by a woman simply being impressed with a man's opinion," Genie says. "Men long to give their opinions and then be admired for their wisdom, clever thinking, and logic. Wise married women need to listen and benefit from these strategies."

I know. I know. I know.

"If a wife often asks for her husband's opinion, a pattern is soon carved in the husband's mind that he is successful in giving his opinion at home. But as you also know, if you ask his opinion and then disagree with it, you are tearing down your husband's desire to want to lead or even discuss things with you, for that matter."

Yes, yes, I know this all too well. Dagnabbit. All *too* well.

"Another idea to help promote spiritual leadership," he says, "is to praise Matthew for any input or ideas. When he suggests a vacation that you like for the family, be sure to say, 'You have great ideas, Matthew. I like when you give your input.' You want him to feel positive about giving his ideas and leadership to the family. And of course, if he gives you a bad idea, review your notes from December 31 (Chapter 16, "What to Do When Your Husband Gives You a Bad Idea")."

Reluctantly, I admit I am the captain of Team I've Got a Better Idea.

"Praise his good ideas and bring them up later," Genie says. "E-mail or text him that you were thinking about his good idea (for example, to take the family biking) and how much you appreciate his having such awesome ideas. One of my mottos is 'Appreciation promotes repetition.'"

I'm still stuck in the "ignore his good things but broadcast his mistakes" mode.

"Now we will move into a more difficult technique to promote Matthew's spiritual leadership," Genie says. "Try not to be the big leader/teacher in front of the children. Of course, you are instructing the children all the time, and this is important for a mother to do. But sometimes a man may feel inferior that's he's not as wise or as quick thinking as the wife. When Dad is around, let him give his opinion. You have more access to the children; you have plenty of opportunity to give them your nuggets of wisdom. Let Dad be the king when he is around."

I don't think there is a tape strong enough to seal my mouth and keep me from telling my children what I think about life. But the idea of not being a herald when Matthew is around is new. I know I sometimes upstage him.

"When couple friends or extended family members are around, don't overshadow your husband with all your wisdom and opinions," Genie says. "And *never* contradict Matthew in front of others."

I contradicted Matthew in front of our friends last month when he gave his opinion about consolidating the school districts in our region. I don't think I want to see a Wife School report card for today's topic.

"Another wise strategy for a wife to promote spiritual leadership in her husband is to ask him to go to a study of the Creator's Word," Genie says. "Remember, you can't ask Matthew for everything, so be intentional what you ask for. Husbands want to please their wives, but they can't do everything. If you ask for a trip to Italy, for him to paint the entire house, for a yard that is immaculate, and to work extra in order to buy new kitchen appliances, you will use up your 'asking points' on those issues. Instead, meet his needs, get under his authority, make him king of your house, make him the happiest man alive, and *then* ask him to go to a study of the Creator's Word or to join a small group where the men love the Creator. Use your 'asking points' on the important issues in life."

I didn't realize there were only a finite number of "asking points."

"You love your children more than life," Genie says. "But the best chance for them to turn out well is when they have a loving, humble, earthly father who loves them and also loves the Creator. Your influence helps develop this kind of man."

This lesson feels heavy and important.

"Ask for family time from Matthew," Genie continues, "but then be sure he *enjoys* it. If he is treated like the king of your home, he will enjoy these events. Ask the children to make sure Dad has fun. Most wives are worried if the children have fun. Of course, you want the children to enjoy family time, but the most important person to enjoy family time is the father."

How I miss these obvious truths is beyond me. Where is my brain? Why have I been so child-focused? Common sense tells me that Matthew is the primary person who needs to enjoy family time so he will want to do it again. I can be a dope.

"Another idea," he says, "is for you to suggest that *together* you join a small group at your church where other couples are seeking the Creator. Don't go to this group and then at home brag to Matthew about the other spiritual men. No, let him soak up the other men's strengths by simply being around them. Nothing will be more effective in Matthew developing spiritual leadership than being around other men who are spiritual leaders in their own homes."

I know we all become like the people we have coffee with.

"And be sure to express gratefulness for whatever steps Matthew takes. Say, 'Thank you for going to that small group with other men, Matthew. The children and I benefit when you make such wise investments with your time.'"

This teaching is not how to do brain surgery, but I know similar amount on both subjects.

"As I've said before, *you must always be concerned about helping a man save face*," Genie says. "You must be careful of his ego and his dislike of being told what to do by a woman. Yes, he appreciates your ideas, but he wants them as suggestions or possibilities, not commands. Young Jessica, Matthew enjoys you being a woman who is bright, driven, and intelligent. Just be sure that even though you are a strong and capable woman that your priority is having a soft heart."

I am a strong woman, and it's nice that Genie sees the beauty in those qualities. However, being reminded of the priority of having a soft heart in the midst of a strong personality is something I need to tape to my bathroom mirror.

It's time for me to take my beef tenderloin to Abigail and then pick up the boys for their dentist appointments. I feel a little weary on these days when a major weakness of mine is exposed. I think Genie senses my discomfort.

"I want to interject two more quick thoughts, and then we're finished for the day," he says.

I was afraid we weren't finished yet.

"Of course, it is of paramount importance that you and Matthew attend a church where the Creator's Word is preached, and in Memphis, there are multiple churches that do that. So find a church where Matthew is comfortable. Don't try to force him to go to a church where the dress code is super dressy if Matthew would rather wear jeans and cowboy boots. If the music is stuffy, find a church where Matthew enjoys the rock band. Again, common sense tells you that if Matthew is comfortable and in his downhill stream, he will want to be more involved."

Matthew has been uncomfortable with our church for years. I guess we'll be visiting that new church in Midtown where the dress code is relaxed, the music is jazzy, and the preaching rocks. I shouldn't need Captain Obvious to tell me these things, but apparently, I do.

"The last idea of the day is to possibly suggest to Matthew that you sign up for a Marriage Enrichment weekend or course at your church. Attending these events can virtually be life-altering for a marriage," Genie says. "There is something about hearing what 'experts' say that penetrates humans' thinking."

Churches in our area have these events all the time, but we never seem to make time to go.

"With jobs, rearing young children, and household tasks," Genie says, "it is difficult to add one more activity to your schedule. Learn to be exceedingly selective and intentional with your time. Couples need margins with unscheduled time. It is imperative to learn to say no to good activities in order to have energy for the best ones."

I need to leave. Isn't he through for the day? Genie needs to learn about sensory overload.

"Rereading the A of Authority is a good reminder that when men are faced with disrespectful and bossy wives, they often retreat instead of lead. A gentle, quiet spirit in a woman communicates she wants to be led and encourages men to do just that."

I knew it. I knew I would eventually get blamed for Matthew being a crummy spiritual leader. Because I've been disrespectful and bossy in the past, Genie is pointing an invisible finger at me. I *knew* it.

"Your own humility and meekness will do more," Genie continues, "to promote spiritual leadership in your husband than any other quality. When you believe that the Creator leads your family through Matthew, your faith will help him step up to his responsibility. But again, women often unknowingly keep their husbands from wanting to lead their families by their critical and opposing comments when the husband attempts to lead."

Genie smiles and then dissolves into the air.

I know I'm a hard case. I'm trying to change. Really, I'm trying. It's hard when you're as strong-minded as me. *Really* hard.

The doorbell rings. I'm late enough already, and if that's my widowed neighbor, complaining again about our dogs barking, I think I'll— Wait, it's not my neighbor. It's ... Indigo! What is *she* doing here?

"I tried to call, but no one picked up," she begins. "Matthew asked me to drop off his laptop for him. He said he wouldn't have time to get back to the office to get it today because he has bowling practice right after work and needs to do some work tonight on his computer at home."

She smiles sweetly. I want to gag. Matthew said nothing about bowling practice to me. She knows his schedule better than me?

She is wearing black leggings, hugging every curve. They are neatly tucked into some low, leopard-print boots with a four-inch heel. Her hair is teased, and her perfume is strong. She is wearing feather earrings, much like the ones Steven Tyler wears on *American Idol*. Her sweater is low, and I can detect some cleavage, even without staring.

I don't like her. I don't trust her. And I'm late getting to Abigail's.

Indigo leaves, and I jump into my car. Dad's name is on my caller ID. He decided by himself that he didn't need to marry a woman who has struggled with alcohol for thirty years. Dad doesn't need me to coach him after all.

"My friend Roy says he is getting older and would like to slow down," Dad says. "He is thinking about hiring an honest, capable person to train and run his businesses. What do you think about Zach interviewing for the job?"

Oh my gosh! Then Allison wouldn't have to move!

To the degree that Indigo bums me out, I am excited that Allison has a chance to stay in Memphis. My life is always a seesaw of the good and the bad. This news about a possible job for Zach in Memphis is a definite thumbs-up!

CHAPTER 23

When There Are Many Things Your Husband Needs to Change

Saturday, March 8

spent some more time on that ridiculous carnival this morning. That annoying event is going to end up taking almost forty to fifty hours of prep time. Mrs. Smith, the principal, calls and wants a detailed list of what's been done and what's still left to do regarding the carnival. I feel a smidge of passive rebellion coming on as I realize I'm not in any hurry to send that list to her.

Some clients gave Matthew four tickets to the University of Memphis Tigers basketball game against Tulsa this afternoon. Brandon and Josh are beside themselves, and it makes me happy to see my boys so happy. Tiger tickets are hard to come by unless you're (a) rich, (b) you know someone, or (c) you don't mind sitting in the nosebleed seats.

We walk into the FedEx Forum and head toward the court for prime seats. I hear the Tiger band, *Go Tigers Go, on to victory ... Fight, fight for the blue and gray.* I feel like I'm nineteen and still in college. Not a bad feeling.

While the Tigers are warming up, the woman in the seat in front of me is fussing at her husband. "Did you pay the Visa?" she asks. "When are you going to change the oil in my car?" and "When are you going to clip those fingernails, Andy?" While the cheerleaders are firing tee shirts into the crowd from a huge blowgun, this poor guy is under fire for all of his inadequacies.

Another couple in front of us, sitting to our left on the aisle, has a newborn. I keep looking at the happy mother, and when I can't stand it anymore, I point in the baby's direction and say to Matthew, "I want one!"

The guy selling popcorn is right behind the mother, yelling, "Popcorn! Popcorn!" Matthew starts digging in his pocket for money and tells the popcorn guy he wants one. I think he is getting the popcorn for himself and is ignoring me. Then when he hands me the popcorn, I look at him, puzzled, and he says, "You said you wanted one." I point to the baby and say, "I meant I want one of those!" We both laugh.

But during halftime, I tell Matthew I am serious about wanting a baby, and he says he is serious, too; that he can barely pay for the two kids we have. I try to not get upset, but it is difficult.

The Tigers win, and we head home. Matthew takes the boys to the park to practice their batting and fielding skills, and I get a visitor.

"Did you write in your Turquoise Journal that not only does Matthew take the family to a ballgame, but he then takes the boys to the park?" Genie asks.

Uh, that would be a no. I forget to write in that Turquoise Journal, yet I know how valuable it is in changing my thoughts when I read it. I need to do better. Matthew does a lot of life right, I admit.

"And did you notice how that woman in front of you flooded her husband with her concerns today?" Genie asked.

I noticed. I felt sorry for the guy.

"Women don't realize that they flood their husbands with their requests," Genie says. "Instead, women should pick one topic from their list of top five to eight concerns in their Turquoise Journal (List 8). Some women want more intimate conversation from their husbands; some want more financial support; other women want more help around the house or a better sex life. The list of what women want is infinite, and the problem is that they want the whole list *now*."

I sure do understand wanting it *now*. Like that baby.

"Let's look from a husband's viewpoint," he says. "Here's a nice, honest, hardworking guy who is content at home with some sex, some food, and not too much emotional drama. Suddenly, he's married to this complex creature who doesn't even know for sure what she wants, but she knows she doesn't want what he's giving."

Ha, ha, I laugh to myself. I don't even know what I want, yet I expect Matthew to know.

"Early in the marriage, the husband often tries to comfort his wife when she complains and frets," Genie says. "He tries to figure out what she wants. But eventually, the husband shuts down because he didn't sign up for this. He signed up for sex, fun, someone to make him feel respected, and a companion with whom to walk through life. But what he got was another mother who tries to analyze and improve him."

I've admitted that. Does he have to keep rubbing it in?

"Men will put their own lives at risk to rescue fellow soldiers who are wounded," he says. "They run mega-billion-dollar organizations. But men feel helpless in the face of a wife who is angry, critical, or correcting."

"Genie, I hear you, but what's a woman to do?" I ask. "Men come into marriage with so many issues that need adjusting."

"If a woman will only ask for change in one area at a time," he says, "while pouring on the Eight A's, most men can handle that. It's the flooding that undoes men."

"Are you saying that if a husband has five or six major offensive things, the wife can only talk about one item at a time?"

"That is *exactly* what I'm saying," Genie continues. "She cannot tell him that she's unhappy with his income, that he doesn't do his share of the work around the house, and that he's not a good father to their new baby girl. That's flooding. Pick one thing, and work on that."

It seems to me that a man should be able to work on two or three things at a time. We women are the supreme multitaskers.

"The Creator made the female with a desire to build her nest, so the wife is repeatedly focused on all that needs to be changed to make the nest more beautiful and functional. That is virtuous in itself, of course. But a wise woman should learn to be content with the status quo while at the same time working on her list of goals—*but only on one thing at a time.*"

Content and working on goals? Such a paradox. I like black and white, not gray.

"Remember, women are the ones who want emotional connection and intimacy to the max," Genie reminds me. "Husbands simply do not have this need or desire. If you want your cat to care, you know you are an idiot. If you want your husband to care like you do, you are equally..." He pauses for me to fill in the blank.

"An idiot," I say and laugh as I think about wanting my cat to care. Our house could be on fire and the cat would still walk at the same pace.

"Take the top five things you want," he says. "Put four on the shelf, and ask for one thing at a time. And usually that's only one thing every few months. Don't flood him. And don't despise him for being a man. You are mad that he doesn't care like a woman? *You* are the woman. *You* are the one who gets to influence him for good. That is *your* job, and wise women do it. Do you complain that you only have twenty-four hours in a day instead of thirty? Of course not. In the same way, stop complaining that your husband is a man and is not as interested in emotional connection and issues like the children and the home. You must motivate him to care more. You start by meeting his needs with the Eight A's."

I need this sermon whether I like it or not.

"Your men are coming in the back door," he says. "Hope they like their dinner."

He vanishes, and the breakfast bar is full of barbeque ribs, baked beans, cole slaw, and potato salad.

"How did you whip this up so fast?" Matthew asks. "You're quite the genie."

No, but I certainly do love it when *my* genie leaves these "happys."

"Jessica, did I tell you that the folks at work are starting a Saturday morning bowling league?"

My insides drop. More bowling? And on *Saturday*? Will Erotic Indigo be there?

Don't freak out, I say to myself. *Get control of your tongue. Self-control, Jessica.*

"I told the guys at work," Matthew continues, "that you and I had negotiated how much time I would be away from the family to bowl. I explained to them I was already at my limit, so I couldn't join the team. Besides, I like being home with you and the boys on Saturdays."

I stare at this man. Matthew? Is that you? Matthew, my husband? Did an alien hijack his brain but leave his body?

"Matthew, you are the world's sweetest husband," I say and hug him. "I can't tell you how much I appreciate your keeping our agreement. The boys and I love our time with you, and wow, here you are, protecting it. This makes me so happy."

And what alien hijacked *my* brain and left *my* body? When have I ever been this sweet?

I can see now that Matthew and I have sailed down this marriage river and have finally turned the bend. When was the last time we have had this kind of conversation? In the first years of marriage? Oh my goodness. My marriage is coming back. It's coming back!

I don't want to ruin this moment, so I won't say anything now. But maybe in a few days, I'll ask Matthew again for the one thing I really want—another baby!

CHAPTER 24

When Your Husband Doesn't Appreciate You

Tuesday, April 1

The carnival is this Saturday. The activities and events are all in order, as are my volunteers. I check the Internet for the weather. Oh no, 60 percent chance of rain. I guess we can always move everything into the gym if it rains.

Sylvia Black's name appears on my iPhone. Sylvia is in charge of renting the inflatables for the carnival.

"Hi, Sylvia," I say.

"Hi, Jessica. I have a chance to go to Heber Springs Lake on Saturday and wondered if you would mind if I was not at the carnival?"

I'm thinking, *Who is going to be in charge of the inflatables if Sylvia isn't there? Me, that's who!* Just what I need—more responsibility on Saturday.

Sylvia must have sensed my hesitation. "If you'd rather I come on Saturday, I will say no to the trip to the lake."

"I hate to ask you to miss a good trip to the lake, Sylvia, but I was counting on you to take complete responsibility for the inflatables," I say. Geesh. I'd like to leave the whole dang carnival thing and go to the lake myself. Or the beach. Or Paris.

Sylvia says she understands and will cancel the lake trip. She doesn't seem annoyed at all. "I was wondering if you had a second to talk about something else?" Sylvia asks.

"Sure," I say. I hope she's not going to beg off anything else.

"I saw how sweet your husband was to you last week, and I have a question about marriage," she says.

What's this? I have a little success with my marriage and people are asking me questions about it?

"Sure, go ahead," I say, even though I know how unqualified I am to give advice.

"My husband, Brian, and I were in charge of leading an all-day youth retreat at our church last Saturday. I organized the event, called all the parents, sent the e-mails, collected the money, and on the day of the event, my husband arrives and runs the games that I had researched and planned. The day was wildly successful, and that night, Brian kept telling me all the compliments he received from the parents on how he handled the games. He never once mentioned my investment and contribution to the day."

I would have a little pity party over this too.

"I made Brian look very successful," she says. "Not that I want the praise of the crowds, but I would like my husband to acknowledge my efforts. However, he didn't even thank me and took all the credit."

I know the feeling of wanting appreciation and praise from my husband. But I certainly don't know how to respond to this complaint. Luckily, I know someone who does. I told her I would think about it and call her back. That will give me a chance to ask Genie.

As usual, Genie overhears through the cosmos and appears. He is sitting on his usual spot, the counter, when I walk into the kitchen. "I heard you talking with Sylvia and her problem with her husband," he says.

"What do I tell her?" I ask. Seems like we should chat and catch up, but this guy is no-nonsense today.

"Most women respond to feeling unappreciated and resentful in one of two ways," Genie begins. "One, the wife says nothing, but, of course, she makes him pay for not appreciating her by either giving him the cold-shoulder or by dropping little critical remarks."

I know this role. *Passive-aggressive* is the term, I believe.

"The second way women respond to the resentment they feel for not being appreciated," Genie continues, "is to confront her husband with angry or sarcastic words. For example, 'I know you think you're Superman, but that event didn't happen without Lois Lane and her preplanning!' "

That remark would be more my style. Sarcasm.

"Instead of either of those two poor choices, a wise wife will join in with the compliments and get on that praise bus. She will think of other things her husband did right and add to the list."

Are you kidding? She adds more praise? To that unappreciative brute?

"When a wife understands," says Genie, "that her husband is the other half of the whole, she will understand that when she helps him be successful, she helps herself."

I'm not ready to teach this stuff. I'm not ready to *live* this stuff. This is Supersonic Advanced Training for Wives!

I remember another friend, Karla, who complained to me about the same issue when we were picking up our boys from baseball practice last week.

"Genie, I have another example of a wife not getting credit or appreciation," I say. "My friend Karla helps her pastor husband, Mark, think of many of his best ideas for programs and for growing the community at their church. However, he never thanks her or tells her how important her ideas are. Mark wouldn't have the success he enjoys if it weren't for Karla's help, insight, and ideas. But she gets no appreciation at all from him for helping him succeed."

"What can I say?" Genie shrugs his shoulders. "When a wife gives her insight and ideas to her husband, they then belong to the husband, and she needs to let them go like you would a kite or a balloon. Most men don't want their success, especially success at work, attributed to their wives' input."

I feel a creepy, irritating surge inflate my chest. Although I know this about men, their egos, and wanting to be Mr. Big Stuff, I can never quite swallow it. It annoys me to no end that wives give their husbands ideas and help and then the wives go unrecognized.

"One of the greatest relationship skills in the universe and one of the rarest is the ability to be humble, that is, to consider others more important than yourself," Genie says. "Women are wise to oil and lubricate the relationships in their life by laying down their rights."

I know what wives are *supposed* to do.

"A wise woman is meek and gentle," he says, "and lets her husband have the credit; the foolish woman demands recognition or sulks."

This seems so unfair.

"Genie, would it ever be alright for a wife to ask her husband for some appreciation?" I ask. Sylvia and Karla are going to want to know. And so do I.

"If a wife is still resentful a couple days later," he says, "and can't seem to overlook the offense, she could consider having some honest dialogue with her husband where she fingertip-tells him her hurt. A wife who is consistently depositing the Eight A's can gently tell her husband almost anything. For example, she could say, 'Honey, I'm so proud of how you ran the games last weekend. I am not looking for any praise from the parents or the kids at the retreat, but it would mean so much to me if I knew you appreciated the work I did to get you ready. *Your* appreciation is what I care about and is what fills *my* tank.' Most husbands are not angered by this kind of gentle remark.

They actually are complimented that the wife wants and needs their appreciation. Do you see that the difference is in *how* a wife communicates, Young Jessica? Truly, death and life are in the power of the tongue."

Sylvia will like this advice. She'll think I'm a genie—I mean, a genius.

"And remember," he says, "whenever a husband is appreciative or gives the wife any credit at all, she needs to be ready to say, 'That's so nice of you to appreciate my efforts. I feel good for hours after you say nice things like that.' Then she adds a sweet kiss on the cheek. It is also wise for the wife to bring up the husband's appreciation later and remind him how important it is to her and how happy she feels when he notices her contributions. *By rewarding a husband with praise when he appreciates you, you encourage him to do it often.*

"My fellow genies in Kuwait are waiting on me to discuss the pros and cons of living inside a magic lantern, so I'm off," Genie says, and, *poof*, he's gone. Never knowing whether Genie is serious or not, I chuckle and pick up the phone to call Sylvia with my counsel.

Starting to dial, I hang up as Jodie White is beeping in on the other line. Jodie and her husband have volunteered to cook most of the food to sell at the carnival. Knowing how responsible Jodie is calms me.

Actually, it is her husband on the phone. "Jodie asked me to call you. Her grandmother died, and we are flying to New Jersey for the funeral. Jodie is sorry that she is leaving you with the cooking for the carnival."

Oh. My. Goodness. What am I going to do about the food? Who is going to cook the food? What am I going to do??

CHAPTER 25
When Your Husband Needs to Be Right

Wednesday, April 2

When I walked into my bedroom after the phone call from Jodie's husband yesterday, a note was on my pillow that read:

I'll have a smorgasbord of food Saturday at the carnival for you to sell, so take the "carnival food worry" off your list. My food will actually be healthy, not the usual junk that carnivals sell. Fondly, Genie

Someday I'll have to go back to real life without a personal genie to intercept my problems, but that's another day. Until then, I'm going to milk this.

Allison's husband, Zach, had his initial interview with Dad's friend Roy, and today he is interviewing again. Allison is afraid to get too hopeful because, of course, Zach might not get the job. I would love for her to stay. Now, with Genie's help, I think I could help her with her marriage, which she desperately needs.

I've got a busy-and-a-half day. The lengthiest task on my "to do" list is to make twenty-five signs for Saturday's events. Why do I procrastinate? At one p.m., I'm supposed to meet with Matthew and our financial advisor. On top of that, today is cleaning day for the upstairs.

Chloe calls. I absolutely don't have time to talk—but, then, it's a sister.

"What's up, Chloe?"

"I'm tired of Chad always thinking he is right," she blurts out.

Uhhh ... make that *two* sisters who need help with their marriages.

"Last night, we were watching some NBA highlight film," she begins. "I told Chad I thought the gold-and-purple uniforms of the LA Lakers were gaudy and ugly. Chad responded in a very unfriendly and authoritative tone, 'You're wrong, Chloe, dead wrong. Those uniforms are dynamite looking and have a champion feel to them.' You'd think I had said that *Chad* was gaudy and ugly."

Uh-oh.

"Chad thinks he's right about *everything*," she adds.

I can understand Chloe's concern. All she was doing was giving her opinion, and she got rudely corrected. Chad is entitled to his opinion, but so is Chloe.

We discuss the situation at length, and she asks me how I would handle the situation if it were Matthew. "Let me think about it some more, and I'll get back to you," I say. Having a Genie answer marriage questions is better than having Dr. Laura live next door.

I walk upstairs to start on the bedrooms and find that the boys' bedrooms are immaculate. Their beds have fresh sheets, the furniture is dusted, the floors are vacuumed, and the rooms are organized. Genie is wearing an apron and holding a feather duster. The comic relief is welcome. "Your twenty-five signs for tomorrow's carnival are on your kitchen table," he says.

Stress leaves my body as I gain back three hours of time. "Are you sure you're okay with bringing the food on Saturday?" I ask.

He winks. "Not a problem at all."

This is another one of those times when I think that this is all a dream and that surely I'm going to wake up. But what a ride this dream has been. I hope I don't wake up until after the carnival is over.

"Today, I would like to talk to you about the need some husbands feel to be right."

Obviously, he overheard my conversation with Chloe. When you get a genie, you give up your privacy. He follows me downstairs where I retrieve my Turquoise Journal.

"A million and one circumstances arise," he says, "when a man and wife differ on how they remember, interpret, or view things. In the 1920s, one of my clients from Argentina went out to dinner with her husband for their anniversary. She remarked, 'You ordered stuffed flounder when we were here last time.' The husband responded with, 'Oh, no, I had crab cakes the last time we were here.' Then the wife continues to explain to him where they sat and what he ate, to which he then reargued his memory of the evening. Before their dinner came, they were annoyed with each other."

This is a common badminton game Chad and Chloe play, arguing over fiddle-faddle.

"These scenarios drain the affection out of a marriage," Genie says. "Therefore, our first principle to consider today is to overlook small topics that don't matter. A wise woman builds her home, and that includes having the humility to let small issues slide."

I still have trouble letting anything slide. And check for Chloe.

"It's certainly not worth arguing over which is the shortest way home from the grocery or if the joke on TV was sexist or not. I've seen couples get heated over who were the best bands or artists of the seventies."

Aretha Franklin, Billy Joel, the Bee Gees—I love and know the music of the seventies. I could get in an argument over that subject.

"Genie, how do women know which subjects to overlook and which to confront? Obviously, who ate what at a restaurant is not a big deal."

"Which brings us to point two, Young Jessica, and that is to review your list of top five to eight concerns in life. Get Chloe to write a list too."

Actually, I have more like fifty to eighty top concerns.

"Pick only the most important things in your life for this list," he says.

I review my list of top concerns. One, my relationship with the Creator; two, our family; three, our health and safety; four, our extended family; five, our friends; six, our church; seven, our finances; and eight, using our gifts to serve others.

"Remember that lists differ from woman to woman," Genie says. "When a woman gets clear on her top values, she can let lesser issues slide."

Arguing with Matthew last weekend about whether fiction or nonfiction was more profitable to read probably doesn't make this top eight to twelve list.

"A woman needs to overlook disagreements about small things," he says. "Common sense dictates that if a woman doesn't bark too often, she'll be more readily heard when she does."

Chloe and I have both barked over minutia.

"For example," Genie says, "pretend you are at the lake, and your eight-year-old son, Brandon, doesn't want to wear a life preserver to swim. Matthew thinks your son is a good swimmer and doesn't care if the boy wears a life preserver or not. Instead of going into hysteria, remain calm, but say in an assertive tone, 'Matthew, safety is one of the things I care most about in life. I know you don't think he needs a life preserver in the lake because he's a good swimmer, but that won't work for me. Please insist that he wear one. I can't move forward until we settle this.' "

I like this. Don't bark often, but when you bark, you'll be heard.

"You can't blow your whistle all the time," Genie reminds me as if he's reading my mind. "A woman who is wise will only blow her whistle when it counts so she will be heard. And even then, she won't explode into a hysterical, angry encounter. Men would almost rather face a bomb threat than a woman's anger. A woman's anger simply undoes a man. It's best to express anger as sadness, hurt, or extreme concern."

Safety is not an issue where I compromise. Containing my hysteria in that lake situation would be difficult. Brandon *would* wear a life preserver.

"I want to discuss another point," Genie says. "When the wife was right and now she wants to tell the husband, 'I told you so.' For example, suppose Chloe and Chad disagreed about whether their son Thomas should play soccer this spring. Chloe's opinion was that she would rather him not so he could concentrate on his school-work, his music lessons, and his tennis lessons. Chad insisted that Thomas can do it all and talks her into signing Thomas up. As the season progresses, Thomas is tired, cranky, and fails several tests in school. It is easy to see that Chloe was right; signing Thomas up for soccer was overkill."

Why don't men understand that we mothers have our fingers on the pulse of our children?

I've got a curve ball in my pocket. Let's see how Mr. Middle-East-Know-It-All will answer this question.

"Genie, Chloe has a degree in finance, and on top of that, she daily reads financial websites and is markedly knowledgeable about the financial world. I've noticed that Chad will act like he knows more than she does about the subject. He even contra-dicted her when we were with them a couple of weeks ago and acted like he was giving the final opinion. I wanted to scream, 'This is Chloe's specialty, and you're an idiot in this area!'"

Genie looks down, rubs his knees, and doesn't say anything.

I'm heated just remembering the incident.

"Genie, not only does Chad act like he knows more than Chloe does about finances, but he also acts like she don't know very much. It's as if he can't stand for her to appear smarter than him."

Genie rubs his knees again and takes a deep breath.

"Young Jessica, what can I tell you? Men who feel insecure by their wife's intelli-gence are usually not made to feel like kings at home. Yes, you can call it pride on Chad's part, and it is. However, most husbands will not feel intimidated by a wife's success and knowledge if she is humble, deposits the Eight A's, and makes him feel like royalty."

Ooh, this stings.

"Women have three choices if a husband feels the need to always be right," Genie says.

I usually don't like his choices.

"One, a woman can overlook this instance and refocus on her efforts to deposit the Eight A's to fill his tank."

I do need to review the Eight A's with Chloe again. And it would be good for me too.

"Choice two, Chloe can sling some mud and harshly confront him about his feeling insecure regarding her strengths. How would that work?"

"Okay, Genie, funny. What's choice three?" Although slinging mud sounds like a choice Chloe would temporarily enjoy, I've been in *Wife School* long enough to know a woman never wins when she begins slinging.

"Choice three is to embrace the discomfort of honest yet kind dialogue. Men are not allowed to treat their wives with disrespect. To begin this discussion with a husband, remember to not react in the moment. A woman might need to table this issue, write about it in her Turquoise Journal, and think sanely and carefully of a wise response. I have noticed that most of the time when women confront their husbands in the heat of the moment, they do a poor job. Therefore, I recommend journaling to form a wise response. When the flaming fire of the moment is gone, a wife can calmly say something like, 'Chad, I don't think you meant to hurt me, but when you contradicted me about finances in front of Jessica and Matthew the other night at dinner, I was hurt and embarrassed. I know you are entitled to have an opinion, but I felt disrespected by the way you contradicted me. I greatly care about how I treat you, but I also want you to treat me with respect.' "

I still can't believe that some women react to mistreatment with such levelheadedness.

"It was fine for Chad to have an opinion about the Laker's uniforms," Genie says. "What was inappropriate was that he didn't allow Chloe to have an opinion. When this happens, women are wise if they gently and calmly say, 'I know you know more about uniforms than me, Chad, but it hurts me when you won't allow me to have an opinion.' A woman is wise to gently tell her husband that she is hurt instead of going down the usual path of becoming offended and angry."

Calm. Direct. Not Chloe's style. And still not my go-to style.

This approach to men is vastly different from what Chloe and I saw growing up. My mother didn't deposit the Eight A's, my father said disrespectful remarks to my mother, and then she responded with what looked like a scene from a battle in *The Hunger Games.*

"Tell Chloe not to argue about whether Chad was right or wrong," Genie said. "Chad is entitled to his opinion. Only react to how he treated her and how she felt. Tell her to do it sweetly, gently, and softly if she wants to be heard. Remember, a woman's hysteria is dismissed by men."

Right now, I'm mad at all this work to deal with men. I'm mad I can't shoot back what I feel. I'm mad, mad, *mad* about all this stupid self-control. I'm even mad that I have to go first and deposit the Eight A's instead of the man going first. I guess all this anger of mine is a pretty clear sign that I still have a lot of work to do in the humility department.

"A woman who goes to such lengths to treat her husband with exceptional care is watering her own garden," Genie says. "He is her husband and her most important relationship in the world. Therefore, she takes the time and energy to water this most important garden with showers of humility and giving. But she doesn't lose herself and never allows him to mistreat her. Engaging in the Ping-Pong game of who is right is ludicrous.

"We've discussed this principle before, but it's so contrary to the human psyche that I will bring it up again. Learn to be a cloud, not a brick wall, when offenses come your way. Being offended easily is a sign of an immature person. Forgive lavishly, exorbitantly, and profusely, as the Creator rewards humility."

This lesson sits on my chest like a slab of concrete. I've had enough for today. Genie must have realized this, as he left rather suddenly.

I walk into my closet to find something to wear to the meeting with Matthew and our financial advisor. There's a pretty red raincoat hanging with an attached hood in my closet with a note pinned to it that says, "Put on this raincoat, as it is misty outside. Also, remind Chloe to put on the coat of humility as she interacts with Chad."

I didn't like this lesson, but I love my new raincoat. I pick up my cell to dial Chloe, but before I can, Matthew calls. I guess he wants to confirm our appointment. "Hi, Matthew."

He's speaking in a low whisper. "Jessica, my car won't start. Chad tried to jump me, but it's dead. The problem is, the only person who is available to drop me off at our meeting is Indigo. I called Robert, and he has another client after us, so he can't push back our appointment."

Instantly, I understand what he's saying. If I pick him up at his office and we go together to the appointment, we'll be late. My mind races for a solution. Matthew riding alone with Indigo in her sexy yellow Camaro with her short skirts sends me into orbit.

"I'm uncomfortable with that scene, Matthew," I say calmly, but I want to yell.

"I know you are. That's why I'm calling you."

"Isn't there anyone else who can drive you?"

"There's not. I already asked," he says.

So what are our choices? Cancel the meeting with Robert? Robert is busy and certainly will not appreciate a last-minute cancellation.

"Well, I guess she has to drive you. I'll see you there in twenty or thirty minutes," I say, and we hang up.

Driving over the speed limit, I want to be in the parking lot when Matthew and Indigo arrive. I park and wait on the yellow Camaro. Finally, there it is, all sleek and sexy.

Matthew gets out, and Indigo drives off. I get out of the car and walk toward him. "How was your ride over?" I ask with a hint of sarcasm.

Matthew looks down without responding as we walk into Robert's office. Right before he opens the door for me, he says, "There's something we need to talk about concerning Indigo."

CHAPTER 26
When Your Husband Is Critical and Complaining

Wednesday, April 9

A lot has happened in the last week. And I mean a lot.

When I drove Matthew back to work after our meeting with Robert, he opened up.

"Indigo has made a few passes at me, Jessica. At first, I thought they were innocent. But she keeps touching me, and her blouses are ridiculously low. This morning, she leaned over on purpose so I could see her exposed breasts. I think I've been foolish to not see that this woman is sending me signals."

I wanted to scream, "OF COURSE, YOU IDIOT, WHAT HAVE I BEEN TELLING YOU??" But I didn't.

"And on the way to see Robert," he continued, "she unbuttoned her blouse one button too low. Her breasts were right there, with her black lace bra. I think you were right. She *is* coming onto me."

I'm shaking I'm so upset. I'd like to take some scissors and cut off all that luscious, dark, thick hair into an uneven, ragged bob. I'm so angry and alarmed that I'm speechless. Tongue-tied. It might be the first time ever.

Matthew continues. "I've got to do something about this. It's not right to you, Jessica. And now that I see it, I know it puts me in a slippery place."

Matthew and I have not stopped talking about the incident for the last week. He says he doesn't know how to fire her. I mean, obviously, she's the most efficient assistant he's ever had, and it would cause a scene to tell everyone at work the real reason.

To be honest, I have trouble thinking about much else.

On Saturday morning, the morning of the carnival, I had to force myself to think about other things. Thankfully, the weatherman was wrong, and it didn't rain. Genie had made authentic Greek, Chinese, German, and French food to sell. No one could believe that an elementary school could have a carnival with food like that!

Daisy came to the carnival as did my dad. Daisy followed him around, gabbing away, not coming up for air. Dad looked like a teenager who was trying to get away from a bossy mother but without being obvious that he was trying to escape.

Halfway through the carnival, I ran into Mrs. Smith. "I don't think we're making much money," she said.

I've worked my tail off for five weeks and lost about fifteen hundred dollars of calligraphy income, so tough toenails to you, I thought. I have never really liked this principal, and her comment confirmed why. At least Brandon and Josh had a blast jumping on the inflatables and shooting baskets to try to win stuffed Spiderman toys.

Later, Mrs. Smith was talking to Dad and immediately seemed to have an attitude adjustment toward me.

"I was telling your father," she said in a singsong voice in front of Dad, "what a fine family you have."

That's not what you said when you told me Brandon was cheating, I thought to myself. For the first time, I looked at her ring finger. Good grief. Ms. Smith was hitting on Dad in a midlife, baby-boomer sort of way. Women, whether they are twenty or ninety, revert to giggly middle-schoolers when in the presence of an attractive man.

Daisy was not about to give up her self-imposed claim on Dad either. She wiggled her way in between Ms. Smith and Dad and said, "Harold, have you tried these sweet and sour Chinese chicken strips? Follow me, and I'll show you where to get them."

Women making advances toward men is one of the present themes in my life. I shudder as I think of Indigo's unbuttoned blouse.

Anyhow, the carnival is over and was a big success. We made *lots* of money. Now I can breathe a huge sigh of relief. But there's no sigh of relief where Indigo's concerned, though.

Allison calls, and I pick up. Last week, Dad's friend Roy offered Zach the job, so the Three Memphis Musketeers are not being disbanded after all.

"Maybe I should have let Zach move to Nevada by himself," Allison says.

Uh-oh.

"No matter what I do," Allison says, "Zach is critical and complaining. I plan a nice relaxing weekend, and he complains that we never go out. I plan a weekend with our friends, and he fusses that I should know he likes to relax without plans on the weekend. Truly, no matter what I do, it's wrong."

Not good.

"When he got home last night," she continues, "he complained that his golf shorts were not in the drawer in the usual place. He also complained that I bought myself a new dress for the upcoming Mahoney wedding. He said surely I could wear one of the dresses I already have."

After some more discussion, I offer to think about her situation and tell her I'll call her back. Whew. Zach is a handful.

I turn around to see my tawny, buffed friend. I guess he has the house wired and listens in from the Middle East.

"Today our lesson is how to respond to a husband who is critical and complaining," Genie begins without even saying hello. Of course, Mr. Eavesdropper knew the topic.

"Let's talk about how to get rid of female assistants who unbutton their shirts in front of your husband," I say.

"Matthew is working on that. Just wait it out," he says. "Now, back to my topic."

Matthew is working it out? How? I'd rather talk about *that*.

"We will discuss this topic of when a husband is critical and complaining by breaking it into two areas. One, how to handle a husband who is critical about life in general. And two, how to handle a husband who is critical of his wife."

I try to change directions in my mind and focus on Allison's situation with Zach.

"I want to preclude our discussion," Genie says, "by making a few comments about men who are complainers. Many times, when a husband is critical or is a complainer, it is because he is unhappy with himself. Most men have difficulty saying to their wives, 'I'm not feeling very manly or confident. In fact, I'm having a lot of fear about my performance. I'm not sure I have what it takes to succeed.' "

Oh, no, he's *not* going to make excuses for these whiners, is he?

"Let's say a husband feels insecure about his intelligence. It is unthinkable for him to say, 'I don't feel as smart as I think I should be.' Whenever a man feels insecure, he is not usually able to express his feelings of inadequacy because they are too painful to him. He will instead often criticize, complain, or be negative."

This does sound like Allison's husband.

"Most husbands aren't even aware of this rumbling below their subconscious," Genie says. "They feel nervous and unsettled inside, and it comes out as complaining and being critical. You cannot solve this man's problem, nor is it your responsibility to do so. Ultimately, this is a problem he must solve with the Creator. But a wise wife can soothe his ruffled feathers to a huge degree."

I knew the wife was going to have a part in this.

"A woman is wise if she can overlook the husband's remarks while she is trying to establish the habit of depositing the Eight A's into his tank. However, I have found very few women who are able to do this, as it takes extreme self-control and focus."

Uh, yeah, like, it would be impossible for me to put up with behavior like Zach's.

"Another point I'd like to make is that a wife must know that too much advice and direction from her can make matters worse," Genie says. "One wife told me how her husband complained how small the seats were in his new Lexus. So she began to tell him the actual measurements to refute his complaint. But that was not what was needed."

"Okay. What was?" I ask.

"The first strategy, as I've said, is to make sure the husband's tank is full of the Eight A's, especially the A of Admiration. Many of his root problems come from a low self-concept, and the Eight A's help heal a low self-concept. Ultimately, a husband needs to find his worth and significance in his relationship with the Creator, but a wife can help in a massive way."

Seriously, does Genie think that depositing the Eight A's are the answer to everything? He probably thinks that if a husband has a receding hairline, giving him the Eight A's will regrow his hair.

"The average husband has a tank that is comparable to a bathtub, as I've said before," Genie says. "Filling up a bathtub everyday with the Eight A's does not seem overwhelming. That is what I've asked you to do daily for Matthew. But needy husbands like Zach who get anxious, complain, and are critical are more like swimming pools. You can fill these swimming pools with the Eight A's, but it takes much more work and time."

What wife wants to do this? Bathtubs are big enough.

"When a wife senses her husband lapsing into his critical state, her first natural response is to talk him out of it," Genie says. "She often explains how much he has to be grateful for. But this only makes him feel misunderstood, and he is likely to get annoyed with her."

I can hear Allison lecturing Zach in my mind.

"The helpful strategy is for the wife to recognize that she has a swimming pool, not a bathtub, on her hands and fill, fill, fill," he says. "Remember, though, it's not the Atlantic Ocean; it's only a swimming pool. The thought of filling an ocean is overwhelming, so a wife would give up before she started. Filling a bathtub is easily doable;

filling a swimming pool requires much effort (but is still doable). But filling the Atlantic Ocean is impossible. The wife needs to understand that she has a swimming pool to fill and not get discouraged when it seems like the Atlantic Ocean."

What about Allison's tank? I should know better than to ask that by now. I should know that the Creator is going to have to fill her tank.

"It may take weeks or months," Genie continues, "before your sister sees a change in her husband's behavior, but I've seen it happen thousands of times. The power of an encouraging wife is inestimable. If a man gets fired or has trouble in his career, you can count on filling that pool for an even longer season (see Chapter 11, "How to View Your Husband's Work from His Perspective"). Also, an abundant amount of stress at work can make the husband critical or complaining. Financial woes are another trigger that can activate fear in a man and will come out as being critical or complaining."

With Zach's new job, he is feeling additionally insecure about the new responsibilities he needs to master in order to run Roy's businesses.

"I agree it is difficult to not let the negative nature of your spouse upset you," Genie says, "but it is imperative. Allison must erect an invisible shield to protect herself from Zach's negative onslaught and, at the same time, deposit the healing balm of the Eight A's. Not only will Zach eventually heal, his affection toward Allison will increase astronomically. *A husband's hard trial is a woman's opportunity to endear herself to him with her cheerful encouragement and consistent admiration.*"

I couldn't take Zach. I just couldn't.

"It's not anyone's first choice to be married to someone with a negative, complaining disposition," Genie says. "However, this was the man Allison was given to love. Even these hard cases will experience much healing with regular swimming-pool deposits of the Eight A's."

Poor Allison. I need to write this down in my Turquoise Journal under "Things Other Husbands Do Wrong."

"When needy husbands begin to whine and complain, most wives see it as a personal attack against them," Genie says. "Instead, it would be beneficial if the wife could see her husband's needy soul and his inner struggle."

I personally have no sympathy for moaners.

"A wise woman will not begrudge the call in marriage to build up her husband," Genie says. "If he has a liver condition, she would not be annoyed at helping him rebuild his health. However, wives are provoked when they are called to help husbands rebuild their emotional health. All marriages require wives to give things to their husbands that are hard. But wives should not resent the call to fill up their husbands. Many a woman has turned a negative, complaining frog into a flourishing, productive prince with her Eight A's."

I can't believe Zach could ever be a prince.

"Wise wives with needy husbands should put on their daily To Do list, 'Fill the swimming pool.'"

"This is the difference between foolish wives and wise wives. *Wise wives do what it takes to bolster their men, which they see as part of their calling.* Foolish wives look at what's fair; at how they are giving more than they are getting. Don't look at what's fair; look at what works, and do what it takes. No one is guaranteed an easy marriage. However, the Creator guarantees that wise wives will build their homes. So encourage Allison to fill up that swimming pool with the Eight A's."

Well, I do like results that work, and so does Allison.

"Just because things are hard," Genie says, "is no excuse to not give Herculean efforts. This is when we see what a woman is made of. Life is about sowing and reaping. Sow extravagantly. Sow profusely. Sow abundantly. Why? Because reaping always follows sowing. Do not begrudge a husband with a swimming pool-sized hole in his heart; focus on your calling as a wife to fill it. Again, though, I reiterate the three exceptions: alcohol or drugs, abuse, and adultery. These problems are not considered normal and need additional help.

"Is there a balance to this teaching, Genie? It seems to me that Zach is mistreating Allison."

"It would be helpful if you again review the teaching "What to Do When Your Husband Mistreats You" (Chapter 14)," Genie answered. "When a husband is rude to his wife, she should look at him and say, 'Remember, you are not mad at me. I would appreciate your being sweet to me.' That is his warning. If that doesn't stop it, say, 'I am sorry you are upset, but you cannot be unkind to me,' and then leave the room, preferably the house. Take a walk or run an errand.

"And it is definitely alright, as we have previously discussed, for there to be a consequence if the husband is unkind. One client of mine, after her husband was very harsh with her, said, 'I am going to read and then go to bed. Maybe you can be sweet to me tomorrow.' The key here is to not get angry or lash out but to be firm in not taking the mistreatment and for the husband to suffer some consequences. An example would be, 'I know I told you I was going to make you strawberry shortcake tonight, but after being treated like that, I am exhausted, so instead I'm going to take a bath and go to bed. I will see you in the morning. I hope you will realize how much you hurt me when you talk to me like that.' "

Allison unknowingly throws gasoline on the fire with her words. But, really, what wife wouldn't want to?

"Genie, Zach and Allison were in a grocery line last week when he asked her a question. She took a second or two to think about her answer, and without looking at her, Zach raised his voice and said, 'Okay, just ignore me. Never mind. You never listen well to me anyhow.'

"Allison was stunned by his comment," I continue. "They're in public, so she's limited to what she can say. When they walked out to the car and she said, 'Zach, I was thinking of an answer and how to respond to you. I wasn't ignoring your question. But you didn't even look at me. That was so unfair of you.' Then Zach started stonewalling. It was horribly upsetting to her."

Genie raises his eyebrows. "It sounds like she has a *large* swimming pool on her hands, Young Jessica. However, her first strategy should be to try to hear what's behind his remarks. She might have said, 'Will you please explain to me why you are so angry?' Sometimes a wife can learn valuable information by asking what's behind the explosion if she can keep her calm.

"If Zach is not able to give a reason why he exploded, Allison could say (and I'm assuming she is depositing the Eight A's when I say this), 'Zach, I love you, and I think you know I try to show you that all the time. I was thinking about how to answer you; I was not ignoring you. That was very disrespectful how you treated me, and I feel wounded. I will have to figure out a way to restore myself.' Then, Young Jessica, *it is important she be smart with consequences.* When they got home, she could tell him she needed to take a nap, a walk, or go on an outing, and that he would need to fix his own lunch. Zach must realize he cannot treat her like that without consequences. *A man cannot adore a woman he can mistreat.*"

Genie isn't through. "After her nap and after Zach fixes his own lunch, Allison must let it be over. Forgive him. Start afresh with a sweet attitude. She may need to do this for weeks and months while filling his tank, uh, I mean, his swimming pool, but persist. A woman who will persevere at this level can really turn water into wine. Not only will her husband learn to treat her like royalty, but he himself will often be healed in his inner man by her love, which is demonstrated by the Eight A's."

I want to believe him, but it just sounds too good to be true.

"Another explanation for a man's negative and argumentative comments," Genie says, "is that he feels guilt over some sin in his life. Humans frequently funnel their guilt into blaming, negativity, arguing, and criticizing."

"Surely, you're not going to blame Allison for Zach's problem with guilt, are you, Genie?"

"No," he laughs. "It is certainly not her fault that her husband sins and has subsequent guilt. It is wise for her to know, however, that humans tend to become like the other humans they are around. Therefore, her purity, gratefulness, and humility draw her husband to a higher level. It is not her responsibility for her husband to be holy or to be happy; it's her responsibility to give him the Eight A's. Now, it *is* her responsibility to be holy and happy."

Genie and I are talking about Allison, but there are takeaways for me in this conversation too.

"I also want to mention," he says, "that when a husband complains about or criticizes something, it is often an opportunity for the wife."

What in the world is he talking about now? An opportunity?

"For instance," Genie says, "if your husband complains that there is a high turnover at his office and that other divisions can't keep employees, it is a chance for you to say, 'The people under you seem to be loyal. You must have some secrets for handling people wisely and generously.'"

"Or when your husband complains, 'It costs so much for the kids to play sports and for us to buy all the right shoes and equipment,' you could say, 'Our children are quite fortunate to have a father who not only is generous but who also makes a good income so we can afford for them to have the necessary money for travel and extra equipment.'"

"Unknowingly," Genie says, "the complaint or criticism is an immature attempt to solicit affirmation or praise. It can be rough out there in the world, and to have a positive, affirming, admiring wife makes the daily grind all bearable and worth it."

Genie leaves, and the doorbell rings. Oh, no, it's Cammey, the mother of Pinching Charlie. She is probably coming to tell me something else that Charlie needs from Brandon.

"Jessica, I wanted to thank you for whatever you've told Brandon," she says. "Charlie says that Brandon gave him some great advice, and now all the guys like him, and he's sitting at the lunch table with them. Thank you so much."

I'm a little taken aback. With all the drama in my life, I haven't given Pinching Charlie much thought, and Brandon and I haven't talked about it for weeks. I'm proud of Brandon for confronting Charlie and helping him socially. And I'm happy for any conflict in my life to resolve by itself. Now what I'd really like to say is, "Well, Cammey, you didn't have to exclude us from the neighborhood Valentine's party, after all, did you?" but I decide to zip it.

While she's gabbing away, my phone rings with a number I don't recognize on the caller ID, but it's good because the phone call prompts her to leave. "Take your call," Cammey says. "I hope we can get together soon."

Yeah, right, soon. Like maybe when our children start having grandchildren. I take the other call.

"Jessica? This is Sue Smith."

Ah, so now Ms. Smith is *Sue* Smith? She must be calling from her cell phone instead of the school phone.

"I was wondering if I could get your dad's phone number? He told me about a reputable place to buy used cars, and I forgot what he said."

Oh, baloney, but what the heck? I give his number to her, and we hang up.

A few minutes later, Dad calls and tells me Sue Smith invited him over for her homemade beef stroganoff and that Daisy called him yesterday and invited him over for her homemade chicken potpie. Women!

I walk into the kitchen to fix dinner. There are two meals prepared: a homemade beef stroganoff and a beautiful chicken potpie.

Funny, Genie.

Now what am I going to do about Infuriating Indigo?

CHAPTER 27
The End of Advanced Training for Wives

Friday, April 11

It's four p.m., and Matthew calls, an unusual time for him. I hope it's not bad news.

"Can you get a babysitter tonight?" he asks.

I quickly survey the night's agenda. I had hoped to start packing for our spring break trip to the beach because we leave in two days. But I stop and think, *Don't react. Be sweet. See what he has to say.* "You sound excited, Matthew," I say. "Did something big come up?" I'm not the queen of flexible.

"I want us to go out to dinner. I have a surprise," he says. "This is important to me, Jess."

I'm trying not to throw cold water on his excitement, but this is not what I had planned. Maybe I won't be able to get a babysitter.

"Let me see if my sister can keep the boys," I say. I start praying that she is busy.

"I hope you can," he says.

We hang up, and I call Chloe. Aw, shucks. Chloe is extra available as her husband, Chad, is out of town. I don't have a good excuse to not go out with Matthew. Chloe tells me to bring the boys over now and let them eat dinner with her so I can get ready without them and maybe sneak in a small nap. Sisters—what can I say?

Matthew and I agree to meet at Osaka on Germantown Parkway. After I shower and take a quick twenty-minute nap, I feel remarkably better and begin to look forward to the surprise. Maybe he got a big raise!

I walk into Osaka and catch Matthew's eye. He is still a handsome man, with broad shoulders and olive skin. His penetrating eyes still excite me.

After we order, Matthew begins. "An account executive at our Dallas branch quit, and they need a new account executive."

I feel a pit in my stomach. Dallas? Why, I know nothing about Dallas except that their cheerleaders should put on more clothes. Dallas?? He got me to come here to tell me that we're moving? I feel lightheaded and shocked all at once. This is *not* how I wanted to get rid of Indigo!

Before I can speak, he continues. "I recommended Indigo, and they hired her! She leaves Monday."

Indigo the Invader is leaving? The woman who has haunted me for eight months is being shipped to Dallas? I feel like I'm Eli Manning, and I just won the Super Bowl! There should be confetti falling from the ceiling.

Matthew looks like an eight-year-old boy who brought home a report card with straight A's.

I pour it on. *Man*, I pour it on. Matthew has *never* gotten such a large dose of admiration and appreciation from me at one time in his entire life! I go *crazy*!

I can't wait to tell Genie. Yaaaayyyy for the Eight A's and Advanced Training for Wives! It works! It absolutely works!

This is a night to remember. My efforts to live the Eight A's have mustered the forces of the galaxy and have pulled Matthew's affections back to me. The thrill of the upward projectile of our marriage gives me an off-the-chart exuberance. Tonight is not a "scheduled night," but tonight, I'm going to light up this pinball machine.

Ten days later, Monday, April 21

Yesterday we got back from our spring break vacation in Gulf Shores. Who can believe the difference in our marriage? I can honestly say I feel closer to Matthew than I have in years. One night while we sat on the beach, watching our boys run around with flashlights, Matthew took my hand and said he was happy being married to such a beautiful, sweet wife. That will be a moment I will remember forever. The crashing of the waves, the moonlight, the happy squeals of our boys, and my husband telling me how satisfied he is with our marriage—does it get any better than that?

The boys are back at school, and Matthew is at work. I finish exercising, and now it's time to dig into the mountain of laundry and start addressing invitations.

"We have now completed Advanced Training for Wives, Young Jessica," says a voice behind me.

Oh, no. Oh, no. Genie's not getting ready to tell me good-bye, is he?

"You have crossed over an imaginary line, Young Jessica," he says. "When a wife gets to this point, even though she will still fail in the future, she is almost guaranteed a fulfilling marriage if she continues walking with the Creator. She has become a giver, not a taker. She has decided she will do what works, not what's fair. She has laid down her demands and instead focuses on meeting her husband's needs."

This sounds like a farewell speech to me.

"The natural tendency of all marriages is to unzip," Genie continues. "The gulf between spouses naturally increases as the years progress. Unresolved conflicts and unmet needs add daily drops of water and, soon, the stream turns into a river. But you now have the keys to reverse this tendency."

I haven't been so happy in our marriage since our honeymoon.

"You know now what you must do when you offend Matthew: ask for forgiveness. Saying, 'I was wrong. Will you please forgive me?' is one of the most important sentences anyone can say in a marriage."

I still need to work on that. I hate saying "I was wrong."

"And remember, as much as you want to grow in the marriage and for Matthew to change and be intimate," Genie says, "he equally wants you to accept him as he is, to have fun with him without having to talk deeply all the time, for you to be an engaged sexual partner, and for you to meet all of his Eight A's."

Hey, I'm doing better here. Why, recently, Matthew and I went to the Regions Morgan Keegan Tennis Championship Playoffs, and I didn't bring up one topic about fixing or changing things in the marriage or in our lives. I was simply a delightful companion. We talked about superficial things the entire time, such as the backhand of Andy Roddick and filling our 401k's. When we got home, Matthew told me how much fun I was to be with. We had had absolutely zero intimate talk, and he loved it. I am still having trouble accepting that men do not need much emotional intimacy and not seeing them as flawed because of it.

"You have been a good *Wife School* student, and I have enjoyed our time together," Genie says.

Oh, dear. This *is* good-bye. Genie's leaving. Oh, dear. He *can't* leave. Oh, dear. I'm not ready for him to leave! Think, Jessica, think. Don't let him leave.

"My sisters and friends have noticed the difference in my marriage, as you know," I say. "But I have no idea how to advise them about their specific issues. How am I going to help them with their marriage problems if you leave?"

I can tell Genie's considering staying.

"Indeed, the best way to master a subject is to teach it," he says.

He's starting to give in. I can feel it.

"Alright, alright, I'll stay a little while longer," he says. "You can continue bringing me the issues of your sisters and friends, and then I will instruct you as to how to instruct them."

What is really funny about this scenario is that I, Jessica, the epitome of a wretched wife a few months ago, will now be counseling my sisters and friends regarding their marriages. Life is certainly unpredictable.

"Next time you visit, Genie, I'll have all sorts of knots from their lives for you to untangle."

As he leaves, the aroma of Mexican fare rises to my nostrils. I turn around to see chicken enchiladas and beef fajitas sizzling on a platter. Also, that pesky mountain of laundry is finished and stacked, neatly folded, on the counter. Since dinner and the laundry are done, I guess I have time to make a call to one of my sisters to talk further about her marriage.

My grandmother used to talk about a column in the newspaper called "Dear Abby" where people wrote in with their problems. Well, lookout, Memphis. Here comes "Dear Jessica!"

PART III
How to Respond to Particular Struggles in Marriage

Unlike Part I and Part II, each chapter in Part III stands alone. Feel free to only read the chapters that are of interest to you (see Contents for complete list of topics).

However, to conclude, please read Part IV, Chapter 41, "The Departure of Genie."

CHAPTER 28
When Your Husband Brags

Monday, April 14

I'm knocking out the wedding invitations this morning. I'm in my zone.

My phone rings, and it is my friend Sarah. "I'm going to be in your neighborhood in a few minutes," she says, "and I want to drop in and return your blue dress."

Sarah had borrowed my dress to wear to a wedding last weekend. She is skinnier than I am with her incessant exercise and disciplined eating, so the stretchy fabric worked for her. Sarah is extremely responsible about returning things. I might, on the other hand, keep a friend's dress until she asks for it back.

"Okay, thanks," I say. "How was the wedding?"

There is a long silence. Then she says, "Jessica, you handle Matthew so well. Would you mind if I stayed a few minutes so you could give me a bit of advice about Brett?"

This morning isn't very convenient, but what can I say?

When Sarah arrives, she tells me how Brett embarrassed her at the wedding with his long storytelling and bragging.

"The group at the table was discussing how the recent golf tournament at the country club lost money," she says. "And Brett said he would have made money because the organization and setup were all wrong."

"What did you say?" I ask.

"I said, 'Brett, you've never run a golf tournament. How do you know that you would have done it well?' "

"And how did he react to that?"

"He blew up on the way home, saying I threw cold water in his face, embarrassing him by challenging him in front of everyone," Sarah says.

This is ugly.

"Later," Sarah continues, "Brett was in a conversation with an old friend, and they were discussing a recent movie they had both seen. Brett told his friend he would like to try his hand at directing a movie someday, saying, 'I think I could do as well as some of those movies that make it to the Oscars.' I was appalled."

I'm afraid to ask, but I do. "So what did you say to that, Sarah?"

"I said, 'Not with any of my savings! I'm not taking a risk on that.' His friend thought it was hysterical, but Brett didn't like it."

This type of marital conflict is deep and knotty. I need Genie.

"Wow," is all I can think to say.

"That's not all," she says. "To really embarrass me, we're talking to our pastor on Sunday, and Brett begins telling him what the problems are with the building project and how he knows how to fix them."

"And what do you say then?" I'm afraid of what's coming.

"I said, 'Brett, you've never been involved with a building project. I bet the pastor's ideas are fine.' "

I feel sick and sorry at the same time for my friend. She thinks she's helping Brett with his bragging.

"I'm going to have to discuss this matter with Brett," Sarah says. "His bragging is ridiculous. But I thought I'd get your advice first."

"Let me think about it, and I'll call you," I say, not having a clue what to tell her. I'm pretty overwhelmed at this interplay. I need a Genie-phone.

Sarah leaves, and then there's an Italian smell floating through my house. Ravioli is sitting on my kitchen counter. **I turn around, and there's my dark-skinned friend.** "I know you don't like Italian food much," he says, "but it is Matthew's favorite."

I rarely make these dishes because the garlic makes my body smell for days afterward. It's true, though, that Matthew loves Italian food. I tend to make food I like instead of food that Matthew likes. I'm still working on the Eight A's myself.

"So you heard my friend's problem, did you?" I ask, knowing this guy rather well by now.

"Yes, bragging and talking too much are common problems," he says.

In my marriage, I tend to be the one to brag and talk too much.

"When a husband brags," Genie says, "he is usually married to a person who is not much of an encourager but rather someone who tends to be practical. She is usually the type of person who is responsible, who gets things done, and points out what still needs to be done. This is good, but she infrequently sees the need to compliment and praise her husband. She does not understand the gigantic need her husband has for his work and behavior to be admired. She tells it like it is, claiming she is a realist, but truly she is frequently a negative person."

This describes Sarah perfectly. "Poor Brett is always looking for affirmation," I say, "and Sarah is the last one to give it to him."

"Exactly," he says. "You can see the cycle. He needs encouragement, and she is annoyed by his boasting, so to put him in his place, she criticizes him even more, trying to get him to be realistic. He feels less and less affirmed by her and therefore brags in public to get the attention and applause he desires from her."

How sad, yet this description is accurate in describing Sarah and Brett's relationship.

"Women think they are giving their husbands a good dose of reality," Genie says, "when they pour cold water on his dreams, ideas, and words. But actually they are doing nothing but burning the affection ropes that tie their hearts together. When a man brags like this in public, it is often because he is criticized at home. A husband who is praised and listened to at home will not feel the need as often to put his net out for compliments like Brett does."

"I see," I say. "Sarah is trying to be realistic, but what she is really doing is starving him of compliments and praise. Therefore, he feels the need to fan his feathers in public."

"A bragging husband cannot be cured overnight," Genie says. "Deep insecurity resides within these men, and often the remedy of praise and admiration from the wife takes weeks, months, and even years to correct it."

Sarah is not going to like this. She's a quick, zip, fix-it-now kind of person.

"Instead of feeling discouraged, though," Genie says, "the wife must remember, 'This is the man the Creator gave me to love.' She must be ready to fill and fill and then fill him some more. Review your notes in your Turquoise Journal on a man's need for admiration (see Chapter 3, "Second A: The Admiration Lesson") before you talk to Sarah. Also review your notes on a man's need for acceptance (see Chapter 2, "First A: The Acceptance Lesson"). The wife of a man who acts like this usually has a critical, correcting tongue. I want to stress the word *usually* because I am not blaming a wife for a husband's poor character. I am simply giving advice that, in most cases, can help heal a man's insecure nature."

I'm not looking forward to telling Sarah these ideas.

"A husband needs to be able to brag when he is alone with his wife," Genie says. "It is not bragging when he is sharing his victories with his other half."

I need to hear this too. Sometimes when Matthew brags about his creative ideas on his advertising accounts, I think he's blowing smoke. But he's not. One of my most important roles is to be my husband's encourager.

"In fact," Genie continues, "even though the wife thinks the husband is exaggerating and needlessly carrying on when they are alone, she should pour on the praise. A wife is wise to magnify the strengths and accomplishments of her husband."

How do I tell this to Sarah without offending her?

"Also, please tell Sarah to especially *not* correct or confront her husband in public," he says. "When a wife fills her husband's tank with the Eight A's consistently, she is able to speak honestly to him in *private* about his indiscretions (see Chapter 12, "How to Correct Your Husband"), *never* in public."

"I'll feel uncomfortable telling this to Sarah," I say.

"Yes, there is a discomfort sometimes with honest dialogue," he says. "Remember, Sarah asked you for advice. It's not as though you are meddling."

I can't imagine Sarah ever encouraging Brett like Genie suggests. Her style is more like using a power washer to scrub the kitchen floor.

Genie was right when he said sometimes there is a discomfort with honest dialogue. I feel a stomachache coming on as I mentally prepare for this difficult conversation. I decide to call Sarah while I am out running errands. I grab Matthew's shoes to take to the shoe shop, a package I need to mail, a card table that I need to return to Chloe that I borrowed for the carnival, and my purse. I stagger down the back steps, trying to make it to the car in one trip, but oh no ... oh no— I lose my balance and fall down the last two steps.

Ow ... owwww ... Here I am, lying on the concrete, and the pain in my right hand and wrist is excruciating. Seriously?

I pick up my phone with my left hand and dial Chloe. "Can you run over and help me? I fell and think I might have broken something in my wrist."

Chloe hustles over to my house and takes me to the emergency room where I have my wrist and hand x-rayed. One of the bones in my wrist is cracked. When I tell the doctor about my calligraphy business, he advises me to give it up for six weeks while my bone heals. Six weeks? That's a lot of lost money and upset clients to deal with.

I call my calligraphy clients. Most of them understand, but a couple of them—as is custom for women involved with weddings—are upset. Like I fell on purpose!

Now I'm having trouble washing my hair, fixing dinner, and changing the sheets on the bed. I need Genie.

CHAPTER 29

When Your Husband Comes Home Grumpy or Doesn't Like His Work

Tuesday, April 22

I am chafed about this bipolar Memphis weather. Last week, we were encouraged that a cheerful summer was fast approaching because of the sunny, seventy-degree weather. Now, the sun and warmth have completely disappeared, and today is cold, gray, and depressive. It's Memphis. What can I say?

The dismal weather somewhat bothers me, but I'm mainly bummed out because the Dallas branch of Matthew's office is having trouble and the agency owner wants Matthew to go for a week to see if he can straighten things out. I must carefully think about what I want to say to him before he goes on that trip and is again confronted by Invading Indigo.

I am driving home from the grocery store when Emma, a friend from church, pops up on my caller ID. "Hey, what's up, Emma?"

Honestly, I have been expecting this call. Emma cornered me at church and asked if she could get some advice. It's as though I have written on my forehead, "Call me if you want to talk about your marriage."

I listen to Emma's complaints about her husband coming home grumpy every night and not liking his work. I tell her I'll think about it and call her back. I begin to unload my trunk full of groceries, anxious to get out of the damp, unpleasant weather.

"May I?" I hear my almost-favorite voice.

With a snap, the groceries are inside and put away.

"I'm trying to think of something special to serve Matthew tonight for dinner," Genie says. "Oh, I've got it!"

With a flip of his wrist, there is crab-stuffed chicken on the counter. The menus at our house used to be like Cracker Barrel; now we're more like Ruth Chris.

"Emma has a dilemma that we need to discuss," Genie says.

I get comfortable on the sofa with my Turquoise Journal.

"Did you hear the conversation, Genie? Emma's husband hates his job. He is a salesman for a large company and comes home moaning nightly about how unhappy he is at work."

Matthew likes his job. Of course, he has the usual challenges, but basically, he likes the work and the people. But thinking of his work makes me agitated about his going to Dallas for a week.

"This is an excellent topic, Young Jessica, and an important one. Men, as you know, form much of their identity from their work. A man and his work cannot be separated (see Chapter 11, "How to View Your Husband's Work from His Perspective"). If a man abhors his job, he will come home depleted every night, and his low energy will have a substantial negative impact on the family."

"Emma said Jacob is in a cantankerous mood most nights," I add.

"Let me separate these two topics, Young Jessica. Some men come home from work they basically enjoy but are still somewhat ill-tempered from the day's pressures. It is normal for a man to need transition time from the stress of work to home life. We will discuss this topic first. But what is not normal or healthy, which we will discuss secondly, is for a husband to intensely dislike his work and feel he is pushing a large rock uphill all day while carrying a backpack of bricks."

I write in my notes, "Topic one: When the husband is grumpy and needs transition time. Topic two: When the husband doesn't like his job."

"Let's discuss a husband's disagreeable behavior upon his return home from work," says Genie. "Maybe his boss was upset. Maybe he's been selling to a hard client without any success. Maybe a coworker admonished him in front of the team. Maybe he lost an account. There are no limits to the pressures that a man feels at work."

"I don't like it when Matthew comes home like that," I say. Occasionally he does come home crabby and sullen.

"You are like most wives," says Genie. "A very wise but rare strategy is for a woman to structure her day so she has some time for herself to be refreshed. All humans need downtime, or free time. A woman needs to get restored during the day while her husband is at work. Getting restored during the day can be many things: having her devotional time, some time to rest, some time to participate in a hobby, exercise, spend time with a nurturing friend, or any number of other restoring activities. The trick is to build margins in your life so you get your needs met so that when your husband comes home, you are 'full' and can focus on him. It is not smart for two needy human beings to come together at the same time."

My friends who work full-time outside the home complain nonstop that they are continually depleted and have no time for themselves. I am extremely grateful for being able to work part-time from home.

I start to speak, but Genie continues. "When your husband comes home, offer him something yummy to drink, get his computer, or run him a bath. A little love and attention go a long way in soothing his ruffled feathers. After a little time, he'll be able to talk, have dinner with the family, and engage with the boys."

When my boys are upset, I nurture them with extra softness and kindness. I never thought that my husband might like that too.

"Wives don't realize that most men need a little time to let go of the day and transition into family life," Genie says. "Some understanding and sweet attention will do wonders for him. If this is a recurring problem, a good conversation to have on a weekend when he is in a good mood is something like this: 'Matthew, I know work is very stressful, and I want to make home a place where you are restored. What can I do each day to welcome you home and let you have a little space to recoup? Do you want me to have dinner ready? Do you want to exercise? Do you want to get on your computer? Can I keep the kids off you for the first thirty minutes? What would be soothing and helpful to you?' "

I never thought of asking Matthew this. I assumed he would be happy to get home to us and never considered that he might need time to dial down from his day at work.

"Emma also needs to understand how to encourage Jacob to become more cheerful," Genie says. "If Jacob ever comes home cheerful, she should praise him and thank him for it. Or if he transitions after his shower, hot tea, exercise, etc., praise him for coming back to himself and remind him how much you appreciate all the pressure he endures at work for you and the kids. A grateful, sweet wife is one of the most satisfying gifts in the world to a husband. It makes all the work and pressure worth it."

Thinking of myself (even though we are discussing Emma), I think I may need to reduce or resign from doing so much volunteer work at school and at church. There are years ahead when we are empty nesters that I can do that. But right now, my own schedule is so packed that I am often an empty tank, not a full one, when Matthew comes home. I'm building a family with this portion of my life, and I want to focus and do it well. It makes sense that a wife with a full tank can soothe ruffled emotional feathers.

"Let's move to topic two, when men don't like their jobs," Genie continues. "This is a more complicated topic. To begin, a common mistake wives make is to become fearful of her own financial security. She will then recite clichés to her husband, such as 'Be grateful you have a job.' Of course, this only annoys him and makes him feel misunderstood."

Emma actually told me she said those very words.

"It is highly beneficial," Genie says, "if a man can find his 'downhill stream' in his career and calling. A 'downhill stream' job is one in which a man's skills, interests, and gifts are used and appreciated. Finding satisfying work is one of the most important tenets of a man's fulfilling life. A helpful wife who is willing and ready to assist if her husband needs a job or career change is crucial. When a man is still in his twenties and thirties, there is not much risk in changing professions, as there is still time for him to find his niche and climb to the top of the profession. Even a transition can be made in his forties if his wife is supportive. However, in the fifties and beyond, wisdom dictates that greater care must be considered in taking on a new risk. But at any age, a wife must understand that the sooner she helps her husband find work in which he finds fulfillment, the happier the whole family will be."

"So, Genie, what does she do to help him?" Emma will want a specific strategy.

"First, the wife will want to help her husband make a list of all of his interests, strengths, and gifts," he says. "Then, she can help him recall times, even back to childhood, when he was involved in any activity where he felt vibrantly alive, when he was in his zone. Maybe the husband loved debating as a kid, and even though he's now in his thirties, he wants to go to law school. Sometimes husbands remember the days when they were president of their college fraternity and how energized they were in that position, thinking that corporate America may be his answer for career satisfaction. Maybe a husband likes to read and think. There are jobs for this husband in the ministry, counseling, teaching, or in writing. Again, a woman is wise to help her husband find his 'downhill stream' career."

"Jacob is an introvert, a reader and thinker," I say. "He is in a sales job that requires him to be gregarious and outgoing all day long. I can see the obvious misfit."

"Changing careers or jobs can be overwhelming," Genie says. "But bookstores are filled with books to help people discover their genius and get in touch with their natural aptitudes. Also, there are career counselors and life coaches who are extremely helpful. I highly recommend these suggestions to Emma and Jacob. The important part I want you to stress to your friend, though, is her confidence in her husband's skill set. Encouragement is worth more than gold in a marriage."

Emma has a sharp tongue. I'm not sure how encouraging she has been. She's had more of a "buck up, buddy" mentality with her husband.

"A wife might need to consider downsizing their home, driving older cars, and/ or eating out less so the husband can go back to school," Genie says. "A sacrifice for a couple of years is worth the effort in order to get her husband excited about his work. *Most men who don't like to work are not in the right field or job*, so an encouraging wife is a lifeboat in this situation. A wife who believes in a man's strengths and praises him for his efforts will fan energy into this man's psyche. Sometimes when a wife thinks her husband is lazy, he is actually a man who has square gifts being squeezed into a circle job. Find the husband's bent and interests and watch this man come alive. One of my clients had a husband in a detailed, computer job who later became a sports announcer. She described her formerly miserable husband as finding the fountain of youth because he regained so much energy."

Emma thought her husband needed B12 shots.

"As a word of precaution," Genie says, "since it is primarily the husband's role to earn a living, he should never put the family's welfare in jeopardy while he is trying to find other work. However, with compromises on both partners' parts, a family will benefit from temporary inconveniences so the husband can ultimately find satisfaction in his work."

Emma is not going to like this advice. She's especially not going to like hearing the word *downsize*. I'd better mosey over to the bookstore and see if I can find a book to give her when I tell her about her husband possibly needing to change directions in his work. This will not be good news to her.

Ah, the bipolar weather is at it again. It's now sunny for my trip to Barnes and Noble.

Ms. Smith is calling me. I don't have the energy to talk to her right now. She probably wants some inside information on Dad, like his favorite cologne or activities. I let it go to voicemail and then listen to her message. "Jessica, please call me as soon as you can. Josh got in a fight at school, and we think he may have broken his arm."

Can't the drama ever push pause for a little while?

Rushing to school, I pick up Josh and Brandon, and we head for the emergency room. Josh now has a cast on his arm.

Matthew was not very understanding of Josh's fight. In fact, he was angry. I know Matthew and I need to deal with Josh's fighting, but I cringe when Matthew gets angry.

I listened to the Love and Logic Parenting CDs, and now I need to figure out a way to ask Matthew to listen to them also. Wise parents don't raise their voices to their children, according to the CDs.

Sometimes I feel I should be further along. Further along in marriage. Further along in parenting. Just further along in life. I need a bunch of genies for *all* of my issues!

CHAPTER 30

When Your Husband Is Not Romantic

Friday, April 25

Matthew calls to ask a question about our income taxes, which are due in two weeks, and mentions that he is interviewing new assistants to replace Indigo. "I just interviewed a woman named Sheila," he says.

"Tell me about Shelia," I say. After that nightmare with Indigo, I am interested in the next hire.

"She's perfect for the job," he says. "Experienced, sharp, articulate."

I want to know what she looks like, not her typing skills. "What else can you tell me about her, Matthew?" I politely ask.

"She's twenty-six, divorced, with a two-year-old," he says.

Twenty-six? Why can't he hire someone his mother's age?

Matthew didn't volunteer any more information about the possible new assistant, so I had to directly ask what she looked like.

"She's attractive," he says.

"Attractive? In what way?" I sweetly ask. Maybe she has an angelic face. Or maybe her looks are innocent and wholesome.

"She's ... uh ... well, she's well-built," he sputters.

Well-built, divorced, and twenty-six. And I'm not supposed to be alarmed? Especially after our recent interlude with Captivating Indigo?

"Yeah, Chad and Tony were ... well ... never mind." he says.

"Chad and Tony were what?" I press.

"Well ... uh, they were discussing ... uh, you know, things men talk about ... you know, she's, uh ... well, you know, good-looking and curvy."

One troublemaker just got deported to Dallas, and now we're thinking about hiring another one? Seriously? Matthew must be brain-dead. How could he not remember what we just went through with Indigo?

"Matthew, Sheila might be a very nice girl," I say, and I really mean that. "But you and I have been so happy together recently. The thought of another coworker who might make me uncomfortable concerns me. Is there any way I could meet Sheila and see if my alarms go off?"

I mean, why do we have to interview and hire only hot women?

"You and I *are* getting along well," Matthew says. He's probably thinking about Wednesdays and Sundays.

We drop the conversation and hang up.

I walk to the mailbox and see my neighbor Heidi outside. We strike up a conversation, and she asks me to come in for a second to see her six-year-old son's room. She found an interior designer who created a cowboy theme for his bedroom.

I need to exercise so I can begin working on my invitations, but since I am thinking about re-doing the boys' rooms this summer, I agree to quickly take a peek.

In the room is a log cabin bunk bed. There is a real child's saddle, a looped rope around the room on the wall, a horseshoe coat rack, and a cowhide nailed to the wall. A sign on the door says, "Welcome to the Ranch." The room is absolutely adorable. I ask Heidi for the name of the designer, and she says, "Elizabeth of Elizabeth Gullett Interiors." I'm going to call her to do the boys' rooms while they are at camp this summer.

As I am leaving, Heidi brings up that she is grieved about the "business relationship" she feels she has with her husband, Patrick. I feel like I'm an actor in one of the new sci-fi movies where my super powers are attracting women with marriage issues. Robert Downy Jr. as Ironman is saving the world, and I'm solving marriage issues in East Memphis.

Heidi confided, "Patrick used to write me long letters about his feelings. We used to take walks in the moonlight, talking about our future, and we enjoyed staring romantically into each other's eyes. Now, we have settled for Little League games and cleaning out the garage."

Relating to the lack of romance in marriage is no stretch for me. I too remember the thrill of being courted and pursued. But now the priority is paying bills and getting homework done.

"What do I do, Jessica, to get the romance back?" Heidi asks.

Since I would actually enjoy more romance myself, I'm anxious to see what Genie has to say on this topic.

"Let me think about it," I stall, "and I'll call you soon."

I workout to an oldie but goodie, P90X. Then as I walk toward the kitchen, I notice my dining room table is set with my best china. The candles are out, ready to be lit. The playlist coming through the speakers is magnificent: "I Will Always Love You" by Whitney Houston, "I Just Called to Say I Love You" by Stevie Wonder, and "The Way You Look Tonight" by Tony Bennett.

Genie is in the kitchen, wearing an apron. He is finishing making chocolate éclair crepe cakes, and there is a prime rib in the oven.

"Today we will discuss what to do when your husband doesn't romance you anymore," Genie says. Seriously, does he travel around on my shoulder? Anyhow, the table and music seem more like *my* getting ready to romance *Matthew*. Does Genie understand the problem accurately?

"As you know, Young Jessica, there are stages in life. Infancy is a stage, toddlerhood is a stage, adolescence is a stage, and adulthood is a stage."

So?

"Courtship is a time in people's lives," says Genie, "when the Creator gives men and women an abundance of hormones that make mating and finding a spouse of paramount importance. Men pursue women with romantic fervor, which of course delights females. Soft words, unexpected gifts, long talks, and extended eye contact all excite the female soul."

I remember. I remember vividly.

"These hormones carry the male like a mighty river during courtship. But eventually, after the woman has been caught, the massive efforts to win her are substantially decreased by the male. This is normal, of course, and even necessary. Honestly, how could any man accomplish anything if his hormones continued to rage at this high speed? A man has gifts he needs to express to benefit the world, children to rear, and multiple other goals to conquer."

I still don't get what he's trying to say.

"Courtship is a season, Young Jessica. Women who bemoan and long for the intensity of the mating days are similar to women who still demand the freedom and fun of their cheerleading days of high school. High school is a season. Courting is a season."

This is pathetic. No wonder we women adore romantic comedies. Women don't want the season to be over. Women still want to be romanced.

One of my favorite movies of all time is *You've Got Mail*. I love the scene where Tom Hanks (Joe) visits Meg Ryan (Kathleen) in her New York apartment while she was sick. Joe leans toward Kathleen and says, "I hope you're better soon. It would be a shame to miss New York in the spring." Every woman watching at that moment wants a special man to show her New York City in the spring.

"I don't want to give up romance," I burst out. I was supposed to be talking about Heidi's marriage, but now we're talking about mine. Whoops.

"You don't have to give it up," Genie says. "But understanding that the intensity of that period was only a season for Matthew will keep you from unrealistic expectations. It doesn't mean your husband doesn't love you; only that the season of rapturous romance has given way to another season. Romance in marriage is more the size of a clutch bag; in dating, romance is the size of a *tote* bag."

I love my Calvin Klein tote bag. I can literally carry my whole life in that thing.

"Wives must learn to give men a break in this area," he says. "During courtship, the Creator gives the man those special burning log hormones that ignite the fire of romance."

"His hormones still drive him to want sex," I say. I used to be embarrassed when I said blatant things to Genie, but the past few months have removed any muzzles I might have previously worn.

"Exactly," he says. "Now he loves you by being faithful and bringing home his paycheck. And the way he mainly experiences romance with you is *through* sex."

Oh, brother. "This looks like one of those seesaws in marriage again, Genie. The wife wants romance, and the husband wants sex."

"Exactly," he says. "So this is another situation where the wife must learn how to teach her husband her needs and desires. The 'logs' that the Creator gave the man to initiate romance might be gone, but Matthew can learn to add his own 'logs.' "

More to learn. More to teach.

"Women have a ridiculous belief that men should instinctively know how to romance their wives. If your husband is going to know how to thrill your soul, it will be through your wise instruction. Especially in this century, women are under the ludicrous notion that if the man really 'got' her, he would intuitively know how to buy her gifts, know what to say, and know how to excite her."

I don't see what's so ridiculous about that. Matthew did it before we were married. And it happens all the time in, uh, in … the movies.

"A married couple still needs to date," says Genie. "After marriage, a wife is equally responsible, if not more so, for the dates. She suggests walks along the river, dinners at a quiet restaurant, or a candlelit picnic. Just remember, however, that most husbands think that romantic evenings should end in sex. I know you don't feel that way, but your husband does."

Men want *everything* to end with sex. "Let's get the weeds out of the garden and then have sex." "Let's watch the Cardinals play baseball and then have sex."

"If the husband is not naturally a good gift-giver," Genie says, "a wife is free to suggest to him what she wants for her special days, or she can suggest that they buy her presents together. Most men are relieved from the responsibility of thinking of what to buy their wives." (See Chapter 36, "When Your Husband Is Unskilled in Celebrating Your Special Days."). Matthew has certainly improved, but the poor thing doesn't know how to buy gifts. I've got enough bath soaps to last me until my great-grandchildren are grown.

"If Matthew gives you new floor mats for your car or a piece of modern art that you detest, try to see the thought behind the gift. Thank him, try to use it, even if ever so briefly, and then realize that you will need to give him a list or go shopping with him in the future."

Matthew gave me a gaudy necklace one year that I was embarrassed to wear. I told him that it scratched my neck, so I needed to take it back. I did notice he seemed discouraged when I returned it.

"Anytime Matthew makes any romantic gesture, like holding your hand when you're out or putting his arm around you in the movie, be sure to let him know. Say, 'I love it, Matthew, when you put your arm around me. It makes me feel special.' As you know, whatever gets appreciated gets repeated."

I'm doing better with that. I used to say nothing when Matthew did nice things and instead criticized his mistakes. Now I pour on the praise when he gets it right and say nothing when he makes a mistake. Hey, I'm learning this stuff!

"Matthew wants to please you, but he can't read your mind," Genie says. "Don't whine that he doesn't send you flowers anymore. Instead, gently and sweetly let him know that the poems he wrote you in the past are some of your most special keepsakes. Demonstrate how much you appreciate his efforts by framing the poems he's written you and putting them on your nightstand."

Genie certainly believes in catching flies with honey instead of vinegar.

"Remember, women are the A students in relationship issues, not men," he says. "Take the initiative yourself to plan outings and dates that will arouse romantic feelings. Be affectionate and sweet. I know you'd like Matthew to concentrate on being more romantic, but again, men are simple, as they like food, sports, work, sex, and hobbies.

They must be lovingly coaxed and taught how important this area of romance is to you. When men fail in this area, it is not personal against you. Men do not instinctively know how much you crave romance."

I still wrestle with the notion that I have to train Matthew to meet my needs instead of his automatically knowing what to do. But that's a little hypocritical of me because, after all, I had to be trained by Genie to meet Matthew's needs.

"Wait until Matthew does something that is romantic and then say, 'Matthew, I especially love the way you framed the words to our favorite song, "Everything" by Michael Bublé. That was the most wonderful present! I know men don't care as much about romance after marriage, but one of the greatest thrills for me is when you still pursue me. Really, Matthew, your pursuing me is one of my life's greatest joys. Although your joys might come from winning a bowling tournament or landing a new huge advertising account, I enjoy when you pursue me romantically.' "

Wow. I understand how Matthew would hear the importance of romance to me if I compared it to his winning a bowling tournament or getting a new, large account. I could say that. I'm going to write that paragraph down in my Turquoise Journal and use it when I catch Matthew being romantic. Sure, I'd rather he be naturally romantic without any instruction, but the reality is that most men aren't. Again, it's fighting the time the sun comes up to be mad that Matthew isn't more romantic. I am at least happy to know there is nothing wrong in our marriage just because Matthew has little interest in romance. And I'm pleased I can teach him about my desire. Sure, it would also be great to have a toned, sculpted body without working out, but that's called wishing, and wishing doesn't bring results.

Genie departs, and I gaze at my beautiful romantic dinner, all prepared. Maybe Matthew and I can take a walk after dinner in the moonlight.

I hear my text ringtone. It's from Matthew. "Sheila is coming back at 2:30 p.m. for another interview with other staff. Want to drop by then and leave the tax forms I need?"

I'm getting to give my opinion about the new hire? Matthew's letting me in? This is pretty romantic in my opinion.

It's already one o'clock, so I shower and put on my cutest outfit. I walk in around 2:40 p.m. to Matthew's office, and there is Sheila. Tight, short skirt. Low-cut blouse. Lots of perfume. Oh dear, oh dear. I smile, greet her cordially, chat briefly, give Matthew the tax forms, and exit.

Matthew calls me as I leave the parking lot.

"You didn't approve, did you?" he asks.

Now that's an improvement. This boy is learning.

"Matthew, she may be the most awesome assistant in the world, but she is sending out signals that she's available with the way she dresses. Would you please look for someone who won't threaten me? I am so happy being married to you, and I don't want anything to change our great marriage."

There's a brief silence on the phone.

"There's another woman who is equally qualified, but the other guys didn't think she looked right. I'll bring up her name again," he said.

When two NBA players make a great play, they run toward each other, jump up in the air, and body slam each other. That's what I want to do right now with Genie.

I feel like I'm flying—and without a magic carpet.

CHAPTER 31
When Your Husband Is Irresponsible

Monday, May 5

Dad calls, extremely excited. "I've got a great idea, Jessica."

I'm listening, but Dad's ideas are not always the best.

"Why don't you and Matthew go on a date tomorrow night with Sue and me?"

Sue? As in Sue Smith, the principal?

"Chloe, Chad, Allison, and Zach are all going. Can you and Matthew?"

How do I get out of this? Why can't he quadruple date with people his own age? Since my sisters and their husbands are going, it will look bad if I say no without an excuse. Think, Jessica, think.

"Dad, I'll check our schedule and call you back," I say. Stalling is a great skill to have in one's arsenal.

Today is a beautiful day, and I decide to burn a few calories by walking in the neighborhood. My friend Jennifer Barkley calls during my walk. Jennifer's husband, Ryan, was a friend of Matthew's in college.

Jennifer asks if Matthew and I are available to go see a movie and get dinner next weekend. Before we hang up, she begins unloading about Ryan. I have become a magnet for women with marital issues.

"We had a date planned last Friday night to go to the Beale Street Music Festival. Jason Mraz was on the program, one of my favorites. I had hired a babysitter and taken extra time to get dressed. When Ryan was twenty minutes late getting home from work, I called and found out he was immersed in some important project at work but had forgotten all about our date night. I ended up sending the babysitter home."

It sounds pretty discouraging to me.

"I wouldn't complain if this was the only time," she continues. "But Ryan forgets to pick up milk when I ask him, he forgets he's supposed to mow the yard, and he forgets when our daughter has a dance recital. His irresponsibility drives me mad."

I don't know what to say. I tell her I will think about it and call her back.

"Good morning, Young Jessica," says Genie, immediately showing up next to me. In addition to his genie garb, he's wearing a pair of Nike Lunar Glide tennis shoes.

"I thought you might like some company on your walk," he says. "Remember, your neighbors can't see me. I overheard your conversation with Jennifer, and I have some advice for you to give her."

"Can you believe how irresponsible that loser Ryan is for forgetting their date night and all those other events?" I ask.

"Now, now, let's not jump to conclusions that he's a loser," Genie says. "I seriously doubt he's a loser or your friend Jennifer wouldn't have married him and Matthew wouldn't like him so much. *Many men who are high in creativity are also subsequently low in conscientiousness.* The traits seem to go together. Is Ryan by any chance extremely creative?"

I am astonished. "Why, yes, he's extremely creative, Genie." Ryan is a brilliant architect, can sing, dance, act, entertain a crowd, and is hilarious.

"I see it all the time," Genie says. "Women are attracted to these men's minds, their fun, and excitement, but then, after the marriage, when it's time to pay the bills and get the yard mowed, well, Mr. Excitement sort of drops the ball."

"That's their marriage exactly," I say, feeling corrected that maybe Ryan is not a loser but rather another example of a man who has both positive and negative qualities.

"My hunch is that this Ryan was attracted to your friend Jennifer because of her organizational skills and dependability," Genie says. "Opposites attract, as you know. But now that they're married, she wants him to carry more of the responsibility in the marriage, and he's resistant to that idea."

That's exactly right. Genie is sometimes spooky.

"This kind of creative man like Ryan," he says, "will often sink or swim depending upon his choice of spouse. If the wife can overlook his lack of attention to detail and appreciate the great fun and excitement that this free spirit brings to her otherwise boring life, the marriage will thrive. However, if the wife moves into the 'mother' role and tries to 'grow him up' by spanking him with her words and withholding her approval, well, you can count on some trouble."

Uh-oh. I think Jennifer has already moved into that mother role.

He continues. "A wife married to a creative yet irresponsible man can help him with a calendar on his bathroom mirror, e-mail reminders, and texts. She can ask questions like, 'Do you want to mow on Saturday, or should I hire a neighborhood boy?' So many women marry this kind of man for his fun and zest, but the second the ring is on her finger, she thinks it's time to remake this man into Johnny Dependable. I also need to tell you that this kind of husband is usually extremely needy for the Eight A's, and when I say extremely, I mean, *extremely.*"

I have noticed Ryan's ego before, bragging about himself (see Chapter 28, "When Your Husband Brags"). I can't wait to tell Jennifer that Ryan is not a loser but a creative whiz with low-conscientiousness.

"Genie, does the wife in this marriage have to take care of the cars, the bills, and most of the organizational details?"

"Probably," he says. "But she's usually very good at this. Getting things done is one of her strong points, not the husband's. His strong points are making life interesting and exciting. Sure, she wants him to pick up his socks and take out the garbage, but are these really issues to fight over? These men make excellent mates to go through life with, if the wife knows how to oil and grease them with the Eight A's. It is wise if these wives take the burden of monotony off their husbands and appreciate what they bring to the marriage, which is fun, life, and newness. Of course, she can pick a couple of things she wants and ask for those important things. But the worst thing she can do is flood him with requests for all sorts of little things, 'Would you please put your dishes in the dishwasher? Would you please not mess up the bathroom mirror when you floss?' She will strip any affection he has for her if she continuously harps on minor issues. This man is a dreamer, and he needs a woman to help him stay organized so he can accomplish great things. If Jennifer does not take Ryan's irresponsibility personally and realizes that she has unlimited influence with him if she can be patient, she can then help him blossom into a fruitful, fabulous husband. Her crabbiness and tongue-lashings, though, will do just the opposite."

Jennifer is a reasonable woman; I hope she'll hear me on this.

"There's a balance to all of this, Young Jessica. The wife who is married to an irresponsible man must let him run his own life whenever possible. If he's late to work, that is his issue. But also remember, a smart wife can always set two alarms, one across the room so he has to get up to turn it off."

Ryan has been in our social group long enough to know that a seven o'clock appointment to him means 7:20.

"The wife needs to remember," Genie says, "that this irresponsible man was irresponsible *before* she married him. Her organizational strength was subconsciously part of the reason why he married her. So she is foolish to resent this. She is not his mother. She does not have to make his dental appointments or take his car through inspection, *but these little gifts to this type of husband are tremendously appreciated.* Tasks like these aren't hard for her at all, but they are like pushing a huge boulder uphill for him."

Sounds to me like she's got a preschooler on her hands.

"Jennifer has to remember to stay in 'girlfriend mode' though," he says, "and not the angry 'mother mode' as she assists him. For example, she can put lists on his bathroom mirror, but she should remember to add at the bottom of the list, 'You are an extremely handsome man, and I love your big shoulders.' "

I've got to write Ryan's weaknesses down in my journal under "Things Other Husbands Do Wrong."

"This wife is loving her spouse, weaknesses and all, and demonstrating it by complementing his weaknesses," he says. "She is bringing her gift to the table, which is organization, and he is bringing his gift, creativity. Great spouses offer their gifts freely to the other spouse and don't keep score."

The idea of making someone's dental appointment seems juvenile to me.

"Whenever Ryan acts mature and responsible for anything at all, tell Jennifer to pour on the praise," he adds. "You know I love the motto, 'Appreciation promotes repetition.' "

Genie vanishes, and I'm finished with my walk.

Time to get out the Turquoise Journal. I write down, "I'm grateful Matthew is on time and makes his own dental appointments."

Dad calls back, and I answer.

"Forget the date tomorrow night," he says. "Sue and I got in an argument over signing a prenuptial agreement. She got furious when I recommended one. I guess she wanted my wallet as much as my bushy hair."

I laugh. But the thought that Ms. Smith is still the principal at my boys' school drains the jovial spirit right out of me.

Life!

CHAPTER 32

When You Want Sex More Than Your Husband Does

Monday, May 19

School will be out in a few days, so I want to finish addressing these wedding invitations for the Wallace wedding before then. I tap "Music" on my iPhone and choose to listen to a new artist, Stephen Gordon, singing, "Over the Line".

Matthew is calling. This is a strange time for him to call. "Jessica, Mom fell, and we think she broke her hip. Can you meet me at the ER?"

Buying stock in our local hospital would not be a bad idea if our family's injuries continue at this rate.

I jump into the car and head to the ER.

Oh, no, I think. *How much time and attention is Daisy going to need for the next few weeks while she's in rehab?* I'm ashamed of my self-centered thoughts.

Matthew meets me at the hospital, and we wait for what seems like hours while they x-ray Daisy. Finally, the radiologist comes out to talk to Matthew and me. "If she did crack a bone, it is so slight that it is not showing up on the X-ray. She should be careful, but she can resume her normal activity when she feels like it."

Daisy actually seems disappointed that it wasn't broken. "Are they sure?" she keeps asking. "I feel like it's broken. Anyhow, I certainly can't walk. What if I recuperate at your house for a couple of weeks?"

I raise my eyebrows at Matthew. If it were necessary, I would be more than happy to do whatever Daisy needed. But this looks like a plea for attention to me.

"Mom, let's see what else the doctor says," Matthew says.

Daisy persuades the doctor to let her spend the night in the hospital. That will give me a chance to discuss her request with Matthew tonight.

I drive home to finish the invitations and get dinner prepped for tonight. The whole day is almost gone now. My phone rings, and it is April, a good friend of mine from church.

April is calling to invite Matthew and me to a small group event at their house this weekend. We chat about trivia for a few minutes and then, unexpectedly, April starts spilling her guts. This seems to be the norm lately. I can't get used to it. Since I have changed how I relate to Matthew, women repeatedly open up to me about their marriages.

"I feel like Eric doesn't love me," April protests. "I mean, he rarely wants to have sex. I'm always the one suggesting it, even almost begging. Isn't he supposed to have the high desire and want me? What's wrong with me? What's wrong with Eric?"

April's husband, Eric, is a superb chef at the Peabody Hotel and is known throughout the mid-South for his exquisite culinary skills. He is popular at church, sweet to his kids, and well, super good-looking. April, too, is hip and chic, and they appear to be the ideal couple.

"Let me think about this and call you back, April," I say.

I go back to making the rub to season tonight's chicken, and, *voila*, as is the norm anymore, the casserole is already made. That means Mr. You-Know-Who is here.

Genie is doing a downward dog yoga pose. He looks very peculiar upside down. "This keeps my six-thousand-year-old back in shape," he says.

I guess he's kidding, but I never know.

"Did I hear that you might need some counsel about sex, Young Jessica?"

"Yes, I do," I say.

"I heard April say that Eric doesn't want sex as much as she does, and she thinks something is wrong in their marriage," Genie says. He shakes his head. "You humans get bent out of shape when you don't understand things. Excuse me, one more pose, and I'm through for the day." He kneels down, arches his back, and grabs his heels. "Camel pose," he says.

I fix us some red raspberry tea with stevia, and we head outside to sit in the sunshine and yak.

"Actually, Young Jessica, about 20 percent of women want sex more than their husbands. It is extremely common, but women are embarrassed to share that they want sex more than their husbands. Like your friend April, they feel their husbands don't desire them because they (the wives) are defective. Or they feel that maybe something is wrong with their husband. But that is not at all what is happening."

I'm certainly not familiar with this scenario. I thought maybe April was right, that Eric found her unattractive or had some hang-ups.

"Sex drive is a function of many things, one being the hormone testosterone. And as you might expect, there's a huge continuum of how much testosterone men have. You know the strong, alpha-male type who dominates most situations, right? He probably has an abundance of testosterone and a very hungry sex drive. But all men do not fit this stereotype; indeed, many men have an average or below-average sex drive. These mild-mannered men often marry go-getter women who are strong, unemotional, driven, and who have a higher sex drive than most women."

As Genie speaks, I think about April's strong opinions, forthright speech, and lack of emotionalism, which is typical of many women. Even after she had a miscarriage, April said there was no use crying over something she couldn't help. I remember her saying that Eric was still a mess over the miscarriage. I also remember thinking how backward that seemed from the way most couples handle such a situation.

"When women realize," Genie continues, "that they are normal, and that they are just one of the 20 percent marriages, they calm down and begin to proactively fix the situation. Instead of the husband putting the kids to bed while the wife takes a bath to relax, in the 20 percent marriages, the wife does what is needed so the husband can relax and get in the mood."

This seemed crazy. I can't imagine my wanting sex more than Matthew.

"What exactly do I tell April, Genie?"

"First, you explain to her that her marriage is normal," he says. "That truth alone will do wonders for her. Secondly, since her husband is the one who has to perform in the marriage act, she will have to work hard to figure out which situations enhance and which situations detract from Eric's best sexual moods. Filling him with the Eight A's will be the first place to start, of course."

Of course. According to Genie, the earth can't rotate on its axis without the Eight A's.

"I am not a sex therapist," he says, "but I have seen women who were terribly upset about wanting sex more than their husbands calm completely down just in knowing that their marriages were normal. Women greatly relax about their husband's lack of sexual desire—and the abundance of their own sexual desire—when they understand that many couples experience this."

Genie departs, and I pick up my cell to call April back. Who can believe that I'm calling someone with advice about sex? I'm a hoot.

April is receptive to the advice. We talk for a full hour. Daisy is beeping in on the other line. April and I are finished, but I let Daisy's call go to voicemail anyway. Then I listen to it.

"Did you and Matthew decide if I can stay with you for two weeks while I recover? I'm certainly not able to take care of myself."

I call Matthew. Daisy had already called him, but he was in a meeting. "I talked to the doctor again," Matthew said. "He doesn't see the need for Mom to stay with us. He said she will be fine by herself. But he did recommend that we get her some help with cleaning and cooking for a week or two until she feels better. I called and told her, but she didn't like it. But what could she say?"

I thank Matthew profusely for handling his mother. I think of at least three or four different phrases of admiration and appreciation. While Matthew and I are hanging up, Daisy's call beeps in again.

"Hi, Daisy."

"Matthew said I can't stay with you, but that you will bring me dinner all week and clean my house. Jessica, the last time you made pot roast, there was way too much pepper in it. Please don't put so much pepper in my food this week."

We hang up, and I walk into the kitchen, wondering what in the world I am going to fix for dinner. On the counter are two beautiful quiches, one for us and one for Daisy. Daisy's quiche has a note attached that says, "This quiche doesn't have much pepper."

CHAPTER 33
When Your Husband Is Emotionally Needy

Saturday, May 31

The boys are out of school for the summer, and they spent last night with Chloe and their cousins. Since Matthew has his fifteen-year class reunion coming up, I decide to add a few highlights in my hair for a little dazzle.

I try a new stylist today, and the idiot puts red streaks in my hair. *Red!* I look gothic. When she sees how disturbed I am, she offers to try another color. I don't ever want her touching my hair again. I feel like crying. What am I going to do about my cyberpunk hair? All I need is a black leather coat, thick black eyeliner, and some chains to complete my look.

I exit the salon and quickly call my friend Hillary who, along with her husband and two boys, is meeting us tonight at the Rendezvous Restaurant. I unload my sad hair story, and she gives me the name of her stylist. I call but can't get in until next Friday.

Matthew, the boys, and I with my cyberpunk hair are now driving to the Rendezvous Restaurant to eat barbeque ribs. The streaks in my hair are the same color as the red squares in the checkerboard tablecloths. We all order, and then Hillary and I excuse ourselves to go to the ladies' room.

"Jack wears me out," she blurts as soon as we get up from the table to go to the restroom. "I had no idea how needy Jack was when I married him. I only have two kids, but it's like I have three."

I thought she was joking, but she is serious.

"He wants to talk everything through over and over again," Hillary said. "His fears, obsessions, and anxieties wear me to a frazzle. I think he is extremely insecure since he is only five foot seven. "

Frankly, I am shocked. Jack is short, but he is probably one of the most kind and honest men Matthew and I know. To hear his wife describe him as emotionally needy is very surprising.

"Do you have any ideas how I should handle this, Jessica?"

What is this? Am I wearing a tee shirt that says, "Tell me your marriage problems"? "Hillary, I have no idea, but let me think about it, and I'll call you next week," I say.

My initial advice is to tell her to tell Jack he can moan from 8:00 to 8:05 p.m. every night and then to zip it up. Hopefully, Genie has better advice than that.

Tuesday, June 3

The boys have left for a weeklong camp at Victory Ranch in Bolivar, Tennessee. Matthew is at work, and I am determined to get my bedroom painted while the boys are away. I am using Sherwin Williams SW6123 Baguette. Spending my week sunbathing instead of painting would be preferable, but such is life.

I change into my painting attire and walk into the room to begin. **Genie is standing there, admiring his finished work with the beautiful SW6123 Baguette.** "I like this color," he says. "I'm talking about the color on the walls, not the color of your hair."

Funny, Genie.

"Let's go lie by the pool and discuss your friend Hillary," he says.

"You heard Hillary complain about her emotionally needy husband, right? What do I say to her?"

I'm very excited to be working on my tan. I put sunscreen on my face, but let my body soak up the nourishing and healing effects of vitamin D from the sun.

"If your child had diabetes," he said, "you would make sure the child got his shots. Although, of course, you'd prefer that your child didn't need insulin, you'd make sure the child got what he or she needed. Hillary has a husband with 'emotional diabetes.' Jack will need her to listen more than an average wife in order to calm and soothe him."

I don't like the analogy. "Genie, a child can't help it if he has diabetes. But can't a husband choose to be more emotionally stable?" As I hear myself ask the question, I know the answer.

"Often, they cannot," he says. "Whatever happened to Jack in the past has created his anxieties. This is the man Hillary was given to love. No one gets a perfect spouse or a perfect life. Some women get a husband who is lazy, and some women get a husband who is a workaholic and is never home. Whatever the husband's issues, the wife is called to come along beside and attempt to plug up the hole."

I normally would say, "Yeah, but who's plugging up my hole?" but I've been in *Wife School* for a while now, so I know the answer to that question.

"When women are confronted with an emotionally needy husband who needs to talk a lot," he says, "their usual tendency is to be annoyed. She often becomes self-pitying and instead of wanting to be home with her husband, she looks for excuses to escape and have time away from him."

If there's going to be an emotionally needy spouse in my marriage, it's going to be me.

"A wise woman knows that her extra dose of love, listening, and care is her calling," he says, "just as attending to a diabetic child would be her calling. She will make galactic strides in helping this man heal emotionally if she is willing to double up on the Eight A's. When Jack wants to rehash a problem he's already discussed multiple times, Hillary's tendency is to say, 'Haven't we been through this enough?' Instead, she should be ready with, 'Sure, Jack. We can talk about that customer as much as you want.' "

Poor girl. A regular dose of the Eight A's can tax me, and yet Hillary is to deposit a supersonic amount into Jack's tank.

"Hillary is rich and doesn't know it," Genie says. "She is rich because Jack is a goldmine of intimacy, relationship, and creativity. He will thrive and bloom when a woman takes care of his emotional needs. Hillary has rich rewards awaiting her if she can mentally see around the river bend."

What a reversal. Here I am feeling sorry for Hillary and Genie says she has a man who is a goldmine.

I take a deep breath while I dial Hillary's number.

"Hey, Jessica," Hillary says as she answers. "I just hung up with my stylist, and she said she'll work you in tomorrow to fix the red streaks in your hair."

I gaze in a nearby mirror and notice that my hair is back to its original color.

"Thanks Hillary, but with a little abracadabra, my hair is now fixed. Would you like to talk about your marriage?"

Abracadabra may work on hair, but *Wife School* is needed for marriage.

CHAPTER 34
When Your Husband Shows Interest in Other Women

Friday, June 6

Matthew calls to say he's coming home early this evening to get ready for his high school reunion. He's extremely excited. He wanted to know if I had ironed his pants and if I was sure the babysitter was coming. I'm nervous too. What if Matthew's old high school sweetheart, Melissa, is there and is a knockout?

Allison calls and says she's a block away and wants to stop by. Even though it's an exceptionally busy day, the Sister Rule trumps again: sisters are allowed anytime for any reason.

Allison stomps into my den, throws herself on the sofa, and lets it rip.

"We're at the Redbird's game Wednesday night," she says. "Alex's whole Little League team went together, along with all the parents. I'm cool with that. I like most of the other parents, except this Kimberly woman."

This story already sickens me. It reminds me of my Indigo days.

"Number one," she says, "she wears the most obscene short shorts you've ever seen. This woman has three kids and dresses like she's for hire. She knows Zach since they both used to work together. She touches him, smiles at him, and laughs ridiculously hard at his bad jokes—it's repulsive. She's looking for attention, I know, but the awful thing is that Zach is such an idiot. He lights up when she's around. I catch her trying to make eye contact with him. I heard her telling Zach she liked his belt. What woman comments on a man's belt? Why is she checking him out and noticing his belt? I could have strangled her."

All women know this sinking feeling in their gut when another woman comes onto your man and he likes it. The wife becomes weak, like Superman around kryptonite.

"It's not like I'll never see her again," Allison says. "Her son and my Alex will probably play ball in the junior league together for years. What do I do, Jessica?"

I felt the same desperation before Indigo was transferred, so I completely understand.

"I will think about it and get back to you," I say. These floozy women drive wives crazy. Honestly, our husband's attraction to them drives us even crazier.

After Allison left, my favorite Mediterranean psychologist appeared.

"Nothing upsets women more than their husbands being attracted to another woman," Genie begins. "Nothing."

I can relate to that. *Nothing.*

"There is much to say, Young Jessica, on this subject. Let's begin with stating the obvious. Men are wired to be attracted to attractive females and especially to those who give them attention. I am not excusing men for flirting with these women. I am only saying that you can't stop the sun from coming up, and you can't stop men from noticing attractive women."

"I'm furious hearing this, Genie. I hate the way men are led by their sex drive."

"Again, I'm not excusing men for any inappropriate behavior," he says. "My purpose in stating this first point is so you will see that men are wired to notice and be drawn to female beauty. To argue about this is to argue that there is a hurricane coming and to then stand and shake your fist at the hurricane instead of heading for shelter. Knowing that men are built this way is very important. It gives you a little compassion and grace for men as well as some ideas for strategy."

I don't want strategy. I want life to not be so unfair to women. I usually love being a woman, but not right now. Right now I see why women want to be liberated. Men. It all stinks.

"Let's not argue over the fact that men are drawn to attractive females," Genie said. "We are not going to argue about this because, like gravity, you are helpless against it *unless you learn aerodynamics.* Today I will teach you the aerodynamics of handling attractive and attentive other women. Be ready because you will not like a lot of this advice."

I don't like this whole topic, even though that Irritating Indigo is gone. This whole subject makes my blood pressure soar.

"The main point today is that husbands infrequently stray if a wife regularly deposits the eight A's," Genie says. "I have said this a thousand times, but it can never be said too often. Also, as I've said earlier, the best way to teach a husband how you feel is to give him a word picture." (See Chapter 13, "How to Explain Anything to Your Husband").

"A word picture? In this situation? Like what, Genie?"

"Allison wants to explain to Zach how hurt she is when he receives the attention of other women," says Genie. "Here is a word picture she might use: 'Zach, I was at the farmer's market this morning. I bought watermelon and cantaloupe and all kinds of produce. There was an attractive, nice man there chatting with me about the blackberries while I checked out, who insisted that he help me to the car because I had so much to carry. So I let him. When we got to the car, he moved in very close and stared at me. He asked me if I'd like to go get some coffee.'"

This sounds more like *Days of Our Lives* instead of *Allison at the Farmer's Market*.

"Allison then needs to pause," says Genie, "and let Zach feel the full emotional drama of such an encounter. After he responds, she should say, 'Zach, that's how hurt I felt at the Redbird's game when Kimberly was falling all over you. Just like you don't like it when I allow other men to pay attention to me, I don't like it when you allow other women to pay attention to you.'"

How does a woman ever think of these word pictures? It seems so difficult.

"When women deposit the Eight A's into their husband's tanks," Genie says, "their husbannds will be able to hear word pictures like these. The truth is, men are often simply untrained, uninformed, and don't think through how they would feel if the situation was reversed."

Untrained? Uninformed? Try stupid.

"Then Allison could say, 'Zach, I realize that men are attracted to women like Kimberly, but I feel it's disrespectful to me for you to encourage her attention. I know you wouldn't like it if things were reversed and I encouraged the attention of attractive men. I want us to be close and affectionate, and I get terribly hurt when you pay attention to her.' "

I like word pictures. Powerful stuff.

"Just a quick reminder," Genie says. "Word pictures don't work as well in a marriage when the wife is not depositing the Eight A's. Her first strategy is always to examine her own behavior to be sure she is doing her part in meeting her husband's needs before she confronts her husband about any inappropriate behavior on his part."

Genie is a broken record about the Eight A's. I would get annoyed at his repetition, but after centuries of helping women, he must know that we need to be constantly reminded.

"On these emotionally charged issues, live the Eight A's, give a powerful word picture that taps into the husband's world and feelings, and then ask directly for what you want. Women have been able to open men's eyes to their blind spots with creative word pictures for centuries."

Tomorrow I'll call Allison with Genie's advice. It's time for me to start getting ready for the reunion tonight.

Matthew comes home early like he said. He showers and dresses, and we leave.

Little hotty-toddy Melissa is there, and after a few too many glasses of wine, she puts her hand on Matthew's chest. He doesn't let her gush all over him, but he is very, very nice to her. *Too* nice. During a brief moment when I have Matthew to myself, I tell him the word picture of *Jessica* at the Farmer's Market.

Matthew hears me and apologizes, saying he would hate it if I let another man flirt with me. I feel rather pleased that he would dislike my accepting the attention of another man. Matthew and I are growing in this marriage, no doubt about it.

CHAPTER 35
When There Is Conflict over Money

Saturday, June 14

Today is Brandon's birthday, and we take the boys to the Shelby Farms section of the Greater Memphis Greenline Trails to ride bikes. Afterward, we drive to Memphis Pizza Café, Brandon's favorite, to get a pineapple and pepperoni pizza. My dad, sisters, their husbands, and kids meet us for a last-minute, informal birthday party.

When we are leaving, by coincidence, Matthew's high school girlfriend, hotty-toddy Melissa, drives by in her white Mercedes convertible. My sisters know the back-story on this wine-sluggin' chick, and that she was a little too friendly to Matthew at his reunion. Just to be funny and silly, Chloe tells the group that she wants to go to her high school reunion in a car like that someday. Although she was just kidding, Chad gets offended because he thinks she is putting pressure on him to someday buy her a car like that. It turns into a huge, ridiculous misunderstanding.

"You want a Mercedes and the moon, don't you, Chloe?"

There is no lightheartedness behind his response. Chloe glances at me and raises her eyebrows, obviously looking for sympathy.

I'm not surprised when I get home and my cell rings. "Isn't he the meanest husband ever? I was teasing you because hotty-toddy Melissa was driving that car. I wasn't saying I wanted Chad to buy me a car like that."

How do these misunderstandings happen?

Chloe and Chad have struggled over money for years. She is the classic spender, and he is the classic saver. Chloe loves gifts, clothes, and furniture. In fact, Chloe loves every pretty thing. And Chad is obviously tired of paying for all her pretty things.

"What would you do if Matthew treated you like that?"

I'm getting good at giving this answer. "Let me think about it, and I'll call you back."

Mr. Roman Nose will know.

Two days later, Monday, June 16

The boys are playing at a neighbor's house, and Matthew is at work. **I head out the door to burn a few calories by taking a short walk and am accompanied by my Palestinian Pal.** He is sitting on a magic carpet that is elevated about three feet off the street that is keeping perfect time with my brisk walk.

"Last night I participated in Line Dancing for Genies," he says. "Today my legs ache too much to walk."

I laugh, but I am very glad to see him, as Chloe has called me back three times.

"Today we will discuss handling money in marriage," Genie said. "It is one of the top areas of conflict in most marriages."

I'm well aware of this.

"There are basically two kinds of people in regard to money: spenders and savers. If savers marry savers, things work out pretty well financially. If savers marry spenders, you can be sure they will have conflict. When spenders marry spenders, I can promise they will have chaos."

The thought of two crazy people both buying frantically and being married to each other is comical. That's like Chloe being married to Chloe.

"Today will be our shortest lesson ever," Genie says.

Did I hear him right? Did he say "shortest"? Did he get mixed up and really mean longest since money is such an involved subject?

"Money is a tremendously complicated and important subject in marriage," Genie says. "Like the subject of parenting, the subject of money must be tackled and learned. I used to spend hours teaching my clients about money in previous centuries. But in this century, one of the Creator's servants, Dave Ramsey, has created seminars and written books that teach couples everything they need to know to get on the same page about money. Attending a Dave Ramsey seminar can substantially decrease and sometimes eliminate monetary conflict that couples have. Even the most financially incompatible couples move toward financial harmony after listening to Dave Ramsey's presentations."

"You want me to tell my sister and brother-in-law to go hear Dave Ramsey? That's the advice I give her?" I'm thinking I might want to go too.

"Exactly. Tell her to sign up for his course called Financial Peace. Many churches in your area offer his course."

This is surprising advice.

"See? A short lesson today. But I need to go soak my muscles in a special mineral salt bath in China," Genie says and then vanishes.

I call Chloe and tell her the advice.

"That's so weird," Chloe said, "because someone suggested to Chad just this morning that we sign up for Financial Peace. I guess I'll get online and see what I can find out."

"Make reservations for Matthew and me too," I say. If I'm going to be an eventual marriage champion, I need to know everything that will help.

I get into my car to do the week's grocery shopping and turn on the radio. Naturally, who is on the radio? Why, Dave Ramsey, of course. I think I detect the scent of a genie.

CHAPTER 36
When Your Husband Is Unskilled in Celebrating Your Special Days

Thursday, June 19

Chloe brings her kids over for the afternoon to swim. Chloe looks more like the kids' big sister than their mom. She has on a pink tankini with big brown polka dots. Ridiculously cute. I wouldn't like her if she wasn't my sister.

Chloe rambles on about her house, her friends, and her kids while making sure I get equal time to ramble about mine. Packing up her towels, sunglasses, and the stray sandals her kids try to leave, she comments on how fragrant my backyard flowers are.

"Speaking of fragrance," she says. "For Mother's Day, I asked Chad for Touch of Pink perfume, and, of course, he wasn't paying attention and only heard the word *pink*, so he bought me Pink Sugar perfume. If he really cared, wouldn't he try harder to get what I really want?"

Chloe isn't the first woman who has complained to me about her husband's gift buying and how he celebrates her special days. "I guess I should be happy I get anything," she says. "But I'm not."

She drives off with her brood in her Ford Explorer. I go inside to do a load of wet towels. Brandon and Josh go outside to play, but I tell them to be back in an hour because we need to get ready to go to summer tutoring. I know the boys hate summer tutoring, but education is supremely important to me.

As I walk inside, I think about Valentine's Day this past February. Matthew was his usual self. We had a gift card we had been saving, so we went out for an early dinner. He arrived late and at dinner, and we talked mainly about his work and then his bowling. I was hoping for a card, some flowers, a small gift, or words about how he married the girl of his dreams. I tried not to think about it as he went on and on about his "clean game" (which means a strike or spare in each frame). Then we went home, and he wanted sex.

My sad thoughts scatter as I notice my favorite genie sitting on the dryer.

"Your little sis doesn't think her husband does a very good job on her birthday and other special days, does she?"

I hate to complain about Matthew because he has much improved as a husband since I've been depositing the Eight A's. However, I am still interested in hearing what Genie says about celebrating my special days. I am still, well, frequently disappointed with the celebrations ... or rather *lack* of celebrations.

"Many men honestly don't care about holidays and gifts," Genie begins. "How can your special days be on his radar if he doesn't personally care about them himself?"

I know Genie is trying to get me to give men some grace here but it's not happening.

"Only a few men are born with natural gift-giving tendencies," he says. "The other men in the world have to be trained. Women are natural gift-givers and therefore think that men should have the same instincts. But as you know, this is wrong. Men are unskilled in celebrating a woman's special days and must be enlightened in how to celebrate the Big Five."

The Big Five? Matthew is already talking about the Big Ten in college football for this fall, but the Big Five?

"The Big Five are birthday, Christmas, anniversary, Valentine's Day, and Mother's Day. Men have to be coached in how to show up for those days in a woman's life," Genie says.

The Big Five. Cool.

"I laugh when women whine and moan that their husbands don't 'get them' or 'know them' because they are terrible gift-givers," he says. "Men don't come with software installed in knowing how to observe a woman's special holidays."

Men don't come with a lot of software installed on relationships, period.

"As we've discussed, men think they are saying 'I love you' by bringing home their paycheck and being sexual faithful. They have no idea what expectations you hold for celebrating the Big Five," Genie says.

He might be right about this. I want Matthew to stop the world and celebrate my special days in a manner in which I feel loved and special.

"There is not a right or wrong way to celebrate your special days," he says. "But I have a few tips that have helped women become satisfied on their Big Five."

I love tips.

"One thing women can do if their husbands are unskilled in gift-giving," he says, "is to tell him you realize that women care a lot about these holidays whereas men do not feel the same way. That takes a little pressure off him right away because you realize he's like most men and therefore not a bumpkin."

And some men want to be good at everything without putting forth any effort.

"Let's say you have tried giving Matthew a list, like Chloe did, and that didn't work. Instead, tell him you realize it is stressful for him to shop for you, and that you have an idea to make it easier for him. Ask if he's interested in hearing it."

Matthew and Chloe's husband, Chad, need a yellow brick road to help them find the right presents.

"Here is an example of what you could say to Matthew. 'Honey, I thought of an exciting way for me to get presents I love and for you to not be stressed about celebrating my holidays. To begin with, we could plan a special night that starts with a good dinner out and ends with sex. In between, we will go shopping. I will pick out something I like for (name holiday). That way, you could take gift-giving off your 'to do' list, and I could have the thrill of an exciting date with you."

The night begins with food and ends with sex. So male.

"Notice I didn't say, 'Let's do this idea of mine since you are so rotten at buying me good gifts,' " Genie says with a wink.

I have said things frighteningly close to that.

"If he agrees or thinks it's a good idea, doll it up," Genie says. "Tell him how excited you are that the big shopping date is only three days away. Dress up that night in his favorite kind of clothes. Wear sexy perfume. Hang on his arm, and tell him what a great time you're having. Talk about some of the things he gives you or does for you that make you happy. Women who are wise can make their men happy and find ways to be happy themselves."

Matthew would like that. What man wouldn't? And it's not dishonest or manipulative. I make sure Matthew's needs are met and I ask for what I want. It's brilliant, not deceitful.

"Sometimes a husband can give good gifts," Genie says. "But he doesn't know that his wife would also love a sentimental card. Asking for what you want is a skill that wives need to learn. Ask with childlikeness, though, not with a disappointed, depressed-woman style. How you ask is everything. Say, 'Honey, I'm like an eight-year-old on my birthday. When I see the wrapped present and the cake with candles, I think I'm going to jump out of my skin. I know I'm still a little girl inside, but I can't help it.'

This will amuse him, not upset him. What upsets him is your unhappiness with life and with him."

Genie keeps saying the same things, but I still need to hear it.

"If all of this advice fails and a husband still ignores your special days," Genie says, "a well-thought-out word picture is in order."

"Can you please give me an example?"

"You could say, 'Honey, imagine there was an annual review dinner at your office where the employees were recognized for their contributions each year. Imagine they begin and then forget to talk about you. Someone reminds the bosses that they forgot you, and then they say, "He's on time most days." They then get back to the other part of the program. You'd be hurt and disappointed, wouldn't you?'

"After you give him a second to feel the sting of the moment, you continue. 'This may sound crazy, but women feel like their birthdays are the annual review for their relationships. They feel that their birthday is when the people who love them show up for them. If my birthday is forgotten or not made much of, I am hurt and disappointed.' "

Matthew would hear that word picture. He lavishes the appreciation and attention he gets at work.

"By the way, that bracelet you want for your anniversary next week is on sale at Dillard's," Genie says. And he's gone.

I thought getting crummy gifts was going to be one of the things I had to lay down or accept about Matthew. Looks like the Big Five have just become the Great Five. I've got to call Chloe later and tell her these tips.

It's time for tutoring. Brandon says he's ready, but we can't find Josh. I call every family in the neighborhood whose home Josh could possibly be visiting. I drive through the neighborhood, yelling and honking for him. I know he was here an hour ago.

Panic sets in. I call Matthew. Then I call the police.

Those were probably ninety of the worst minutes of my life. Josh had gone into the forest behind our house where he is not allowed. He accidentally stepped into a deep hole and fell into a ditch that he could not climb out of. No one could hear him yell, but the police helped us find him. I am still weak from the ordeal and am trying to recover.

Sometimes I need to get things—like how my birthdays are celebrated—in perspective. This scare with Josh did just that.

CHAPTER 37

When Your Husband Doesn't Want to Spend Quality Time with You

Friday, June 20

My blender broke, so I gather the boys, and we drive to Target. They head for the sports department as I head for the appliances.

Oh, heavens. Am I seeing right? Is that Indigo looking at the makeup? What is *she* doing in town? Matthew didn't say anything to me about her visiting. But he did say he would be home late tonight because he had some new clients in town. I feel my fear escalate.

Carefully, I avoid Indigo while I pick out a blender and then check out. When I get home, I call Matthew.

"She's not in town, Jessica," Matthew says. "She's in Dallas. I talked to her earlier on the phone today."

"I saw her at Target."

"I've got to go. My clients are waiting on me. We'll talk later," and he hangs up.

Is something going on? Is Matthew pulling something over on me, and I'm just a dumb duck?

Some friends and I are meeting at the Memphis Zoo for a playdate with our kids, so I try to put these issues out of my mind. But it is difficult.

The grizzly bear feeding is at one p.m., and the polar bear feeding is at two. We also want to see Gina the elephant who is about to give birth. That should make me feel skinny, looking at a pregnant elephant.

My friend Sophie is here with her girls. I've never seen girls with such huge bows in their hair. Maybe I'm just jealous because I don't have any "sugar and spice and everything nice" darlings.

Sophie decides to follow me through the zoo. She chats about her life and especially her husband, Tony. I still can't get over how I'm now bait, drawing women with marriage problems to myself.

"For example, Tony is out again tonight," Sophie says. "He's actually with some men from our church helping to feed the homeless at the Memphis Union Mission, so how can I complain? He's not at bars or casinos, but he's also not at home. It's always work, church, hobbies/sports—but not me. He puts everything ahead of me."

I hear her pain. I remember the nights of Matthew working late and bowling until midnight. Thoughts about my Target errand and seeing Indigo barge into my mind and feel like a kick in the stomach but I push the thoughts back out of my mind.

"What should I do, Jessica?" she asks.

I want to scream, 'Get your own genie!' but that would not be nice. I guess I'm in a bad mood from the Target run.

I push "play" on my verbal tape recorder. "Let me think about it, and I'll get back to you." I can't wait to get back home and sit inside with a glass of ice tea. The Memphis sun can be pretty rough in June.

Inside my den, Genie is napping on my sofa. The boys can't see him, but it still makes me nervous. They go outside to swim.

"I've spent many a day in the sun in the Arabian desert," he says. "But that's no match for your Memphis summer."

He's got that right.

"I saw Indigo at Target," I spit out.

Genie looks at me, puzzled. "How is that? She's in Dallas."

I have to get to the bottom of this later. I *saw* her. But I decide to let it go for now.

"Did you hear my friend Sophie while we were at the zoo, Genie?"

"Of course I did," he says. "Are you ready for her advice?"

I'm really not. My insides are still upside down, but I see my dinner of shrimp alfredo pasta on the counter. I also notice that my laundry has been done again. How can I refuse?

"Today we will discuss what to do when a husband puts everything else in his life ahead of his wife," Genie says.

My brain is fighting, not wanting to cooperate and listen, but I wrestle it down.

"Let's begin with discussing that people have different appetites for quality time together," Genie says. "Just like couples have different appetites for sex or for saving money, individuals have different desires in all areas. When couples have the same appetites, we say they are compatible. If both couples want a lot of sex, there is not a problem. It is only when one spouse wants something frequently and the other is not interested to the same degree that there is a problem. Did you know that some couples have sex once every two to three weeks, and they are both happy with that? It is because they are compatible in that area. Being incompatible in appetites is not a deal-breaker, though; it simply calls for some strategy."

"I get this, Genie," I say. The strategy of scheduling sex was a lifesaver for Matthew and me.

"If Sophie's appetite for quality time is higher than Tony's, she can explain the difference to him as one of appetites, not that he's a horrible family man who doesn't love or care about the family."

My pre-Genie thoughts were that Matthew was a horrible family man. I now see how wrong I was.

"It has been common for centuries for spouses with an independent nature to vex the other spouse," Genie says. "One spouse wants to roam around unleashed, and the other spouse feels left and uncared for."

It's the pits being the one who is left.

"Sophie must realize that her husband has many interests," he says. "It does not mean he does not care about her. I'm sure Tony's active life was attractive to her when she married him. The two of them simply have different appetites for quality time together. Obviously, hers is high and his is low."

Unquestionably.

"Here is an example of what other women have said to their husbands in the past. 'Honey, I love the way you have many interests. It makes you a fascinating person. I think you and I have a few different appetites that I think we should discuss. For example, I think your appetite for sex is higher than mine, and I'd like to discuss a way we could negotiate that discrepancy so you will be happier. I also think I have a higher appetite for quality time than you do, and I'd like to negotiate the discrepancy in that appetite also.' "

This sounds more like a labor union discussing wages and vacation time than a man and wife discussing their marriage.

"Another thing Sophie could say is, 'If I knew each week when we were going to have quality time together, I could relax and enjoy your participating in other activities. Actually, Tony, this is a way for me to be satisfied and for you to have me off your back.' Husbands like deals like this."

Don't we all?

"Women begrudge asking their husbands for quality time," Genie says. "They feel their husbands should naturally want to be home. But that's crazy. Spouses are different and have different appetites and needs. Don't be mad at your husband for a difference in appetite but negotiate so that each appetite is satisfied. Sex, quality time, a desire for nice clothing, a desire for an ample savings account—all different values and therefore different appetites. Once spouses see that there is no right or wrong but rather a difference of, say, blue or orange, they stop attacking each other and move into negotiating."

Matthew and I have negotiated his bowling time, sex, how we spend Christmas, how much time we spend with his family, our spending, the kids' schedules, and a million other topics. I should have been a lawyer.

"I'm going swimming in Belgium this afternoon. That will cool me off," Genie says as he leaves.

I pick up my phone to call Sophie with the new advice, but before I finish dialing, Matthew beeps in on the other line. "Guess who you saw at Target this morning?" he asks.

I know who I saw. Exasperating Indigo.

"Indigo's twin," he says. "Indigo called again about some business and happened to mention that she is coming to Memphis next weekend to see her twin sister."

I feel kind of stupid—but definitely relieved.

We laugh and hang up. Glad that's cleared up. I have been upset all day, thinking that Indigo was in town, and that she and Matthew were seeing each other. I wonder how much unnecessary time I waste worrying about the wrong things?

CHAPTER 38
When Your Husband Lies or Is Deceitful

Wednesday, June 25

Today we arrive at the Beach Club in Gulf Shores, Alabama, our annual vacation spot. We unpack and go down to the beach before getting ready for dinner. One of the highlights of the whole vacation is our meal at The Restaurant at The Beach Club, which is outside on the patio and is about forty yards from the ocean. We watch the sun set as we eat filet mignon and Caribbean Maui. Tonight the management has hired a musician who is playing my parent's music, Carly Simon and James Taylor. Now he's playing a little Bon Jovi. Oh, there's Michael Jackson. The musician is doing a march through the last forty years as he's now playing Justin Timberlake and Maroon 5.

Matthew and I share a long look and smile at each other. Life is good.

While we were in the car on the way here, my friend Sarah, who asked for advice last April about her braggart husband, called. Now she has more drama to deal with.

The boys are poking at each other, but their play is harmless. Both boys need a haircut, but hey, it's summer. Their big appetites remind me to be grateful that they are healthy, and healthy makes me happy.

After dinner, Matthew and the boys run down to the beach for one more game of Frisbee before dark. Content and enjoying the sunset, I meander along the boardwalk.

"**I need that recipe for Caribbean Maui,**" a familiar voice says. "Was that Jamaican Jerk seasoning?"

"Glad to see you," I say to my best friend, Genie. "I guess you heard my phone call with Sarah earlier?"

"I was enjoying the beach, too, but on the Indian Ocean," he said. "But yes, I heard."

Sarah was wound up in a tight wad when she called because she found out Brett was hiding some money from her. He had bought some new golf clubs but had lied and said a client gave them to him. Sarah was suspicious, so she went to the pro shop where Brett golfs to snoop around. A conversation with the pro leaked that Brett bought the twelve hundred dollar set last week.

"It was bad enough to be deceitful about the money," Sarah had said, "but he *lied*. He *lied*."

"I felt sorry for her, Genie. How terrible to not be able to trust your husband," I say. I think of all the times I did not trust Matthew with Indigo. I'm a head case.

"One breach of honesty does not make a dishonest man," he said. "One breach is only a honest man who made a mistake. A truly dishonest man has a pattern of being dishonest, and this does not describe Brett."

I am shocked at this statement. I thought one lie meant you were a liar. Actually, I have lied before, and I don't want to be labeled a liar, so I might need to think about this.

"As far as Sarah knows," I say, "this is his only instance of deceit. But of course now she wonders what else he has lied about."

"You humans are weak," Genie says. "You make many, many mistakes. Your mistakes do not define you. Sarah may feel frantic about her husband being untrustworthy, but I will give you the best tactics for any wife to take when confronted with a husband's dishonesty or deceitfulness."

I hate the thought of someone lying to me. Hate. Hate.

"Of course, as I have said a thousand times, Sarah needs to control her hysteria. Naturally, her alarms are set off, and she is experiencing severe emotional turbulence after learning of her husband's deceitfulness. Self-control and calmness are needed when she communicates with Brett. Very few wives remember this, so I continually repeat it."

My alarms are set off, and it wasn't even my husband who was deceitful. I want to scream at Brett too, so I can imagine the force of emotion that Sarah feels. He *lied*! The bum.

"The first thing Sarah should communicate is her shock," Genie says. "But she should tell him that she's shocked because she believes that deep down he is an honorable man. She should say things like, 'It's so unlike you, Brett' and 'That's not who you are.' "

What? What??

"Other good sentences Sarah should say to Brett are: 'I count on you to be honest; that's who I married.' Also, 'You had a momentary lapse of mind; that's not the real you.' Or, 'I know what kind of man you are, and it's one of honor and integrity; if you made a slip-up, it was a moment of insanity. It's not the real you.'"

Granting Brett such grace and attributing his mistake to a momentary lapse of mind does not set well with my judgmental, uncompassionate heart. Of course, if *I* make a mistake, I want others to give *me* grace and believe in my better nature. I am struck by the realization that I have one set of standards for how I want to be treated and another set of standards for how I treat others. Sometimes I'm a slimy rat.

"This belief in a man's true virtue is important to him," Genie says. "It allows him to save face, straighten up, and get back on the bus. Men crave their wives' admiration, and a woman who is depositing the Eight A's wins a man's heart and attention. If he makes a mistake like this, he will be relieved you don't think that this is the real him. He will be happy you believe that he had a moment of insanity and that you're ready to forgive him and move on. He wants to be a man respected for his honor and integrity. No man wants to be a scalawag. Hold up the ideal. Tell him that's who he is."

When I get home, I'm going to write in my Turquoise Journal, "Be grateful Matthew is not a liar or a scalawag."

"Brett has a conscience; he knows deep down what he did was wrong," Genie says. "A wife helps a man by telling him this is just a temporary lapse, and again, it is not who he is. Sarah should say she knows the real Brett, and that was not him. 'All men make mistakes,' Sarah should say to Brett. 'So you made a mistake. It's alright. It's not who you are. I forgive you.' This utter belief in the man's integrity enables him to forgive himself and get back on the straight-and-narrow path."

I like Matthew to keep right in the center of the straight-and-narrow path.

"And Sarah is not to later remind Brett of this mistake," says Genie. "Wise wives only remind husbands of their virtue and accomplishments. Throw your husband's mistakes into the deepest part of the ocean and let them sink to the bottom because love does not keep a record of wrongs."

I can't imagine throwing Brett's lie into the ocean. I would want to frame it and put it on the mantle so I'd have an obvious record of the wrong.

"Now we will move into what only the most mature women can handle," Genie says. "After Sarah calms down, she will need to explore why Brett felt the need to hide the money from her."

"Oh, Genie, come now!" I blurt. "You're not going to blame Sarah for Brett's lying, are you?"

I feel angry at Genie for even insinuating this.

"No, Young Jessica," he says in the most calm voice. "I am not blaming Sarah at all. But true humility always examines itself. True humility takes blame and gives credit. I am not saying it is her fault, but a wise woman would ask herself questions such as, 'Is it possible that my husband feels I am so controlling with money that I would not want him to have a nice set of golf clubs?' She should examine herself, and then, when she is ready, she could approach Brett and ask him gently and sweetly if he felt the need to hide the purchase because of anything in her."

I am mad. The bum lies, and now the wife is going to see if she is partly at fault? I feel like resigning from *Wife School*.

"Wise women build their homes and humility is the foundation," Genie says. "Don't ever be afraid of hearing how others truly feel. Explore how others perceive you. Be willing to hear hard things from others."

We were talking about lowlife lying, and now the wife is exploring how *she* might have contributed to the mess? I don't think I can take this.

"The Creator gives grace to the humble. I am not trying to excuse Brett or blame Sarah. I am only telling you that wisdom dictates that we forgive others and examine ourselves. You are not very receptive to this, Young Jessica. I am going back to the Indian Ocean now. You can think on this. I will see you back in Memphis next week."

Genie leaves, and I see Matthew and the boys walking toward me. I am still mad. It will take a little time to digest this lesson. I will have to chew on it before I talk to Sarah. There must still be much pride in me because I am unwilling to easily forgive others and examine myself.

I put the whole conversation with Genie on a shelf in my mind. It's time to return to enjoying my family. Time to get flashlights and look for crabs.

As we start scouring the beach with our flashlights, I realize, however, that I am probably the biggest crab on the beach as I think about my refusal to easily forgive others.

CHAPTER 39

When Your Husband Doesn't Help Around the House

Friday, July 4

After stuffing the last deviled egg to take on our picnic, my cell rings and it is Crystal, one of my favorite calligraphy brides. I finished her invitations yesterday, and I bet she wants to come over and get them.

"Hi, Crystal," I answer.

"He broke the engagement, he broke the engagement!" She wails, hardly able to speak.

At first, I feel terrible for her, but shortly, I begin to worry about getting paid the $650 for the work I did. We hang up, and of course, she didn't mention paying me. I know she's devastated over the broken engagement, and to her, my little fee is nothing compared to her heartbreak. But that was thirty hours of my time.

I begin to think how devastated Crystal must be. It would be traumatic to have your fiancée break your engagement six weeks before the ceremony. My compassion for her arises while my annoyance of losing $650 diminishes. Diminishes, not disappears.

We are late for the preliminary activities at the Germantown Fireworks Extravaganza in Germantown, a suburb of Memphis. We load up the car and try to drive there quickly, but the traffic is horrific. When we finally arrive at the park, we are each given a little American flag. Matthew is pulling the cooler, and I am transporting the lawn chairs. We look for an empty space on the lawn to set up our picnic.

The Germantown Symphony Orchestra is playing "God Bless America." While I set out the broiled chicken and deviled eggs, the orchestra plays "Yankee Doodle" and

"This Land Is Your Land." The crowd is surprisingly aroused as everyone rises to their feet, wilding waving their flags and singing, "This land is my land, from California, to the New York Island."

Matthew and I smile at each other as we experience the exuberance of this patriotic moment. Matthew is not the emotional type, but he is waving the heck out of his little flag. The crowd erupts into applause. This is America, home of the free and the brave.

Our friends the Barkleys ramble in with their four young children at the end of the song. Jennifer is the friend I counseled early in May about Ryan being irresponsible (see Chapter 31, "When Your Husband Is Irresponsible").

Today, Jennifer is visibly upset. When the men can't hear, she whispers to me, "I have to do everything around the house. Ryan is worthless to help. Sorry we were late." She asked if I would go to the restroom with her, as she obviously wanted to get me alone to talk.

"It seems like Matthew helps you so much," she says. "How do you get him to help around the house?"

Is it Dr. Phil? Dr. Laura? No, it's Dr. Jessica, the new marriage counselor in Memphis.

I tell Jennifer my usual LMTAIAIGBTY ("Let me think about it, and I'll get back to you").

While the fireworks are blasting, Matthew and the boys rate each explosion. "That's an eight." "That's a nine." "That's a one." I feel a surge of contentment as Matthew tussles Josh's hair as they playfully argue if one display was an eight or a nine.

I notice that Jennifer and Ryan hardly speak to each other. I remember the cold days of resentment. Maybe I can help her.

Three days later, Monday, July 7

The boys are with Daisy for the afternoon. The three of them are going to a movie and then to Sheridan's Frozen Custard to get smoothies. Daisy does try to be a good grandmother sometimes.

I sit down to address wedding invitations for my client Kelley, who is probably the sweetest bride I've ever worked for. A grateful, kind bride like Kelley can make up for eight to ten bridezillas.

Anyway, I like addressing invitations. The repetition relaxes me, similar to how some women enjoy knitting. I think of Crystal and the $650 that I'll probably never see. Oh well, such is life.

I walk to the table and find all five hundred of Kelley's invitations done in the most beautiful calligraphy I've ever seen. **"Arabian calligraphy," Genie says.** "Also, we need to talk again about your friend Jennifer."

Sympathy arises as I think of frazzled Jennifer at the firework display.

"Today we will discuss what to do when a husband doesn't help much around the house," he begins.

I didn't see any food on the counter. I wonder if he's going to abracadabra something for dinner. I think I'm getting a little spoiled.

"A helpful fact to keep in mind," Genie begins, "is that even though there is a large surge on the part of working women to get husbands to help more around the house, men still feel basically the same about housework as they have for centuries, which is they don't want to do it."

I'm a little shocked. Many of my friends work and expect their husbands to help around the house. This is reasonable, of course. What's wrong with men?

"A major difference exists between how women and men perceive housework. Women are burdened until the work is done whereas most men don't even see what needs to be done. Laundry can be piled a mile high and dishes falling out of the sink and still many men's antennae won't pick up there's housework to be done. A man can be enthralled with the preseason New Orleans Saints special on TV and never consider that the dirty kitchen floor needs mopping."

"Genie, that's selfish and inconsiderate of men," I say.

"No, it's men," he says. "They don't have an antenna that alerts them that housework needs to be done. It's similar to how men don't hear babies cry in the night, but the slightest whimper wakes up the mother."

I never knew if Matthew was faking being asleep when the boys were babies or if he really didn't hear them, like he said.

"I will let you in on a little secret, Young Jessica. Most men have a secret fantasy about their home life. They want a happy, fresh-looking wife to meet them at the door with a hot, home-cooked meal on the table. They want the house to be clean and picked up and have their laundry done. They want the children to be well-behaved, quiet, and respectful. They want to walk in from a hard day at work and the family run to get his pipe and slippers. I'm not exaggerating."

This isn't *Leave It to Beaver*.

"Men would never ask for this, but I am letting you in on their secret fantasy."

I've got some of my own fantasies, Buster.

"Knowing that all men tend to be like this helps women give husbands—"

"I know, I know. Grace and slack," I say. It is true that when a husband's offense is common to most men, the offense does not sting as intensely.

"Women must be wise in knowing how to ask for help with housework," Genie says, "because the husband is naturally reluctant to give help since he thinks it's the wife's job. A well-worded word picture is often a good strategy." (See Chapter 13, "How to Explain Anything to Your Husband.")

I think Jennifer should just call Merry Maids and give Ryan the bill.

"Wise women don't expect men to read their minds. If a wife would like the husband to do more, the two of them should sit down and make a list of everything that needs to be done. Cars regularly need oil changes, the refrigerator needs monthly cleaning, weeds need to be pulled from the flower beds, children need to go to the dentist twice a year, and so on. All jobs can be listed. Then the couple can agree as to who does which job, how often, what they should hire out, etc."

More negotiating. I like negotiating.

"You are familiar, Young Jessica, with many of the attempts women use to plead with husbands for help. A list that is posted in a common area is a typical strategy."

Why should the wife even have to make the list? Oh yeah, most men are brain dead regarding housework. Actually, Matthew does help me quite a bit. I need to write that in my Turquoise Journal.

"A good tactic," Genie says, "is for the wife to give the husband choices about work around the house. An example would be (after establishing together that the dining room needs painting), 'Do you want to paint the dining room, or should we hire someone to do it?' "

Ah, questions that offer choices. I know that trick.

"Sometimes it amazes me how little foresight some women have," Genie says. "For example, if a woman has a husband who does not like yard work, why does she insist on buying a wooded lot with a huge yard to build a house on? Or if a woman has a man who does not like to participate in decorating for Christmas, why would a woman plan to extravagantly decorate her home since she is going to be doing it solo?"

Obviously Genie doesn't realize how important holiday decorating is to women.

"If no one wants to do the cleaning jobs around the house, choose to keep other expenses low, such as limiting eating out, deciding to drive older cars, etc., so you can afford weekly or biweekly cleaning help."

Oh, my! A maid? Is he recommending a maid? I want a maid.

"If the wife works or is overrun with many little children," Genie says, "and the husband does not want to participate in the weekly or daily housework schedule, a cleaning service or a maid can take a lot of stress off the household."

I only have two children, and I seem to get my housework done. But poor Jennifer! She's got four little rugrats, and Ryan doesn't want to help. A weekly or biweekly housekeeper could be a lifesaver for her.

"Some men are opposed to getting household help," I say. "Even though we could have afforded it, my father used to say that housework was mom's work."

"Funny," Genie says. "Those same men often have secretaries and hire a neighbor boy to mow their lawn. Humans are prone to blind spots. If a woman needs household help and her husband doesn't want to give her the help or hire out for it, she should simply say, 'Honey, I know you love me and want me to be happy. I also know you don't think I should get a maid and that housework is my job. But I want you to give me a maid just because I want it. Not because I deserve it but because you love me and want me to be happy. I have found where we can save money in the budget, so we can afford it. I try not to ask you for too many things, but this is something that is very important to me. Maybe you can give that to me for Christmas, my birthday, and our anniversary, all rolled into one.'"

"There is nothing wrong with a woman asking for something simply because she wants it," Genie says.

Well, I'll be danged. Ask just because she wants it. Love, love, *love* it. I don't need a housekeeper, but I can't wait to call Jennifer and give her Genie's advice.

There is a knock on the door. I see that it is Crystal, that sweet girl with the broken engagement. Her whole face is filled with sadness. She hands me a white envelope. "Here is the $650 I owe you for the invitations," she says. Her eyes begin to moisten.

I know Crystal's family, and they are not rich. It is impressive to keep your word, especially in difficult situations.

I open the envelope and see several twenty-dollar bills. I close it back up and hand it back to her. "You don't owe me any money, Crystal. Consider this a gift. I can't imagine how painful it would be to have your engagement broken," I say.

What if Matthew had broken our engagement? The thought of my going through life with anyone besides Matthew is grievous.

Crystal left, deeply grateful for the cancellation of her debt. Although I lost $650 dollars, my having a faithful husband who helps me around the house makes me a wealthy woman and cancels any negative feelings I have about the loss.

Crystal's broken engagement makes me sad for her, but it is true that other people's troubles often make us aware of our own good fortune.

CHAPTER 40
When You Work Outside the Home

Monday, July 14

Daisy walks in the back door. She is picking up the boys to take them to a movie. When Daisy makes grandmotherly gestures toward the boys, I soften toward her.

Matthew calls while Daisy is still here and says that his boss is loaning us his ski boat this Saturday.

As I hang up, Daisy asks, "What are you so excited about?" She asks too many questions, but this one seems harmless.

"Matthew's boss is loaning us his ski boat this Saturday. We are going to take it to Heber Springs Lake for the day."

She gets the most pitiful look on her face and says, "I haven't been to the lake in years. I used to love the lake when I was young."

Who hints at inviting herself like this? Who? *Who?* I know she's lonely, but instead of asking her to join us at the lake, which would spoil my day, I ask her to come to dinner tomorrow night.

"How fun," she says. "Can you invite your father, too?"

Next day, Tuesday, July 15

Against the boys' will, I make them go with me to the library to get more books for them to read as well as books for me to read to them. I get *A Wrinkle In Time* by Madeleine L'Engle, *The Lion, the Witch, and the Wardrobe* by C. S. Lewis, and *Charlie and the Chocolate Factory* by Ronald Dahl. I loved these classics as a kid. Even though

I try to read out loud to Brandon and Josh every night at bedtime, it is a struggle in the summer because they would rather play kickball or four square outside with the neighborhood kids.

As we're checking out at the library, I run into Heather, the mother of a friend of Josh's. She is frantically searching for her keys, talking to her office on the phone, and corralling her energetic boys. "You are so relaxed, Jessica," she says in a too-loud-for-the-library voice. "Look at me. I'm insane, and you're calm."

She notices the difference in our inner peace; I notice the difference in our clothing. She looks like she just left Neiman Marcus. My shorts and tee shirt are several years old.

It is true, however, that I keep margins in my life so I'm not frazzled. Granted, she works full-time. But look at her expensive clothes, her big diamond, and the new Lexus SUV she drives. It's obvious we have different lifestyles.

"Maybe I could call you sometime, and we could talk about how to get off this treadmill," Heather says. "I thought I could have it all, but I'm miserable trying to work full-time and rear these kids at the same time."

I want to say, "Don't call me. I barely know you!" But I know better than that. I'm supposed to share Genie's wisdom with others. Sometimes I can be a selfish clod. "Sure! Want to put my number in your cell phone?" I ask, gaining control over my self-centered impulses.

The boys and I then get groceries and head home. They help me lug in the two hundred dollars worth of food and then run outside to play with the neighborhood gang.

"Would you like some help with that?" I hear, and instantly, my kitchen is cleaned up. Chicken salad is on the counter as is a cut-up watermelon, fresh corn on the cob, strawberries, and celery, carrots, and cucumbers that are ready for dipping into the homemade hummus. A beautiful summer spread. Beautiful, healthy food is one of my favorite delights on Earth.

"I barely know Heather, and she wants advice from me, Genie. That is weird," I say.

"People can often sense who has good counsel and can help them," he says. "I want to talk to you today about when women work outside the home."

Of course that is the topic. I grab a piece of watermelon and sit down to listen.

"I don't want you to think I'm a hardnose here," he says. "I know some women have to work to put food on the table, and I have much compassion for those women."

I get up to get more watermelon. It's so yummy and sweet.

"I want to start by saying I have seen many women work full-time outside the home when the children are small where it has worked beautifully."

I'm a little surprised to hear him say that, but I'm listening.

"The first situation where it works for the woman to work full-time when her children are small is when a couple has fabulous childcare, such as grandparents," Genie says. "A second situation that works well is when the husband doesn't mind picking up the slack. We will discuss this more in a second."

That wouldn't be Matthew. He likes to have me at home taking care of the homestead while he's out slaying wild Indians and bears.

"The third scenario when it works well for the wife to work away from the home," Genie says, "is when women are genetically human Energizer Bunnies. These women seem to be able to do more than the rest of you."

My cousin Olivia is like that. She can do it all while whistling Dixie.

"Let's begin today's discussion with listing many of the responsibilities a woman has in caring for her household. As we discussed on July 4 (see Chapter 39, "When Your Husband Doesn't Help Around the House"), most husbands have a fantasy that the wife will take care of all the domestic responsibilities. For women to be able to work outside the home successfully, her husband would have to agree to take on some of the domestic work or to hire it out. That is not just laundry, cooking, and cleaning. Birthday and Christmas shopping must be done, school projects for the children have to be completed, and trips to doctor appointments as well as rides to baseball practice and Boy Scouts must be scheduled."

I know this long list.

"There have to be margins in the family, too," Genie says, "so dad has time to fix bikes with the boys. And moms want to have margins to teach little Suzy how to bake. As you demonstrated this morning, parents need time to read out loud to their kids."

Ah, a stroke of approval from Genie. I'll take it.

"Surprisingly," he says, "the commodity that is most rare in families is time, not money. A mom may work so the family can live in a bigger house and wear designer shoes, but if there is a scarcity of time and energy for the family, the family suffers."

I think of my Aunt Mollie, who worked full-time and her boys turned out beautifully. But again, she was an exception because she was a human Energizer Bunny *and* had a husband who was willing to help.

"If families cut back their expenses," Genie says, "by not eating out, by driving older cars, and by living in smaller houses, they would be shocked at how much money they could save."

Matthew insists on buying older, used cars and paying cash for them. He would never have a note on a depreciating item. Thank you, Dave Ramsey.

"Again, some women can do it all," he says. "But the majority of women needs ample time to cook healthy meals, to walk in the sunlight, and to plan family outings."

It takes a lot of time to chop up onions and to mince fresh garlic.

"Even when women cut back their hours of working to part-time," Genie says, "a huge change can occur in the family. Mom is happier, and that happiness trickles throughout to the entire household."

When this mama ain't happy, *everybody* should take cover.

"One helpful thought is to know that your desire for an expensive lifestyle comes from comparing yourself to your peers. If you can find some friends who value the mom staying home with young kids (and possibly having a home business instead), you will be substantially free from trying to keep up with the Joneses. If all of your friends are wealthy, eat out frequently, and have the latest gadgets, you will find yourself compelled to compete. Having a social network where other couples are careful about their spending will help you be comfortable with a less expensive lifestyle. Ultimately, you will have an enriched life because of less stress and more margins."

I am grateful for my middle-class life.

"Every year, Young Jessica, you attend the local Vesta Home Show where home builders display their spectacular new homes. And every year you marvel over the details of the wood floors, the eight-inch crown molding, the brick treatment behind the breakfast bar, and the beautiful, opulent light fixtures in the foyer."

Those new homes do wow me.

"Just like the builders invested enormous time and energy into building those houses," Genie says, "the wise woman invests enormous amounts of time and energy into building her home and family. There's only so much energy and time in life. So don't be foolish and waste your finite energy and time. Give it to your most important earthly priority, your family. Give it to make a rich, lush, overflowing garden of a family. If a woman can work full-time and still build this house, well, kudos to her. I certainly understand how important it is for a woman to express her gifts in the world, but that is secondary to the most important and, ultimately, the most satisfying of all endeavors to a woman, that of successfully building a family that is pleasing to the Creator."

Genie certainly gets my soul at its deepest level. I have many goals and concerns in life, but nothing, absolutely nothing, rivals my love for my family.

"I understand that women want a low-maintenance, high-return marriage and family," he says. "But they need to give up the lie and the fantasy that a low-maintenance, high-return marriage and family even exists. It doesn't."

I start to contradict him and give him some examples, but the only ones I can think of are—again—in the movies.

I pick up the phone to call Heather and realize I don't even know her last name. I feel ridiculous calling this woman I barely know and giving her advice about her life.

"Jessica, I've been waiting for your call," she says. "Tell me everything you think might help me."

I tell her everything I can remember. Oddly, she's tremendously receptive.

Tonight Daisy is coming to dinner, and yes, I invited my father. What else could I do? I warned Dad that Daisy would be here.

Daisy walks in. It is obvious she has gone to a lot of trouble to look nice. She had her hair and nails done and is wearing a new outfit. But Dad comes to the door with a surprise: Sue is on his arm!

When Daisy sees Sue with Dad, she pretends that a huge migraine is coming on and leaves. I get Dad alone in the kitchen and ask him what he is thinking, bringing Sue to my dinner party, uninvited, and especially when he knew Daisy was going to be here.

"I thought maybe it was a good way for Daisy to finally realize that there's no chance that she and I are going to get together," he said.

Men! Why couldn't he just tell her instead of all these not-so-subtle hints? Now I'm the one who is going to suffer for Daisy's humiliation. I love my dad, but he needs a *Genie School* for men!

PART IV

Conclusion

CHAPTER 41
The Departure of Genie

Monday, August 4

The house is quiet because the boys left for a weeklong church camp. My cell rings, and it is Matthew. He is frustrated with his new secretary who spends more time on her computer picking out her bridal registry than she does doing her work. I listen attentively, stopping what I'm doing so I can concentrate. Then I give him sympathetic understanding. "That's a lot of pressure to have to think of the brilliant ad campaigns and also handle the personnel. I'm not sure how many men could handle that much responsibility so well," I say.

Next, I admire him. "Matthew, you're so good with people. Remember how well you handled the situation with Tommy, the junior account assistant who was stirring up gossip in the office? You'll figure out what to do in this situation too."

I am a changed woman. I surprise myself.

"If we don't have plans tonight," Matthew says, "there's something I'd like to do."

Oh no, I think. *He wants to go see a baseball game or some other equally boring sporting event.* I prepare myself to answer wisely.

"I want to take you out," he says, "and buy you something that you've been wanting. A new outfit or something for the house."

My jaw drops. How romantic and adorable is that? Since Matthew is not a gift person by nature, his gesture is underlined, in bold, and italic. He is filled with affection for me and is offering to demonstrate it.

"And maybe I shouldn't tell you this on the phone," he says, "but I know you want a third child. On the way to work this morning, I got hit with the thought that children are a blessing, so why would I want to say no to blessings? And since you're such a fabulous mom and wife, I enjoy making you happy."

My eyes fill with tears. Wow.

"Jessica, are you still there?"

He's not used to my being silent.

"Matthew, I-I ... don't know how I-I ... ever married such a wonderful husband. I mean, you are the sweetest husband in the world." And I mean that. I really, really mean that. I can't believe how Matthew has changed. I can't believe how my feelings have changed for Matthew. I'm in a little bit of a shock.

After hanging up, I walk around my house in sort of a daze. Matthew said I can get pregnant. Another baby. *Another baby.* My eyes fill with tears again.

"I heard your phone conversation with Matthew," Genie says as he appears.

"Can you believe that he has changed his mind about having another child?"

"Oh, I can easily believe it, Young Jessica. This doesn't surprise me at all."

"And he wants to take me out to *buy* me something?" I say, still flabbergasted by his offer.

It's not that I am seeking gifts. Of course, I do love gifts. But this unusual demonstration of affection by Matthew is huge because it confirms that I have succeeded in meeting his needs, making him feel admired, and winning his love. The Eight A's have broken through his bulletproof vest and penetrated his heart.

"I am extremely proud of you, Young Jessica. You have beautifully learned the lessons in *Wife School*. It is therefore time for me to depart."

"Depart?" I ask. "For good?" First, Matthew makes me so happy I cry, and now I'm so upset that Genie is leaving I want to cry. I feel like I'm six years old and learning to ride a bike. The training wheels are off, and my dad is getting ready to let go of the bike for the first time. I'm afraid I'm going to fall.

"Are you sure I'm ready?" I ask. "Isn't there more I need to know?" The thought of being on my own terrifies me.

"Yes, you are ready, Young Jessica. But I have three final remarks in conclusion," Genie says.

Only three? He's going to condense the last eleven months into three remarks?

"One, be sure to read your Turquoise Journal frequently," he says. "Just like your hair and body must be washed every day or they become unclean and unattractive, your mind needs to be frequently bathed with Matthew's virtues. You understand daily regimens. You fix your family's food daily. You brush your teeth daily. You don't have to review the principles daily, but you must do so frequently. The best insurance to keeping these principles centered in your mind is sharing and discussing them with others. Teaching others has always been the best way to learn a subject."

I was hoping to be through with being Memphis' newest counselor, but I guess I'm not.

"Secondly," Genie says, "your marriage will not be determined by a once-a-year anniversary trip to Italy. Of course, these moments may be the highlights of your year. But the real work of marriage is done when you daily demonstrate the Eight A's."

Men need air, water, food, and the Eight A's.

"You demonstrate the A of Acceptance when your husband again forgets you don't like to watch seven hours of football on Sunday."

Matthew does love Peyton Manning and Drew Brees and can get sucked into football marathons.

"The real work of marriage is done," Genie says, "when you fix your husband breakfast and give him the A of Admiration by telling him how attractive he looks in his suit and paisley tie."

Matthew *is* gorgeous in his new charcoal-gray, pinstriped suit.

"You give Matthew the A of Appreciation," Genie continues, "when you bring home a carload of groceries and then say to him, 'How nice it is to be married to a man who makes sure there's always money in the bank to buy healthy food for our family.' "

I do like money in the bank.

"You fill Matthew's tank with the A of Attention by noticing how he loves the crab cakes at Bone Fish Grill and then go online to find a copycat recipe so you can surprise him."

How would I live without Google?

"Matthew will be delighted with the A of Activities as you plan things you both enjoy instead of letting the fun and play drizzle out of the marriage," Genie continues.

Matthew and I have loved the concerts we've attended. Recently, we sat in the center of the third row at the Chris Tomlin concert. "How great is our God, sing with me."

Genie is still going at smokin' speed. "Matthew will enjoy the A of Approval when you are exceedingly careful with your complaints and criticisms."

Still working on muzzling the mouth.

"The A of Affection will be demonstrated to Matthew when, even though you're tired," Genie says, "you choose willingness because, after all, it's a 'scheduled night.' "

I'm still growing in that area of the marriage, but I'm light-years from where I was a year ago.

"And last and most importantly," Genie says, "you realize that the A of Authority is from the Creator. It was designed to bless and protect you, not confine you."

I feel like I should now be that chess or marriage champion, but deep in my heart, I know I have far to go in consistently depositing the Eight A's.

"Okay, Genie, and the third and final remark?" That second remark was a killer.

"The third and final remark is that your strength dries up easily, Young Jessica. All human strength easily evaporates. Therefore, be a tree planted by a stream of water so your roots can receive continual nourishment."

Does he expect me to understand what that means? What tree? What water?

"The stream of water is the Word of the Creator," Genie says. "Be in His Word so you can be nourished and fed."

I know the feeling of being parched and wanting Matthew to fill me.

"Our time together is now over," Genie says. "Be sure to give my lamp to someone else who needs me."

What if something comes up and I don't know what to do? I feel a mini-panic episode coming on. Immediately, though, I remember that the Creator isn't leaving. I will miss Genie, but I am not being deserted.

Genie twirls and swirls into a hurricane of energy and reenters the brass lamp.

Gone. Vamoosed. Just like that.

There should be a bugle playing taps. Or maybe, more appropriately, a loud Oriental gong. Something. Something to signify this moment.

For my last "happy," there is a beautiful standing rib roast on the counter along with broccoli and cheese soup, and homemade whole wheat rolls with honey butter. Saying good-bye to these "happys" will be a feat in itself.

I put the lamp back in the mahogany box. I wonder to whom I should give it? Each of my sisters comes to mind.

My thoughts trail back to Genie's teachings. I have learned how to meet the needs of my husband. Giving to Matthew in a language he can hear is now a skill I possess. Secrets to understanding, loving, and honoring my husband have been divulged to me. And now Matthew is turning more and more toward me. This gift is priceless. *Priceless*.

The memory of my throwing a fit because Grandma left me an old wooden mahogany box crosses my mind. I was mad to the moon and back that there were not stocks and bonds in that box.

I had no idea what true riches lay inside that brass lamp.

THE TURQUOISE JOURNAL LISTS

List 1: Strengths, Gifts, and Qualities I Admire in My Husband (Chapter 2)
List 2: Things Other Husbands Do Wrong (Chapter 2)
List 3: Unmet Expectations I Have of My Husband (Chapter 2)
List 4: Nice Things My Husband Says or Does (Chapter 2)
List 5: Things My Husband Might Find Difficult to Accept in Me (Chapter 2)
List 6: One Hundred Things I Appreciate about My Husband (Chapter 4)
List 7: Activities My Husband and I Might Enjoy Together (Chapter 6)
List 8: My Eight Top Concerns/ When to Use My Appeal Coupons (Chapter 9)

ACKNOWLEDGMENTS

The person I would like to thank first is the most important person in the world to me, my strong, honest, and kind husband, David. His integrity and sacrificial love has been a picture of Christ to me since the day we married. My many knots have been untangled by his years of devotion and care. I would never have attempted to write *Wife School* without his support and confidence. I know he got tired of my talking about this project, but he listened well to all I had to say, just as he has listened well to everything for over thirty years. I remember the cold night in January when I read the first chapter out loud to him and his eyes got moist. I still don't know what that meant exactly—I just knew it meant something good. "Something good" is what he has given me for the entirety of our marriage. I have always told him that on a resume of my life accomplishments, my best accomplishment will always be "Married Well."

The next person I'd like to thank is Elizabeth. During her recuperation from surgery, she read the first draft of this book, and her positive comments and laughter gave me hope that other young women would laugh too as they learned how to love their husbands. Elizabeth's comments changed the story in this book. Her drive and independent nature are superseded by her gentle and quiet spirit. Her precious husband adores her, and her brothers are looking for a girl like her to marry.

Michelle comes to mind next. Michelle has been a great encourager and willing to talk as long as I needed to sort out the issues in this book. Michelle is an once-in-a-lifetime friend. She is a wonderful wife and mother, and her wisdom and godliness were important compasses to me as I wrote this book. Michelle is the type of friend who is faithful *no matter what*. She is dearly loved not just by me but also by all of her friends

Leslie is my lifelong friend who gave me some much-needed feedback that reshaped this book on the second rewrite. I can always depend on her to be a great Bible thinker and communicator. She's been a comforting and wise friend for twenty-five years. What a gift her friendship has been to me.

Karen is a lovely friend with a huge heart who was very encouraging about this manuscript. Her repetitive kindness to my family has also been tremendously appreciated. I have learned so much about family from watching her.

I'd like to thank Kendall next. I remember the first phone call I received from Kendall after she read the first rough draft. Her enthusiasm and confidence delighted me to no end. I have told Kendall repeatedly that I could not have written this book until we became friends. I had to see how she modeled the Eighth A before I could finally write about it. Kendall is a beautiful example of a godly woman and a great friend. We have spent untold hours discussing how to help other women with their marriages. I cannot believe how much I have learned from Kendall.

Early in my marriage, I had another friend who shaped who I was in a significant way. Although I don't see Carrie as much as I would like to, her godliness and early influence are everywhere in my life. I respect her greatly and still have very tender memories of her.

This book would not have been written had it not been for Suzanne. I thank God for sending her to our family.

There were many other initial readers who critiqued this book, but three stand out: Emily, Jenny, and Elizabeth. Your encouragement to me personally and to write these principles has been unbelievable. I have changed many things because of your comments. You will always be deep in my affection.

Other proofreaders who stand out are Holly, Emily L., Faith, Jennifer, Sheri, Sherri, Shannon, Amanda, Lauren, Michal, Lisa, and Selwyn. Thank you all for your comments.

And lastly, this book was mainly written for my precious granddaughters, who are all still in the mind of God. How I love you all. I can't wait to have slumber parties and to go get our nails done.

ABOUT THE AUTHOR

Julie's own happy marriage of thirty-two years is to a very patient man, David, who says he is the rat in her marriage laboratory. David and Julie's six children, ages 31 to 21, are Elizabeth (married to Trent), Stephen (married to Elaina), Joseph, Jonathan, Benjamin, and Samuel. *Just like you*, love of family is at the top of her list. You can see a picture of Julie's family at her website, JulieNGordon.com.

But next to family, Julie's passion is helping women with their marriages (*Husband School, Where Men Learn the Secrets of Making Wives Happy*, co-authored with David, is now available), helping women with their weight problems (*Weight Loss School: Where Women Learn the Secrets to Finally Get Thin Forever*), and pursuing her newest topic, refuting the teaching of the New Atheists.

On any given day, you can find her writing in her bedroom, meeting with women, cooking (Paleo), going to the gym (still an effort), or texting her kids (even if they don't always text back).

Go to www.JulieNGordon.com for new information, other books to be released, blogs, etc. E-mail Julie with your comments at JulieNGordon2012@gmail.com.

May God richly bless your marriage!

The End

Made in the USA
San Bernardino, CA
05 January 2018